Belly Up

ALSO BY WALTER STEWART

NON-FICTION
Shrug: Trudeau in Power (1971)
Hard To Swallow (1975)
As They Can See Us (1977)
Strike (1977)
Paper Juggernaut (1979)
Canadian Newspapers (1980)
Towers of Gold, Feet of Clay (1982)
But Not in Canada (1983)
True Blue: The Loyalist Legend (1985)
Uneasy Lies the Head (1988)
Wrong End of the Rainbow (with Eric Kierans) (1989)
The Golden Fleece (1992)
Too Big To Fail (1993)

FICTION
Right Church, Wrong Pew (1990)
Hole in One (1992)

Belly Up

The Spoils of Bankruptcy

by

Walter Stewart

Canadian Cataloguing in Publication Data

Stewart, Walter, 1931-
Belly up: the spoils of bankruptcy

Includes bibliographical references and index.
ISBN 0-7710-8304-1

1. Bankruptcy – Canada. 2. Bankruptcy – United States. 3. Corporate debt – Canada. 4. Corporate debt – United States. I. Title.

HG3769.C34S74 1995   332.7′5′0971   C95-930363-4

The publishers acknowledge the support of the Canada Council and the Ontario Arts Council for their publishing program.

Typesetting by M&S, Toronto
Printed and bound in Canada on acid-free paper

McClelland & Stewart Inc.
The Canadian Publishers
481 University Avenue
Toronto, Ontario
M5G 2E9

1 2 3 4 5   99 98 97 96 95

For Joan, again, with love

CONTENTS

Belly Up

Gather Ye Creditors While Ye May

"As long as everyone takes a whipping like little ladies and gentlemen, the company emerges from bankruptcy and survives as an ongoing business." – Stratford P. Sherman, 1991[1]

$

Many years ago, as a financial reporter, I interviewed a Toronto businessman who had gone into the electronics industry, did well, expanded too fast, and went bankrupt. He was discharged by the courts, in due course, for a payment of, as I recall it, about forty-five cents on the dollar. Then the poor sap worked at any job he could get until he had paid off every cent of his original debt. And *then* he went back into the industry and did quite well the second time around. How droll! He clearly had no understanding of the bankruptcy process. He regarded it as merely a stage of stepping away from his creditors until he could reorganize, so that he could get his feet under him and pay them all back, instead of as a place to scrape away all his old debts and start borrowing again.

At the time, I admit, I rather admired this man, who felt that, because he had been advanced the money, he should repay it, no matter what the courts said. I have learned better. Not long ago, I heard Jim Smith, a poet, being interviewed on Vicki Gabereau's CBC Radio show, explaining that he had been through a personal bankruptcy and, "I shed about $25,000."[2] Gabereau giggled. I'll bet none of the creditors giggled, but never mind, this man – a writer, a member of my own tribe – knew what bankruptcy was all about. Shedding debt. Or getting back at someone. Or stiffing an opponent in a lawsuit.

If you want to meet a man who knows how to use bankruptcy, meet Michael E. Chodos of Thornhill, Ontario. The master. Chodos is a lawyer who, away back in 1981, undertook a wrongful-dismissal case on behalf of Soel Szarfer, who had been fired from his job in a hairdressing salon. Szarfer had smashed his wrist in an accident and was not as adept as he had been, so his boss threw him out. Szarfer didn't like it much, and he sued. While the case was dragging on, as these things do, Szarfer's wife began to do some part-time secretarial work for Chodos, and it was she who typed up the documents for the legal case. These documents showed that one result of the injury to her husband, and his consequent unemployment, was that the marriage was in difficulty.

So, Chodos seduced the woman one evening in his office. A subsequent court would say that "he used confidential information for his own purposes in order to obtain the delights and benefits of the affair."[3] The affair lasted six weeks, until Szarfer found out about it, by accident. The end result was the breakup of Szarfer's marriage and the loss of his two children, who went with their mother. At the same time, Chodos's handling of the wrongful-dismissal case led to *its* dismissal. Under the multiple strains, Szarfer suffered a breakdown and required psychiatric help.

Szarfer then sued Chodos for breach of fiduciary duty and placing "his personal interest in conflict with his duty as a solicitor by engaging in an adulterous relationship with Mrs. Szarfer."[4] In due course, which is to say in 1986, Szarfer won and was awarded $43,660. Mr. Justice

D. H. Carruthers found that Chodos had taken advantage of Mrs. Szarfer's vulnerability, and that this constituted "professional negligence."[5] This is very naughty, and the Law Society of Upper Canada duly looked into the matter, and a discipline committee recommended that Chodos be disbarred, but that came to nothing.

As to the verdict against him, Chodos simply filed an appeal and ignored it. In 1988, he lost the appeal, upon which he took a series of actions to protect himself, and then went into bankruptcy. While the appeal was pending, he gained $65,000 on a successful investment, but paid not a cent of this over to Szarfer. The gains simply disappeared.[6] He liquidated between $29,000 and $30,000 of Registered Retirement Savings Plan (RRSP) certificates and gave the money to his wife, who had a full-time job as a social worker. He set up an investment company with his former law partners and put money in trust through this venture, in an attempt to insulate it from Szarfer. Then he declared himself insolvent and hid in bankruptcy for two and a half years, while paying Szarfer not one thin dime, although the debt had now risen, with interest and costs, to $210,000. He owed other creditors $146,000, including $42,700 to Revenue Canada for unpaid taxes, as well as taxes on the RRSPs he had cashed.

During his bankruptcy, Chodos was spending $8,148 a month, or just under $98,000 a year, on, among other things, a full-time nanny for his two children, who were twelve and sixteen and hardly in need of a nanny. He also paid $500 a month for "lawn cutting" at the Thornhill house owned by his wife. And, these were only his expenses; his wife, the social worker, covered other costs, such as $2,000 a month in the summer for the kids' camp. Mr. Justice Dennis Lane, who heard the Chodos bankruptcy case, expressed a feeling of "severe unease" at the fact that "he has made no effort nor given any instructions to his family and his housekeeper to reduce his family expenses."[7] There was no need to, he was doing fine.

In the meantime, Szarfer, the man to whom Chodos now owed $210,000, was destitute. His total income was $2,000 a month, from a disability pension and workers' compensation, out of which he paid

$600 a month for child support and $935 a month to the Royal Bank, to repay loans he had accrued during all this torture. He had $465 a month to fritter away on himself.

Chodos ignored a summons to appear as a judgment debtor, and refused to deliver all his property to the trustee in bankruptcy, as required by law.[8] He treated his unsecured creditors, including Szarfer, with contempt, and would make no offer to pay them anything at all, although he did suggest that they might try to collect $120,000 that he said his law partners owed him. Then, he applied for discharge from bankruptcy, and got it, on January 22, 1992, on condition that he would agree to pay to all his creditors a total of $100,000. By this time, the debt had swollen to $386,000, including the $210,000 owed to Szarfer.

In granting the discharge, Mr. Justice Dennis Lane wrote that, "He [Chodos] is every bit as indifferent to Mr. Szarfer as he was in 1981. . . . It appears to me from all the evidence that his primary motivation in going into bankruptcy was to avoid having to pay Mr. Szarfer anything upon this judgement."[9] Just the same, "A major objective of the *Bankruptcy Act* is the return of bankrupts to productive economic life. After two and a half years in bankruptcy, it is certainly time for Mr. Chodos to be returned to full productive membership in the economic community. This is true notwithstanding the disgraceful conduct which led to his bankruptcy."[10] This was also true, I guess, despite the fact that Szarfer, his victim, was not returned to productive economic life; but, of course, it was no part of the Bankruptcy Act to worry about that.

So, in return for wiping out debts of $386,000, Chodos was required to pay $100,000, of which Szarfer (owed about 60 per cent of the debt) could reasonably expect to collect $60,000. However, that's not how it works. Revenue Canada, as a "preferred creditor," collected about half of its $42,700 right away. But the money owed to other creditors was covered by a consent judgment, which Chodos signed on April 3, 1992. Under this, he was required to pay to the trustee in bankruptcy $500 a month – the same sum he pays for lawn-cutting – between July 1, 1992, and June 1, 1995. Thereafter, he has to pay $750 a month until the debt is discharged. The $500 represented interest at

6 per cent annually between January 22, 1992, the day of his discharge from bankruptcy, and June 1, 1995. [11]

The $750 Chodos is now paying monthly, out of an estimated income of somewhere around $200,000 a year, [12] just covers the interest on the $100,000 at 9 per cent and makes no provision for repaying the capital; that repayment is not mentioned in the document. Szarfer gets about $450 a month from the trustees.

His share of the $210,000 owed him before Chodos ducked into bankruptcy, if he ever collects, is about $60,000; he lost $150,000. Chodos gained – by paying $100,000 instead of $386,000 – $286,000, and he is getting rid of the $100,000 by paying the man whom he so grievously wronged less than he pays his gardener.

Now, that's the modern way to use bankruptcy.

Under the Canadian bankruptcy process, the creditors recover, on the average, between two and four cents out of every dollar originally owed. Now there's a figure to contemplate. The trustees in bankruptcy recover about twenty-six cents of every dollar claimed by creditors, on the creditors' behalf, but twenty-two to twenty-four cents of that disappears in the process of collecting and administering the bankrupt estate. [13] What the creditor gets is four cents, or less. You go into bankruptcy owing $100,000, you emerge owing nothing, and the people you borrowed from get $4,000 to share around. If you really want to damage someone, get him to lend you a lot of money, and then go belly up. You will nail the sucker.

I don't mean that bankruptcy as a process is entirely beneficial; it hurts some people, such as working stiffs who lose some of their wages when their employer dives for shelter, plumbers and other subcontractors who can't collect when fly-by-night developers disappear over the horizon with their back pockets bulging, and, of course, the creditors. But for every loser, there is a winner. And his lawyer.

Insolvency law teaches us many lessons, but the greatest of these is the one propounded decades ago by Bob Edwards in the Calgary *Eye-Opener*; he wrote, "Bankruptcy is when you put your money in your hip pocket and let your creditors take your coat."[14] Or, to put it another way, bankruptcy is the game in which cheaters ever prosper. Financial failure is something that can happen to anyone, but going for broke – forging ahead regardless of the consequences to others, or, worse, deliberately engineering a bankruptcy in order to gain thereby – happens most often to the supremely greedy, superbly stupid, wilfully arrogant, or monumentally crooked. Our courts treat them all about the same. Indeed, under North American bankruptcy law today, the man who takes these things seriously, who worries about his creditors, feels shame over his debts, struggles with anything like persistence against the obligations he took on, that man is no more nor less than a sucker.

Take Bernie Cornfeld; he was no sucker. Bernie was the Swiss-based American guru who set up an international mutual-fund poker game called the Fund of Funds, which asked the musical question "Do you sincerely want to be rich?" and then proceeded to pick the pockets of most of those who sincerely answered in the affirmative. Bernie incorporated three of his companies in Canada, because he had noticed a certain playful looseness in our approach to these matters, and he, at least, became rich. When his mutual-fund scheme, which was essentially a pyramid game, finally collapsed, and most of the companies went bankrupt, Bernie was grabbed by the authorities in Switzerland, who do not share our broad and flexible outlook, and spent eleven months in jail before he was able to beat the rap. The charges against him were quashed on technical grounds, and he moved into the Los Angeles mansion that once belonged to Douglas Fairbanks, Jr., and opened a chain of health-food stores.[15] His sidekick, Robert Vesco, who managed to slip away from the wreckage with $225 million, was, when last heard from, bouncing around the Caribbean somewhere and not seeking interviews with the press. His other sidekick, Norman LeBlanc, Montreal's gift to the world of accounting, is now an adviser to what the *Financial Post*, always a humorous newspaper, described as "some rich but unidentified Costa Rican businessmen."[16]

But, you ask yourself, are these bozos really happy? Oh, my, yes. Why shouldn't they be?

What I am getting at is that the way the bankruptcy system operates contains some flaws. All too often it rewards the crooked and penalizes the trusting; it shelters the extravagant and plunders the innocent; it wreaks fearful havoc with anyone naïve enough to want to pay off his accumulated debts, and turns loose the skiptrace and scofflaw with a cheerful wave and a pat on the back. More and worse, this state of affairs appears to be just what the framers of our laws intended. It isn't that the system doesn't work, but that it does, that causes the damage. In his judgment in the case of Michael Chodos, Mr. Justice Lane went to great pains to show that he was merely following the precedents in Canadian law. The reaming of Soel Szarfer and the rewarding of Chodos were just part of the system.

Bankruptcy, which was once a plunge into ruin, despair, and even slavery, gradually became less onerous, until, in our own day, it has often become first an escape hatch, then a haven. What was a disgrace is now, in many cases, a saving grace. In the United States, the process has gone one step further; bankruptcy has become a gold mine. In Canada, we have not yet reached the gold-mine stage; in this country, going broke is somewhere between a serious hindrance and a blessing. However, for the rich corporation, it can be the stoutest shield of all. Canadian corporations are likely to push it further, in the direction taken by the Americans, for the obvious reason that, nowadays, a corporation in bankruptcy protection has great advantages over one not so shielded. Among other things, all interest payments are suspended, along with any civil tort lawsuits directed at the company for killing, maiming, or otherwise inconveniencing the general public. There is also the lure of globalization, or free trade; if we do not give our corporations the same advantages that our competitors in the United States have, the argument goes, they cannot compete in the global marketplace. Perfectly true, too; it is part of the larger thesis that whatever the Americans do, however dim-witted, immoral, or scummy, we must imitate, or perish.

The tool of choice in the United States is Chapter 11 of the Bankruptcy Code, but we already have our own version of Chapter 11, the Companies' Creditors Arrangement Act, available only to large corporations, like Olympia & York Developments Ltd. of Toronto, which used it to transfer billions of dollars in debt to others less deserving, namely the shareholders of Canada's large banks. They, in turn, passed it on to the rest of us in various ways, including increased service charges. In Canada, the new Bankruptcy and Insolvency Act (BIA), which came into force in late 1992, is a distinct improvement over the old one, as far as personal bankruptcies go, but it does not touch the main issue, which is the way in which, as *U.S. News & World Report* noted in an awestruck headline, "IT PAYS TO GO BROKE."[17]

The crucial, revolutionary change came when the American Bankruptcy Act was rewritten in 1978 (the new version was called the Bankruptcy Reform Act, which is a little like calling acid rain "clean-air modification"). The new law cleared the way for Chapter 11, the section of the act covering corporate bankruptcies, to be turned into a kind of superfund for megacorporations.

The best wrinkle of all in the reform was that it dropped the need to show that you were insolvent in order to seek bankruptcy protection. Companies with billions in the bank could, and did, creep into shelter by claiming that they might, sometime in the future, run into trouble. And then they could take advantage of the shelter to stiff their creditors, before emerging, shed of debt.

The new American act even dropped the word "bankrupt" to describe those who had become insolvent; they were now merely "debtors." Hell, we're all debtors; that's no disgrace. Under this legislation, special bankruptcy courts were established, where, until then, the regular courts had dealt with the subject. We must not say that many of the bankruptcy judges wound up in the pockets of global corporations; we merely note that quite a few of these judges seem to have lint in their ears. This change, by the way, was in clear violation of the U.S. constitution. (These judges would become, in practice, full federal-court judges under Article 111 of the constitution, without meeting the other criteria for such appointments.) So what the courts did was simply to stall a legal challenge to the amendment until Congress could shove through another amendment to bring the law onside.

We have not followed the United States this far along the trail, but we are getting there. Rick Orzy, of the legal firm McCarthy Tétrault, one of the nation's most-respected bankruptcy practitioners, tells an illuminating story about a recent conference of bankruptcy specialists in the United States. An American lawyer read out a newspaper editorial that complained that the law worked to the great advantage of debtors and against lenders. Then, to appreciative chuckles, he read the date on the editorial – well back in the eighteenth century. The speaker's point was that "in this country, the law has always been debtor-friendly." Orzy recalls thinking, "Yes, but that's the American tradition, the American background. Our philosophy has been quite different. Why are we making the Canadian system over to follow the American one?"

The answer to this crucial question appears to be "because that is the kind of nation we are becoming." We are moving more and more towards the American kind of two-tiered medical practice, with one system for the rich and another for the rest, although it is the most unjust and unworkable in the advanced world. We are bending ourselves into pretzels to meet the demands laid on us by the Free Trade Agreement and the North American Free Trade Agreement, whose advantages seem to accrue to megacorporations and whose disadvantages fall on the rest of us. We seem to operate on a national premise that, if the Americans have it, we want it, and that if we don't give our corporations what their corporations get, they will walk away and incorporate elsewhere. There is enough rough truth in this last supposition to make anyone who contemplates the riches the huge companies can reap through Chapter 11 worry that this is the way we will go, whether it makes sense or not. There is also a good deal of evidence, as we will see in Chapter Five, that our judges are beginning to work to the same rules, or absence of rules, as American judges, with many of the same results.

There was a provision in our 1992 reform of the law that, after three years – that is in late 1995 – the whole issue would be returned to a parliamentary committee to study what has happened, and what changes should be made as a result. This process will, going by the past record, take a few years. Obviously, then, this is a good time to review the legislation, measure what we have, and see what might be done by way of improvement before our bankruptcy law is set in concrete. It took more than twenty years to work through the last set of reforms; what we do in the next couple of years will set the business and financial agenda for this nation for the foreseeable future. We ought not to go ahead without some understanding of where we are, and how we got here, and what lies ahead. Because, as in so many matters, we appear to be following the Americans in our approach to bankruptcy, we will gain some illumination of our subject by looking at developments below the border, and trembling.

The glaring fact that leaps out at any student of this subject, besides the tiny amount of money that is gleaned from the bankruptcy process (four cents on the dollar, forsooth, I can't get over that), is the wondrous way our corporations and individuals have learned to play the system like a zither. Under modern bankruptcy law, debtors in Canada and the United States have recently gone belly up, not for the obvious and usual rationale – to shed unbearable debt – but for what might be called the Dozen Dandy Reasons to Go for Broke:

1. **To void union contracts.** Wilson Foods, the first to follow this route, went into Chapter 11, cancelled its collective agreement, cut wages by 40 to 50 per cent, and emerged a year later with no union and fat profits. Management then voted itself raises of 36 per cent. Wilson was the largest pork processor in the United States when it pulled this trick and showed no signs of being in serious financial difficulty.[18]

2. **To cut costs and cheat suppliers.** Once in bankruptcy, a company is freed of the obligation to pay for goods it has already received and can even cancel contracts and leases it doesn't like and renegotiate them downwards. Suppliers may be paid off, years later, at a few cents

on the dollar, while the bankrupt firm emerges to pile up profits. You might think that, in these circumstances, the suppliers would just stop shipping when a firm declares bankruptcy, but they would be foolish to do so. Debts incurred during bankruptcy have priority in payment, so suppliers are better protected when they sell to a ward of the court than to a company outside of bankruptcy; they may not get paid on the old goods, but they will on the new. That is why Federated Stores, owned by Robert Campeau, was able to keep goods on the shelves long after he had shoved it into insolvency.[19]

3. **To frustrate a legal obligation.** In light of the Chodos case, I cannot imagine why any Canadian who loses a large lawsuit would ever pay it off in full, or even attempt to. Simply stall, then go bankrupt, and walk away smiling. The case is not unique. In another instance, a Toronto truck driver got into an argument with another driver over a parking space at a mall, and beat the other driver so badly that he was hospitalized. The victim launched a civil suit for assault against the truck driver and his employer, and won a decision of about $300,000. The driver went into personal bankruptcy and avoided payment, although his company was forced to pay part of the settlement. In due course, he was discharged and free to start again, clear of all debts. These are the rules. If you lose a lawsuit, dive into shelter and let somebody else pay.

4. **To void a lease.** A company in bankruptcy protection can get out of a long-term lease by paying a penalty of six months' rent – even if the lease runs for twenty-five years. More and more retailers are using this provision to whipsaw landlords into renegotiating their leases downwards. If the landlord doesn't like it, the tenant can just nip into bankruptcy and pay nothing.

5. **To block lawsuits.** One of the provisions of the Olympia & York Developments Ltd. restructuring – and it is the case in almost every large bankruptcy – was the voiding of all lawsuits against the Reichmann brothers of Toronto, who owned the company, or against Olympia & York, for all their previous actions.[20] Not ruination, but absolution.

6. To escape the costs of having killed or maimed thousands of people. Two of the key cases in this category, those involving the Dalkon Shield, the intrauterine contraceptive, and asbestos, will be dealt with in much greater detail. In brief, in each case, a giant corporation put itself into bankruptcy to shed thousands of liability lawsuits and emerged hundreds of millions of dollars richer. The victims all over the world, on the other hand, are still suffering and dying.

7. To gain market advantage. Companies in protection don't have to pay interest on unsecured loans. At the same time, banks will advance them money, because, as with suppliers, this repayment comes out of the cash flow ahead of earlier debts. In 1990, Eastern Airlines, using this protection, was able to slash its airfares and, in turn, plunged Midway Airlines into insolvency, as it tried to keep up.[21]

8. As a negotiating tactic. Texaco Inc. was nailed by a Texas jury for its illegal interference in the sale of Getty Oil Company to Pennzoil Company. Pennzoil had made an offer to buy Getty, which was accepted, then revoked after Texaco came up with another offer. Pennzoil sued, and won. The award was for $7.3 billion in actual damages and $3 billion in punitive damages.[22] When it lost its appeal of this mammoth award, Texaco went into bankruptcy and remained there for eight months. The chairman of Pennzoil, J. Hugh Liedtke, likened this to the occasion when his daughter threatened to hold her breath until she got her way.[23] But it worked. Pennzoil was blocked from enforcing the judgment, while Texaco was freed of interest charges while it was in hiding and continued its operations without change. It saved about $1 billion in cancelled stock dividends and unpaid interest charges. Pennzoil, faced with years of waiting and, perhaps, never collecting anything, settled for $3 billion, and Texaco emerged from bankruptcy. It had never, incidentally, disputed the $7.3 billion in actual damages, just the punitive award. Texaco gained somewhere in the neighbourhood of $5 billion by going into Chapter 11; in addition, it was allowed to retain ownership of Getty Oil, the object of the exercise. Part of the fallout of this case was the sale of all Texaco stations in Canada to raise cash.

9. To fend off an unwanted suitor. A company in protection cannot be taken over without the permission of the supervising court, and the supervising court nearly always follows the wishes of the present management, so one way for the company bosses to keep their jobs when a hostile takeover threatens is simply to plunge the company into bankruptcy. The costs will be borne elsewhere.

10. To get a tax break. One effect of the Johns–Manville bankruptcy was to give the re-emerging company, the Manville Corporation, an immediate $100-million U.S. tax refund and a tax shelter of more than $700 million, since the law allowed the company to show an accounting loss of $700 million plus for a single year,[24] creating a huge paper loss, even though the money was to be paid out over a period of years. The shelter could be, and has been, applied to future Manville Corporation profits. The company is doing very well, thank you. The taxpayer, not so well.

11. To shuck off environmental costs. Galactic Resources Ltd. owned a moribund gold mine in Summitville, Colorado. Starting in 1986, the company raised $200 million by the aggressive promotion of an untried mining methodology, which, as a matter of fact, did not work very well. When leaks from cyanide-containment barriers began to destroy the countryside around, the environmental authorities wanted Galactic to clean up the mess. Instead, in 1992, the company went bankrupt and abandoned the mine site. The Environmental Protection Agency took over and has been spending $40,000 a day on the cleanup. The total cost will come to $100 million or more.[25] None of it will be paid by the people who made the decisions that led to this disaster.

It is not clear whether a Canadian company can get rid of the costs of damaging the environment by going belly up; in Alberta at least, it cannot. When Northern Badger Oil and Gas Ltd. went bankrupt in 1987, the provincial Energy Resources Conservation Board ordered the receiver to clean up seven wells, at a cost of $200,000, before paying off the secured creditors, for the very good reason that there would be nothing left in the estate for the cleanup if they were paid first. A debenture-holder went to court to get the money instead, and won. The court held that "the protection of the secured creditor was not to be lost because of the Board's order." [26] In effect, the Bankruptcy Act had to be followed before provincial environmental legislation.

However, the environmental authority appealed, and the Alberta Court of Appeal held that the board had "wide powers to ensure environmentally safe operations, including abandonment of wells." [27] The court noted that it was hard to reconcile this duty with the provisions of the bankruptcy law, which gives the secured creditor precedence, but "this did not amount to a subversion of the scheme devised by Parliament for the distribution of the assets in a bankruptcy." Sooner or later, the Supreme Court will have to sort this one out, and then we'll know whether our law is more progressive than American law.

12. **To protect illegal gains.** Edward Carter, a Vancouver-based stock-scam artist who made $9.5 million by bilking a mutual fund, avoided having to repay the money after he was convicted of stock manipulation by declaring bankruptcy, while maintaining memberships in two Vancouver clubs, owning a condominium in Florida, and spending $4,500 on tickets to Blue Jays baseball games. His Toronto house is in his wife's name and safe from seizure. He once had $5 million in an RRSP, but it disappeared. He had a bank account in the Bahamas in the aptly named Hideaway Trust, with $1.8 million in it, but that, too, mysteriously vanished. He was ordered to pay $3 million in compensation, but the bankruptcy made the order unenforceable. [28]

There are still those foolish enough, tender enough, honest enough, to shy away from bankruptcy, especially at the personal level, but the really clever, with-it movers and shakers of our society have come to recognize that going belly up, especially if you happen to be a large and ruthless multinational corporation, can be a positive blessing.

The implications of the change in bankruptcy law are not merely a matter of sociological interest. Canadians and Americans pay billions of dollars every year, directly and indirectly, not merely to keep the whole system creaking along, but in tax benefits to the corporations that have gone broke and to the creditors who loaned them the money. In all the Canadian bankruptcy cases closed in 1993, creditors registered valid claims of $6.6 billion and received $147 million, or just over two cents on the dollar out of the estates;[29] the difference of over $6 billion represented potential tax write-offs to the lenders of – depending on their tax brackets – anywhere up to $3 billion. Send not to ask for whom the bill tolled; in the cases of the Principal Group, the Canadian Commercial Bank, the BCCI, Johns–Manville, or Texaco, it tolled for the taxpayer.

In addition, the costs of all these failures are transferred, by the lending system, over to the innocents. On the heels of the O&Y débâcle, small-business loans were cut sharply, and Canadian banks hoisted their service charges to replace the billions that went glimmering during that escapade. It is an inescapable fact that the creditors have to make up their losses by charging them to the customers who do pay their bills; they have no other source to tap.

The purpose of this book is to look at how we got ourselves into this fix, to examine some of the most illuminating – and disturbing – examples on the record, to consider the differences and characteristics of personal and corporate bankruptcy, to compare the Canadian and American systems, and to discuss what, if anything, we can do about what might be called the ruination of the ruination business, while we still have time to fix it.

CHAPTER TWO

The Broken Bench

"If a man owes you money, and he is unable to pay, do not pass before him." – *Haggadah*, Palestinian Talmud, 4th century

$

We are in Venice, in the latter part of the eighth century, in the marketplace. Around us there are the stalls of farmers, vendors, and artisans selling their wares. Suddenly, the busy bustle of commerce is overlaid by the deeper, uglier sound of angry shouts and stamping feet, as a milling mob of merchants descends on the small stand operated by Luigi, the bootmaker. Luigi is deep in debt; he has obtained hides, and tools, and laces, and even food, on credit from the other marketers around him, but, due to a temporary recession, no doubt brought on by free trade with Florence, he has been unable to sell the excellent footwear he turns out at his little workbench. The outraged creditors swarm into Luigi's stall, seize the implements of his craft, round up and bear away his supply of hides, tanning materials, and dye, and, to mark their displeasure, destroy his workbench before his very eyes. Seems a little rough. I mean, the poor sap has enough troubles, right? And along come these goons and express themselves in a violent manner.

But you have to see it from their point of view, too. They strongly suspect that the reason he can't pay them is not due to a falloff in business, but because he has been socking the proceeds away safely somewhere. Moreover, they have been through other incidents in which the forlorn bootmaker, sobbing out his grief because he has not been able to discharge his honourable obligations, and is therefore forced to make them swallow the loss, has bobbed up, soon after, a few miles away, with a smile on his face and a sockful of cash.

So it is with no regrets and much vigour that they take their axes to Luigi's workbench, rendering him, in a phrase of his time that will become familiar to our time, a *bankarupta*, or "broken bench."

Although the word "bankrupt" developed this way in medieval Italy, the concept, and the legal instruments to sort out disputes between debtors and creditors, have been with us since Roman times. They were, until recently, rude and crude. Under early Roman law, a creditor who could establish that his debtor was unable to pay was allowed to seize the debtor and put him into chains for sixty days, pending payment. If that was not forthcoming, he could sell the poor sod into slavery, and keep the proceeds, or put him to death.[1] There may be modern creditors who look on this period as the good old days. Much later, the law was amended, so that the borrower who could prove that his inability to pay was due, as we say, to "circumstances beyond his control," was able to avoid execution by surrendering all his assets to his creditors. The dishonest debtor still got the chop.

The early Roman approach embodied a concept that lasted from at least the fourth century B.C. until well into our own century: the notion that the person who had contracted obligations which he could not meet was not merely a financial failure, but a criminal who should be punished. He could be discharged from his disgraceful condition, and returned to his workbench, only after his debts had been paid and he had been subjected to personal humiliation.

There was a built-in difficulty to this approach, of course, for, once Luigi had been deprived of his workbench, he could no longer make boots. No boots, no money, and no way to pay off his creditors. It seems that they didn't much care, or, if they cared, the pleasure of making Luigi suffer for stinging them outweighed the pain of realizing that they had now deprived him of the only means by which he could make right his financial deficiencies.

For the next eleven hundred years, things did not change much in this line; lenders tended to take it out of the hides of borrowers when they couldn't pay up, by seizing their goods, or their persons, or both. Of course, if the borrower was too big, or, say, too royal, for this treatment to work, it was hard to apply. For centuries, the kings of England, France, and Spain made a habit of getting money from Jewish bankers, since Christian doctrine forbade the extraction of interest as being unclean and ungodly, right up until the time when capitalism came into its own, at which point it became as clean and godly as all get out. (Deuteronomy 23: 19-20 prohibits taking interest from any person, but explicitly allows the lender to take interest from a foreigner. Ezekiel 18:13 lists the taking of interest as one of the sins worthy of death, and leaves no loophole for foreigners. One presumes that the really godly don't collect on their GICs.) In the meantime, it was the Jews who loaned the money that allowed the royals to hire the mercenaries to go out and hack up the peasants on the other side, for the glory of it all.

Every now and then, fed up with paying interest, the royals would resolve to curb the deficit, but they did it in a more straightforward manner than the rulers of today. They would suddenly discover that interest was ungodly again, call in the preachers, mount a religious crusade, cancel all their debts in the name of Christ, and rouse out the mob to murder a few hundred, or a few thousand, Jews. Henry III of England tried to get a handle on things by passing a law that limited the interest that could be charged to two pence per pound per week.[2] That works out at 43 per cent per annum and shows what high rates the lenders felt they had to charge against the day when their business would come to an abrupt halt. Henry's son, Edward I, who inherited his father's debts and disposition, expelled all Jews from England in 1290, thus wiping out his debts.[3] He also seized all their estates, so that he would have had the money to pay them if they hadn't taken off like that. The Lombards, papal bankers and wool exporters, took the place of the Jews as royal creditors;[4] they were made to herd together on Lombard Street in London, still a centre of finance. As a means of curbing the deficit, croaking your creditors beat the GST hollow, although it tended to make the lenders a trifle shy next time out. On the other hand, it avoided the perils of bankruptcy, at least for the king.

Commerce became more sophisticated with the passage of time; Christianity embraced capitalism, including its dependence on finance and interest, and paper money, bills, bonds, and share certificates replaced barter trade – not just for the upper crust, but for the emerging middle class, as well. Debt and credit became matters that affected a much wider segment of society, and there was a need to establish some method to allow creditors to collect on a wider and more regulated level than just hiring a mob or buckling on your personal sword.

The first law dealing with debtor default was passed during the reign of Henry VIII, An Act Against Such Persons As Do Make Bankrupt. It provided that, once the debtor was shown to be insolvent, all his property was delivered up to the sheriff, sold, and the proceeds distributed among his creditors. Then, he was discharged from his debts, even if they weren't all paid. This act of 1542 was amended, in 1571, to limit the right to bankruptcy to "persons engaged in trade"; all others were subject to imprisonment until friends or relatives satisfied the creditors' claims.[5]

This was the beginning of the debtor's prison. You got the authorities to bung the bankrupt into jail. Even if you never collected, you had the pleasure of knowing that the son-of-a-gun was suffering for his sins. A free vote of some of the former investors in, say, the Principal Group of companies, might conclude that a small spell in the slammer would do a world of good for Donald Cormie, founder of that conglomerate, in place of the nice time he appears to be having at his mansion in Arizona. But we know better; we know that the moral satisfaction associated with the debtor's prison was no compensation for the damage done, not only to the person who racked up the bills, but to society as a whole.

The road to debtor's prison followed one of two familiar routes, whether in England, the United States, or Canada. In the first, a creditor demanded payment of an overdue debt, and, when he could not collect, he filed a lawsuit. If the trial court upheld the demand, it issued a judgment, providing for the seizure and sale of the debtor's assets. If the defaulter could not discharge the debt even after all his goods and real estate were sold, he was slung into jail on a writ of execution and left there until he could.[6] The difficulty with this approach, from the lender's point of view, was that the debtor might do a midnight flit before the bailiffs came to call. We have not really solved this problem to this day, and it was much more difficult in the seventeenth and eighteenth centuries, because the court before which you had to haul the debtor might not meet in your particular area for some months. It gave the rascal too much time to pack his bags.

In Britain, where our commercial law arose, our ancestors had a stab at blocking the midnight flit through the second approach to debtor's prison, a process called *mesne*, a term from ancient French, meaning "intervening." The creditor got the sheriff to intervene by complaining to a court official either that a debt was overdue or that the debtor intended to abscond. The court then directed the sheriff to seize the debtor, and, if a subsequent trial proved the claim against him, he was sent to jail until he paid the money. By common law, the creditor could, under this procedure, seize either the debtor or his property, not both. The presumption, which often turned out to be mistaken, was that the debtor would give up his estate to secure his freedom.

In the late seventeenth and early eighteenth centuries, the laws were changed to allow an insolvent merchant or trader to surrender himself to the court for examination on his obligations and deliver up his property to his creditors, rather than waiting for them to take action against him. The property would be sold, and the money split among the creditors, in proportion to the debt owed. Once this was done, the debtor would be granted a discharge, provided he had not committed any fraud or attempted to conceal any assets, in which case he would be hanged.[7]

The granting of a discharge before all the debts were paid was a solution that only applied to a merchant or trader. For the general run of debtors, there was no bankruptcy and no discharge; if found insolvent, they were jailed. The bankruptcy law was not extended to cover general debtors until well into the nineteenth century. Moreover, for these people, the process worked backwards. Where a merchant could approach the court and ask for an examination, the ordinary debtor could not; he had to wait until he was petitioned into bankruptcy. Then, he would be imprisoned, and his goods surrendered to a court of bankruptcy, which would distribute them to the creditors. But if there were few or no assets, there was no relief. The rule was: reimburse or rot. Or, in the words of Justice Sir Robert Hyde in the mideighteenth century:

> If a man be taken in execution, and lie in prison for debt, neither the plaintiff, at whose suit he is arrested, nor the sheriff who took him, is bound to find him meat, drink or clothes; but he must live on his own, or on the charity of others; and if no man will relieve him, let him die in the name of God, says the law; and so say I.[8]

A tough baby, Robert Hyde. The debtor who died in prison was buried in a pauper's grave, and that was the end of the matter. Well, it was rather hard to lure out the credit on which all great enterprises are founded, when the price of failure lay in the debtor's prison and the pauper's grave. Credit, as they say, is the lifeblood of commerce, but few people were actually willing to bleed for it. Two solutions were found: the first was the development of methods to share the risks, the second was a change in the attitude towards and treatment of, debtors in general.

On the first count, business developed the joint-stock company, and then the limited corporation, as the principal means of financing commerce. Joint-stock ventures, such as the Company of Adventurers into Hudson's Bay, pooled the resources of a number of partners, who each put up some of the money required for a trading voyage, or other enterprise, and shared in the proceeds according to their share in the risk. This was a huge advantage over the single merchant or partnership approach, but it still carried the danger that, if the venture failed and lost more than was originally invested, any creditor could take action against any of the joint-stock owners for the entire amount of the debt. If the company owed a million pounds, the whole amount might be demanded from someone who had originally invested ten pounds in a stock certificate. This meant that only the very rich could participate in these emerging corporations. The middle class that was being thrown up by the Industrial Revolution would never invest in someone else's business. Would you buy into the Bank of Montreal if you faced the prospect of having your house sold out from under you because of the money it loaned Olympia & York?

This gap was closed with the invention of limited liability, in 1855.[9] Creditors could no longer come after each and every one of the owners of an enterprise to collect money owed; their liability was limited to the amount they had invested in the first place, the amount they had used to buy shares.

The second solution to promoting credit was a gradual change in the treatment of those imprisoned for debt, as it became clear that the process simply didn't work. For one thing, more and more debtors opted to protect their assets, when seized under the *mesne* process, by simply remaining in jail. The creditor, when he realized that he had nothing to gain except, perhaps, malicious satisfaction, would withdraw his complaint in return for a partial payment or even the promise of payment. There was also the problem that the debtor's dependents were thrown upon charity, friends, or the public purse. At the same time, the community was deprived of the debtor's work. It did not do the creditor much good to have the children of his debtor consigned to the work house, and it might even cost him money, by way of local rates.

Accordingly, borrowing from Roman law, the British began to allow some categories of debtors, usually single men and women who owed less than a certain amount, to substitute indentured service for imprisonment. At least the creditor got something out of it. Again, some petty debtors were released on taking an oath that they were indeed impoverished; this did not provide any money for the creditor, but, like the modern computer-based record of bankruptcies, provided a warning to the general public, and other potential lenders, that this person was a poor credit risk. Finally, certain assets, such as tools, eating utensils, bedding, furniture, and clothing, were put beyond the reach of the creditor.[10] This was not because of a sudden softheartedness on the part of the owning classes, but to prevent the total impoverishment that would throw the expense of caring for the debtor's family onto the community.

Of course the larger debtor was not helped by any of these changes; his debts were too large to be worked off by indentured labour, he would not be forgiven simply because he took a poor debtor's oath, and a handful of tools, or a bed, wouldn't solve his problems, either. Indeed, the large debtor was in a bind. As soon as word got out that he was in difficulty, there would be a rush to the courthouse by his creditors, each of whom wanted to seize as much of his assets as possible before the others turned up with their claims. This was so manifestly unfair that, in 1869, a revised Bankruptcy Act in Britain established a new method for distributing the assets among the creditors. Instead of the court taking on the job, a trustee was appointed to take over the debtor's estate and to administer the liquidation and distribution of the assets. The trustee was supervised by a committee elected by the general body of creditors. Unfortunately, this system did not work too well, because it led to endless battles over who got how much, and a modification was introduced in which the control was shared by creditors and court officials.

The 1869 act also abolished imprisonment for debt, except where a person with assets wilfully refused to turn them over, in which case he was jailed for contempt of court. The effect was to continue imprisonment for debt under a different guise, because debtors were often put in, or kept in, jail on contempt charges based on little more than a creditor's complaint that he hadn't been paid, and therefore the debtor must have hidden the loot. For thirty years, these prisoners were sent to the first division of the British penal system, where they were exempt from hard labour and lived in relatively greater comfort.[11] However, in 1899, parliament changed its mind again, and lumped all prisoners together, although debtors were allowed to wear their own clothes rather than prison garb, if it was "sufficient and suitable."[12]

For all the fiddling around the edges, the fundamental assumption of the law had not changed from Roman times; poverty was a crime, and, especially, being in debt was a crime.

The Americans started with British law, but gradually moved in their own direction. The development of the hinterlands required men to take great risks, including financial risks; moreover, in such a growing and turbulent society, the midnight flit was rather easier to execute than it was in downtown London. Finally, the American colonies were far more diverse, and far less subservient, than either the British or their colonists in Canada, and, as a result, there was a far wider range of laws among the American provinces, or, as they became after the Revolution, states. For one thing, in many of the more conservative states, imprisonment for debt did not even begin to be abolished in law – although it had faded in practice – until 1922, while other states had a liberal approach to creditor and debtor rights from the beginning.

Many of the American colonies extended relief to all insolvent debtors, not just merchants and traders, as far back as the early eighteenth century.[13] The defaulter petitioned the legislature, or the courts, with an offer to exchange his assets for a discharge from jail and protection against arrest for the same debts. In some colonies, all creditors had to accept this proposal for it to become binding; in others, once a given proportion of the lenders – usually one-half to three-quarters – accepted, the arrangement applied to all of them, and a trustee took over the assets, liquidated them, and divided the take, in the form of a dividend, to all qualified creditors, according to the size of each claim. The debtor might be out of prison, but he was not clear of the debt, in most colonies. He could only be discharged as a bankrupt when all the amounts owing were paid.

By and large, as in England, only traders and merchants could gain relief from debtor's prison via bankruptcy, although Rhode Island allowed any insolvent, male or female, merchant, trader, farmer, shopkeeper, or labourer, to apply for relief. [14]

A major difference between American and British practice was that in most colonies, it was the debtor, rather than the creditor, who could initiate the action. In Britain, most bankruptcies were involuntary – the lender hauled the borrower before the authorities and began the process, because payments had stopped, or because he thought the debtor was in danger of becoming insolvent, or was concealing assets, or was about to abscond. Furthermore, once bankruptcy had begun, only the creditor could begin the process of discharge.

These rules didn't work too well on the frontier. Many insolvencies were caused when a highly dependent, staple-oriented economy was ravaged by crop failures, wars, or political or economic crises that disrupted trade. No one was to blame, despite the tenor of the law. In the second place, in a scattered society, the first creditor to the courthouse could seize all the assets before anyone else could even get a claim in; this favoured local creditors at the expense of those further away and discouraged lending from the centre to the outlying areas, where it was most needed. In Canada, it may be argued, this lesson has never been learned.

It was also hoped that allowing the debtor to act would reduce the incidence of fraud; if he came forward before he was entirely wiped out, he might be able to save something from the wreckage. The alternative was to try to conceal assets or simply to disappear.

For the most part, as in England, the general thrust of the law was to punish the debtor for his insolvency and to refuse to discharge him from his obligations until all the money was returned. The general belief was that any relief given to debtors would only encourage extravagance and undermine the fabric of the nation. Lawyers, who made a good part of their incomes as debt-collectors, were in the vanguard of every attempt to block reform. Insolvency was wickedness, however caused, they stressed, and we must not reward the wicked by allowing them to escape their obligations, or they will only go out and do it again, with the consequent ruination of society – to say nothing of walloping the rich, whom God has ordained to rule over us. This perverse logic, like so much that is given us by our communal leaders, and especially our lawyers, was able to withstand the evidence that punishing honest debtors did not in fact bring money shoaling out of the ground to pay back the creditors; it only made matters worse for debtor and creditor alike.

However, until well into this century, the assumption underlying the law in Britain, the United States, and Canada was that bankruptcy should not be an escape hatch through which the debtor could slip; he would have to work his way out by paying back the money.

In general, Canada followed British law, although there was one period during which the Province of Canada, before Confederation, seemed to lean more in the direction the Americans had taken. An Act to Provide for the Relief of Bankrupts and the Administration of Their Estates, passed by the legislative assembly of the Province of Canada in 1851, did allow a debtor – provided he was a merchant or trader – to file a declaration that he was "unable to meet his engagements."[15] This was a voluntary bankruptcy. He could also make a deal with his creditors, what would today be called a "proposal." However, the main ground of bankruptcy was this one: "Every such trader who shall be arrested by the *mesne* process . . . shall be deemed to have thereby committed an act of bankruptcy."[16] This 1851 law also provided for the discharge of the bankrupt "after he had made full disclosure and delivery of all his estate and holdings." Clearly, the law only envisioned personal bankruptcies, and the whole process came unstuck if the rascal had lost at gambling. There would be no discharge "if such bankrupt shall have lost, by any sort of gaming or wagering, in one day twenty pounds" within the year preceding the insolvency.[17] This quaint act, more liberal than the British law, was blamed by contemporary writers for spreading ruin, because traders were allowed to weasel out from under their debts without suffering imprisonment. The law was wiped out by Confederation, in 1867.

While the British North America Act gave the federal government jurisdiction over bankruptcy, it gave control over property rights to the provinces, with consequent confusion all around. The courts compromised by looking to British practice as a guide. The Insolvent Act of 1869 applied only to traders and included both voluntary assignment and compulsory liquidation, but in 1875, a new act wiped out this provision and bankruptcy became, as in England, enforceable only by the compulsion of a creditor. The creditors were pleased; a contemporary pamphlet noted, "The mercantile community of this Dominion may well congratulate themselves that this enactment, ruinous to their honourable reputation as a class, as well as in a pecuniary point of view, has been repealed."[18]

Any single creditor owed $500 or more could petition the debtor into bankruptcy on the grounds of his "absconding, secreting, fraudulently assigning or procuring execution, being imprisoned in a civil action, refusing to appear for examination as to his debts," allowing any judgment against him to be unsatisfied for fifteen days, or "having acknowledged his insolvency."[19]

There was no substantive change in Canada until the passage of the Bankruptcy Act of 1919, by which time, a whole new commercial phenomenon had come to dominate business.

Yes, but what if the debtor was not a person, but a corporation? Since 1855, limited liability had given us a whole new class of persons – for that is what the corporation is, in law – who could not be hoisted into the hoosegow for non-payment of debt, or even for contempt of court. If it is true, as a British judge once complained, that "a corporation has no soul to be damned, and no body to be kicked,"[20] it is also true that it has no *corpus* to haul off to jail. You could suspend it, but you couldn't jug it.

When a creditor moved against a company, seizing the assets, the first thing that happened was that it could no longer operate. If you folded up the firm, the assets were usually sold for much less than they were worth. The grand prices at bankruptcy sales are not particular to our time. The creditors, who were very often other companies, might realize very little out of this process and might, indeed, go broke themselves while trying to collect. It might be better, in the long run, to try to keep the company going, bringing in cash, and to use that cash to pay off at least some of the debt.

Now, this would not work unless the insolvent firm's owners or managers, or both, could see a way out. They were not going to work themselves to the bone just to pay back the money to somebody else. Bankruptcy had to carry with it the promise of release. It took a few decades to work that one out, but we finally got it. And, once the application to companies became clear, and the value of the process became obvious, the same logic was slowly applied to personal bankruptcies, as well. It was the development of the corporation, not a sudden avalanche of amiability, that began to take the punitive sting out of bankruptcy.

Along with the development of the corporation came the growth of a body of rules to distinguish between secured and unsecured debts, a distinction which remains crucial, not merely in bankruptcy law, but in the whole area of creditors' and debtors' rights. A secured debt is one which is backed by a particular asset or assets. A mortgage on a home, for example, is a secured debt; so is a corporate bond, when it is backed by a particular asset in the corporation. A lien, pledge, charge, or privilege written against the property of the debtor, whether a person or a corporation, is a secured debt.[21] The secured creditor does not have to put the debtor into bankruptcy to collect. If you have a mortgage and fail to pay your monthly amount, the bank, trust company, or other lender can force you to pay, if necessary by foreclosing, selling the property out from under you, and taking the cash from the proceeds – or by sending in a receiver to seize the assets covered by the security. Bankruptcy may or may not result from this action, but the lender, in effect, is simply realizing on the asset, as he is entitled to do. That was the deal you made when you signed the mortgage, lien, or bond.

The philosophy behind this arrangement is quite different from the pay-up-or-be-punished approach; when the debtor falls behind in payments, the asset may be seized and sold. If it realizes more than the debt, the difference goes to the borrower; otherwise, he or she may still be in debt to the extent of the shortfall, but this is a matter of equity, not punishment. The explosion of consumer lending in the fifties, sixties, and seventies was built on this approach – the car was security for the loan with which it was purchased – as was the huge edifice of bonds and debentures that supports the corporate structure. The company borrows money from a bank, another company, or the general public by issuing bonds. (A bond is a debt instrument bearing interest, and the principal is repaid at the time specified on the certificate. Usually, it is a specific debt, such as a mortgage bond, secured by the real property of the company. A debenture is a similar debt instrument, but backed by the integrity and name of the borrowing corporation, rather than by any specific asset.) Bonds are secured claims and, in the event of a failure, come ahead of all the unsecured debts, including debentures, by virtue of the ability of the creditor to insist on realizing on his security. Most importantly, the Canadian Bankruptcy and Insolvency Act (BIA) provides a temporary stay of proceedings to block all creditors with claims against the bankrupt (so they can't send in the bailiffs to seize the assets), but secured creditors are exempted from this stay after a series of deadlines have been passed (in the United States, matters are arranged quite differently; see Chapter Four).

However, people, and more especially companies, may have large outstanding debts that are not secured by any particular asset. Everyone who uses a credit card is an unsecured borrower from a bank or trust company, as is everyone (almost everyone) who has arranged for a standing overdraft on his or her bank account, but we are pikers in the borrowing line, when compared to corporations. They not only have a "line of credit" with one or more banks, they borrow vast amounts of money on what is called "commercial paper," in effect, the company's IOU, raised with a bank, a trust company, other corporations, or the general public. These loans are secured by the goodwill of the firm, sometimes on little more than a smile and a handshake. Olympia & York Developments Ltd., once the world's largest privately owned property company, managed to persuade banks all over the world to lend it billions of dollars, based on what turned out to be a misplaced trust in the company's ability to repay.

For the purpose of this discussion, the crucial point to fix on is that secured creditors are, in a general way, able to act outside the scope of the Bankruptcy and Insolvency Act; they can shake the tree at any time when the money is not forthcoming, or even when they have reason to believe it will not be forthcoming. It is the unsecured creditors who have to go to law to collect.

The gradual change in all these aspects of debtor and creditor relationships was reflected, with mind-numbing slowness, in the development of the legislation governing bankruptcy. Canada's bankruptcy law of 1919 began to reflect the realization that revenge might be sweet, but it did not pay the rent, and that honest debtors ought to be allowed to escape once the courts and their creditors were satisfied that they had made an honest effort to discharge their debts.[22] Bankrupts could also make a general assignment to creditors to escape liquidation – voluntary bankruptcy was back with us. However, this act dealt with business debts only, whether they were individual or corporate; consumer debt, in the modern sense of that word, was rare.

The 1919 act contained the usual rigorous injunctions against the midnight flit. "The court may, by warrant addressed to any constable . . . cause a debtor to be arrested" if there was probable reason for believing "that he has absconded, or is about to abscond," or that he was "about to remove his goods."

Moreover, the debtor could be "committed to the common gaol . . . for any term not exceeding twelve months" if he refused to appear for examination on his debts or "refuses to make satisfactory answers to any question asked of him."[23]

Under those rules, our jails today would be plugged to the brim. The law was amended from time to time over the next thirty years to make bankruptcy gradually less onerous, to distinguish between personal and corporate bankruptcy, and to bring more outside supervision into the liquidation of assets and the dispersal of the dividends, at each stage. In 1949, the act was rewritten "to clarify and simplify the procedures,"[24] ho, ho, and became undecipherable to the lay mind, a condition it retains to this day.

It was amended again in 1966 to reflect the fact that finance companies and, later, banks were lending money to consumers to buy cars, appliances, and just about everything else, on credit. More and more, the only way to clear away the debtloads thus created was through the process of bankruptcy, so the practice of law was broadened accordingly. The 1966 amendments also tried to deal more effectively with fraud in bankruptcies, although fraud, like poverty, continues to be ever with us.

Because it had grown in such a helter-skelter way over the years, the act had become sadly out of date, and a tussle began in 1970 to rewrite the legislation from top to bottom. In the end, it took twenty-two years and seven different bills (most of which died in committee) to get a major amendment, not a new act, passed in 1992.[25] What follows is a primer on the law as it developed once we got over the punitive obsession.

In modern bankruptcy law, the major thrust of the legislation is to provide a way to allow the insolvent person, or corporation, to survive or, if that is not possible, to start over again.

In Canada, a debtor commits an act of bankruptcy if he or she:[26]

- Voluntarily makes an assignment of his property to a trustee. The debtor assigns his property to a licensed trustee in bankruptcy (nearly always a chartered accountant) for the general benefit of his creditors. This is done on a simple one-page form, available from the official receiver in the area, and submitted to that receiver. There is a sworn statement of the property owned by the debtor and a list of creditors, with their names, addresses, and amounts owed.

- Makes a fraudulent conveyance of his property. For example, the debtor transfers assets to an offshore haven before they can be grabbed.
- Involves his property in a fraudulent preference. If a person is about to go broke, and sells his valuable antiques for a dollar to a friend, he has committed an act of bankruptcy.
- Does a midnight flit. This, of course, is not the exact wording of the act, which is incomprehensible to the lay mind. In this case, for example, the section reads, "if, with intent to defeat or delay his creditors, he departs out of Canada, or, being out of Canada, remains out of Canada, or departs from his dwelling-house or otherwise absents himself." Midnight flit.
- Permits an execution against him in which his property is seized. The debtor has fourteen days to clear away a legal seizure of any of his assets; after that, he is a bankrupt.
- Indicates to a meeting of his creditors that he is insolvent.
- Attempts, even if the attempt fails, to dispose of or secrete any of his property with intent to defraud, defeat, or delay his creditors. This is one of many new sections of the act designed to try to curb increasing fraud. It will make lawyers rich, just on the phrase about "intent."
- Notifies his creditors that he has suspended or is about to suspend payment of his debts.
- Defaults on any proposal made to his creditors under the act. Where a debtor wants to make a deal with his creditors, he can suggest a proposal, usually an extension of time, or a partial payment, or some other composition of the debt. This is filed with a licensed trustee. The debtor

is not technically bankrupt unless and until he fails to meet the terms of this proposal.

Or, the biggie:

- Ceases to meet his liabilities generally as they come due. When the person or company cannot meet ongoing obligations, any creditor may file a receiving order in court, which must contain two allegations: 1. that the debtor owes the petitioner at least one thousand dollars and; 2. that the debtor has committed an act of bankruptcy within the past six months. The easiest and most obvious act of bankruptcy to prove is failure to pay.

You can jump, or you can be pushed, and you can jump in one of two ways: by making an assignment of your assets or by making a proposal to your creditors in a formal way, under the act.

The debtor, whether a person or a company, must be insolvent before jumping. And, before you say, "Well, of course," take note that, in the United States, under Chapter 11 of its Bankruptcy Code, a corporation does not have to be insolvent to file. You are insolvent if you cannot meet your obligations, or even if you get yourself in a position where the aggregate of your property would not be sufficient to meet your debts, due and accruing.

The Bankruptcy and Insolvency Act is not the only law governing insolvency in Canada, and, in fact, it does not apply at all in the cases of the insolvency of banks, insurance and trust companies, or railways, all of which have their own laws – and the federal Winding-Up Act – to lead them into oblivion. Moreover, creditors cannot use the act to force farmers or fishermen into bankruptcy, although these two classes may make an assignment in bankruptcy. They can jump, but not be pushed, under the BIA. This provision is not, as many farmers and fishermen can testify, a hell of a lot of use in practice, because the normal way to advance money to these people is by way of a demand note, callable at any time, and secured by the assets – all the assets – of the lender. When the price of wheat droops, the bank yanks the loan, demanding full payment within a short period of time, and, when the debtor cannot come up with the money, the bank moves in, sells off the security for whatever it can get, and presents the debtor with a bill for the rest.

He isn't bankrupt, merely destitute. Then his other creditors gang up on him, and he goes into bankruptcy on his own.

However the bankruptcy comes about, whether voluntary or forced, the government official involved is the "official receiver," who represents the federal superintendent of bankruptcy and oversees the actions of the trustees. Every province and territory constitutes a bankruptcy district, and within each district, there are several divisions, each headed by an official receiver. In Ontario, there are seventeen such divisions. The receiver conducts an examination of the bankrupt's conduct, the causes of bankruptcy, and the way in which the assets have been handled. He also acts as chair of the first meeting of creditors, in the cases where there has been either a voluntary assignment or a petition into bankruptcy. In the case where there has been a proposal, the receiver does not chair the meeting, since this is a private matter between the debtor and the creditors. If the proposal is rejected, bankruptcy automatically follows, and the receiver would then step in. [27]

The official receiver is in an entirely different position than the private receiver installed by a creditor to protect the assets involved in a secured loan. This receiver represents the creditor, not the public; his or her duty is to get the money back, or as much of it as possible, for the people who put him in there. The official receiver's job is to see that the provisions of the law are met and to oversee the bankruptcy.

The non-government official involved is the "trustee in bankruptcy." In Canada, this is nearly always a chartered accountant (in the United States, it is usually a lawyer) who is licensed by the superintendent of bankruptcy. The trustee represents all of the creditors of the person or firm involved, under the general supervision of the official receiver.

The trustees are the backbone of the business, the ones who actually take charge of the "estate," as the sequestered assets are called, and administer it. He or she is required, among other duties, to:

- take possession of the debtor's assets, inventory them, and insure them;
- make a list of the creditors and the debts owed;
- prepare a detailed statement of the affairs of the bankrupt, and a report to the creditors on the causes of the bankruptcy;
- discover and report on any "questionable transactions," such as a bankrupt who has paid off one creditor while ignoring others or sold assets at knockdown prices before the bankruptcy;
- sell the assets in the estate and distribute the proceeds;
- review the claims against the estate and disallow those over which there is a dispute (the courts, not the trustee, must settle these);
- prepare a report to the court when the time comes to apply for a discharge from bankruptcy (i.e., when the debts have been paid – this is rare; when the creditors accept a proposal from the debtor; or, when it becomes clear that there is no more to be gotten from the debtor, and therefore no reason to prolong the bankruptcy);
- report to the court on the administration of the estate and apply for his or her own discharge from the post of trustee.

The trustee is paid out of the estate, and the wise trustee makes sure he gets paid first. The amount is set by a meeting of the creditors, but in Canada, it is usually related to accountancy charges, not – as in the United States – to legal charges, which are much higher. If there is no arrangement for his pay, the trustee can charge up to

7.5 per cent of what is left in the estate once the secured creditors have been paid. In the case where there may not be enough money in the estate to cover the trustee's work, it is considered wise practice to persuade one of the creditors (or, in the case of a personal bankruptcy, a friend or relative) to put up some money in advance, so that the trustee gets paid. There is nothing in law to force a trustee to act in any particular bankruptcy, and without this seed money, the matter may remain unresolved.

We, unlike the United States, have no special kind of court and judges for bankruptcies. In Ontario, there are three bankruptcy court offices – in Toronto, London, and Ottawa – but these are really the homes of the registrar in bankruptcy and the deputy registrars, who look after the administration of the law. The registrars hear unopposed bankruptcy petitions, make interim orders in matters of urgency, fix costs of administering the bankruptcy, hear any appeals of the decision of a trustee who has disallowed an unsecured claim, and rule on matters of procedure.

A handful of judges specialize in insolvency matters, and they are often referred to as the bankruptcy court, but, officially, there is no such thing. These judges rule on all appeals from the registrars and on disputed petitions for receiving orders, hear any cases where the discharge of a bankrupt is opposed or the approval of a proposal is opposed, deal with any questions of disputed priorities of claims, and hold any trials of bankruptcy issues directed by any other court. They also have a crucial role to play in the overseeing of the Companies' Creditors Arrangement Act, as we will see in Chapter Five.

The way in which the creditors are paid off follows a line of protocol as rigid as the one that ordains that the wife of a count shall shove in to dinner ahead of the wife of a mere baronet. There are classes of creditors, and each class must be paid off in full before the next class gets its nose in. This is the order of precedence:[28]

1. Secured creditors. If they have realized on their security, and are still owed money, they collect here.

2. Unsecured creditors. These are divided into three subgroups, the

preferred, the ordinary, and the deferred – something like the good, the bad, and the ugly. Again, each category must be paid off in full before any of the remnants of the estate passes on to the next class. The preferred come in nine categories:

a. Funeral expenses.
b. The costs of administering the bankruptcy, beginning with the expenses and fees of the trustee.
c. A special levy on the estate, in an amount fixed by order-in-council, to help defray the expenses of the office of the superintendent of bankruptcy.
d. Wages, salaries, and commissions of any employee, owed for the period of six months previous to the bankruptcy, up to a maximum of $2,000, and $1,000 for the expenses of a "travelling salesman."[29]
e. Municipal taxes.
f. Any arrears of rent for a period of three months before and three months after the bankruptcy, if owed under a lease.
g. Any indebtedness of the bankrupt under the Workmen's Compensation Act, the Unemployment Insurance Act, or the Income Tax Act.
h. Claims resulting from injuries to any employee of the bankrupt not covered by workers' compensation.
i. Claims for unpaid income tax, unemployment insurance, and Canada Pension Plans.

Only after all these claims have been paid in full do the ordinary unsecured creditors get to collect. The remaining assets are lumped together and divided among them, in proportion to the amount owed. That is, if the final payoff came to four cents on the dollar – which, as we have seen, is normal – a debtor owed $1 million would get $40,000, and one owed $10,000 would get $400.

Two of these classes require some explanation, classes "d" and "i." Before the 1992 revisions, the amounts under "d" were limited to $500 and $300, and in many cases, even this pitiful amount could not be collected, because the money was long gone before it reached these points in the queue. However, some provinces had passed legislation to protect these amounts. Ontario, for example, has a Business Corporations Act, which allows the worker to launch a lawsuit for up to six months' wages against the director of a bankrupt firm if he or she sues within six months of the insolvency. Unless, that is, the director has taken the rather elementary precaution of resigning within six months before the collapse.[30] This awkward and expensive remedy was marginally better than nothing, but created obvious inequity. If your employer went broke in Ontario, you had a better chance of collecting owed wages than if the nosedive took place in Manitoba.

In 1990, the Mulroney government advanced a proposal for reform which was a good idea then, and is a good idea now. To protect the wages of employees, there was to be a new Wage Claim Payment Act, which would cover up to $2,000 in wages and vacation pay per employee, plus up to $1,000 in expenses for travelling employees. Where the employer was in bankruptcy or receivership, the employee could file a claim with the superintendent of bankruptcy, who, once the amount owing had been verified, would pay it. In effect, the law said, the wage-earner deserved protection, and if the bankrupt firm's assets could not provide him or her with a minimum payment, the public purse must do so.

To provide the money for this purpose, the act proposed setting up a fund into which employers would pay .024 per cent of insurable earnings, about ten cents per employee per week.[31] Corporate Canada, with some exceptions, screamed bloody murder. It was another tax. Not a big tax, but a tax. The scuffling around this proposal dragged on and on, and it was finally smothered in the report of the Standing Committee on Consumer and Corporate Affairs in October 1991. Ten cents a week was too much for our corporations to pay, or, at least, too much for the business lobby to swallow, and they lined up enough Tory mossback MPs to threaten the entire legislation. The end result was the $2,000 and $1,000 compromise, but "d" is given "super priority" in the distribution of assets. It is unclear what this will mean in practice, since the change has not been in effect long enough to be licked into shape by the courts.

The other section worth a look is "i," the one dealing with Crown claims. What happened here is that, over the years, the various governments, federal and provincial, worked out ways to ensure they got theirs ahead of the secured creditors. The logic went this way: An employer is required to withhold income tax and set it aside on behalf of the employee. In real life, no employer ever does, but what has life to do with law? This money was said to be "in trust" for the government, so it didn't ever come into the bankrupt estate.

As Uwe Manski, president of the Canadian Insolvency Practitioners' Association, put it to me, "Governments have tried to elevate themselves from unsecured creditors to super-secured creditors. The government says that money you were supposed to put in trust is located in whatever assets you have – it is a deemed trust. Every level of government did this. Our association studied this and found thirty-eight statutes that said that various levels of government were in line for deemed trusts on any free assets. The king comes first is a little archaic, but that's what we had."[32]

A small measure of common sense finally suggested that, if we went on this way, no one except various levels of government was going to collect anything from any bankruptcy, and the redrawn act wiped out at least some of these deemed trusts. However, as Manski says, "The power of the Crown is dissolved except in the case of federal and provincial income tax and the employee's share of the income tax, Canada Pension Plan, and Unemployment Insurance. They just couldn't give up on those."

Finally, there are the deferreds, those who are put off until all other claims are met, such as the spouse of a bankrupt claiming for a debt owed or the wage claims of officers and directors of a bankrupt corporation. They come last, and in the normal course of events don't stand a chance in hell of collecting anything.

There is more, much more, to the BIA, which rambles on for 123 pages in the original, plus 100 pages of 1992 amendments, and another 108 pages of regulations, but I think we have enough now to get the flavour of the thing, which is that of a dog's breakfast or, at the very best, a dog's luncheon. Well, call it a feast for lawyers. A Toronto law firm, going through the act – and, probably, rubbing its hands with glee – noted seventy-five items in which it was not clear what the law meant, or intended, and which the courts, in the fullness of time and billable hours, will have to decide.[33] By dint of hard work and application, legislatures from 1919 to 1992 have managed to refine and simplify Canadian bankruptcy law to the point where you have to be rich to go broke, just to look after the legal aspects. Frank Bennett, the author of the standard text on these matters, estimates the fees for petitioning a debtor into bankruptcy at "$4,000 to $7,500 for services rendered up to the first meeting of creditors."[34] These are the trustee's fees, and the legal fees begin where these leave off. And, of course, where the business is complex, the trustee may have to hire his or her own legal counsel to provide advice. (Summary bankruptcies, which we will deal with in Chapter Ten, come much cheaper.)

However, take heart. We have certainly come some distance from a broken bench in a Venice market, we have closed the debtor's prisons and managed to remove most of the element of punishment from the process. Bennett notes, "Not long ago, bankruptcy was considered a disgrace and a social stigma to many. Today, there is no longer any stigma attached if the debtor is unable to pay his or her debts. The debtor who has many debts should take advantage of the relief provided for under the *Bankruptcy Act*."[35]

This, of course, is the legal view. Some of us think the pendulum may have swung too far and reopened a vein of dishonest ore that rogues have been able to mine for centuries. We will look at some of the most interesting historical cases in the next chapter.

CHAPTER THREE

Historical Bellyflops

"Everybody in Vanity Fair must have remarked how well those live who are comfortably and thoroughly in debt; how they deny themselves nothing; how jolly and easy they are in their minds." – William Makepeace Thackeray, *Vanity Fair*, 1848

$

I want to look at some of the great collapses in financial history for three reasons. The first is that they are so often fascinating stories in themselves; the second is that they contain lessons which can still be applied, if we are not too dense to get the message; and the third is that there is, I believe, what might be called an evolution in bankruptcy that has given us, as evolution so often does, a new and more adaptable creature. Not more attractive, though, just snakier. We saw in the last chapter that the theory of bankruptcy changed from a process to punish the debtor to one which was at least as likely to punish the creditor, instead. We are evolving towards a system in which society at large bears the punishment, shared with the creditor, and the bankrupt prospers as the green bay tree. I don't think we mean to do this; I don't think we are even aware of what is happening. I think we ought to stop and ponder the next step, in the light of the lessons of history.

In this chapter, I will deal with a number of cases that contain a high level of roguery, but they are, I would argue, of a different kind than, say, the collapse of the savings and loan associations in the United States, or the nosedive taken not long ago by Johns–Manville Company Ltd.. The rogues I am dealing with in this chapter are clearly labelled, and they knew themselves to be rogues, and they were recognized as rogues, when the slow-grinding wheels of justice eventually caught up with them. (The notable exception is Sir Walter Scott, who believed himself to be a wonderful chap and foisted that view on history; as you will see, however, he was really a rogue, and not the least of them.)

Then, in Chapter Four, I want to deal with the changes that enshrined the new approach to bankruptcy in legislation, when we shuffled off the notion of original sin in these matters and embraced the Dr. Feelgood approach, on the heels of, and because of, the changes that had been made in the United States.

With this under our belts, we will be able to go on to look at some of the more recent financial stumbles, to see how the new laws are affecting the practice, not merely of insolvency, but of finance itself. We will see, in the case of the American S&Ls, and a number of similar cases on this side of the border, first the erosion of the notion of responsibility for debt, and then the use of indebtedness as a weapon to gain a competitive edge – and even to make huge amounts of money.

We need to know how the business of going broke worked in an earlier time to understand how it works today, and how it is likely to work tomorrow, to follow the argument that we seem to be going in a direction no one planned – and that most of us would reject out of hand.

The most outstanding financial bellyflops in history show an astonishing similarity in many of their aspects, no matter when they occurred. These similarities run through two areas: what might be called "no fault" bellyflops and the more interesting cases of failures in which the damage was obviously inflicted by specific human agents who are readily identifiable.

There have always been, and always will be, bankruptcies occasioned by events completely outside the control of the bankrupt person or firm, or in which persons of ordinary foresight simply did not see, in time, the fates that would flatten them. Buggy-whip manufacturers who failed to hear the rumble of the automobile rolling up the road to run them over; whale-oil merchants who were sure the public infatuation with kerosene was a temporary aberration; bustle-makers who could never embrace the notion that enough buttock was enough. There were, too, changes in law – the Corn Laws, the Enclosure Acts, and, in our own day, the establishment of the Free Trade Agreement with the United States – that thrust hundreds of thousands of honourable, intelligent people into insolvency. Perhaps they ought to have seen the looming danger, but these legal changes are always accompanied by reassurances from the various governments that the adjustments will be painless, or that the pain will be temporary, or that – in the case of the Free Trade Agreement – today's pain will lead to tomorrow's gain, somewhere. Possibly the steelworkers chucked out onto the street in Hamilton, Ontario, or the furniture manufacturers bankrupted in southern Quebec, take comfort from the fact that jobs are springing up in Mississippi and Tennessee. Or, possibly not. In any event, these law-induced calamities, like those brought about by changes in fashion and technology, are unavoidable so far as the individual bankrupt is concerned, even though they are of human origin.

Then, the operation of events outside any human control – the consecutive failure of potato crops in Ireland, the dustbowl that accompanied the Great Depression, the onslaught of Hurricane Andrew on the southeast seaboard in the autumn of 1992 – has often brought economic calamity to victims who could never have predicted the disasters that were about to overcome them.

But these recurring themes are not what interest me so much as the cupidity, stupidity, and larceny which run like silken threads through the financial history of industrial civilization, and which show no signs of diminishing or being brought under effective control.

One of the most interesting of these outbreaks, and one which sets a pattern we are still following today, was the phenomenon referred to as "Tulip Mania," which overwhelmed the Republic of the United Netherlands in 1635. Not coincidentally, Amsterdam was the seat of the world's first permanent stock exchange, opened in 1631,[1] where a robust futures market was fed by, and catered to, some of the wildest speculators in history. Tulips had been imported into western Europe from Turkey in the sixteenth century, and huge fields of the flower covered a stretch of forty miles, between Amsterdam and The Hague, by the early part of the seventeenth century.[2] The flowers were first popular and then fashionable – all the best homes had them – and then profitable. In the beginning, the bulbs were sold individually, at ever-increasing prices (twelve hundred florins, or about $480, for a single specimen of a bulb called "Semper Augustus," in 1624); later, entire beds were sold. The usual way to sell the bulbs was by weight, and the unit of measure was an *aas*, about one-twentieth of a gram; a common sales contract covered one thousand *aas*. The futures market developed when buyers began to bid for the "excrescences," or outgrowths, on the sides of the bulbs, which could themselves develop into bulbs. First, a premium was paid for bulbs with excrescences, and then the bumps themselves were bought and sold.

The bulbs were normally taken out of the beds in June, and replanted in November, so the selling season was limited to the summer months, and the bulbs were paid for and taken on the spot. However, with the excrescences, it was necessary to leave the outgrowth attached to the main bulb for some months, and it soon became the practice to buy and sell these at any time in the year, for delivery when they were judged to be healthy enough to survive on their own. You never knew whether the promising little bump on the bulb would flower, after you had paid a few hundred florins for it, so there was a high element of risk in this trade. But then some genius, working from the model of futures markets already established, realized that he could buy excrescences for, say, two hundred florins each and sell them for three hundred florins to some other speculator, without ever taking them into his own possession. What he sold was the right to future delivery of the little bumps. When this trade was joined by outside speculators, and was no longer limited to professional growers, the stage was set for ballooning growth and inevitable collapse.

By the end of 1634, the trade in tulips had taken off, and new ways of marketing were introduced; you could now trade in pieces, in thousand-*aas* lots, in pounds, baskets, beds, and whole gardens.[3] Prices shot up; a pound of a rare kind of bulb called "Witte Croonen," bought for the equivalent of $50, sold soon after for $1,440. By the late fall of 1636, the speculation had gotten entirely out of control, with bulbs selling for hundreds of times their value of a few months earlier, and buyers mortgaging their homes, and lands, to get in on the action. Inevitably, the market reached saturation and reality set in. The following winter, for the first time, sellers offered bulbs for which there were no takers. The collapse came as quickly as the boom, plunging thousands into financial ruin. Of course, there were others who had managed to get rid of the bulbs, or the bits of paper representing bulbs, before the crash came, but when the balloon burst, many more were damaged than had prospered during it ascension. As with any financial market, as soon as the prices started down for current transactions, future prices, which are always based on the expectation of an increase, plunged even more precipitously. Middle-class citizens found themselves holding paper pledging them to pay hundreds of thousands of florins for goods that would only be worth, when the time came to take delivery, a fraction of what they had paid. The classic road to ruin.

Not surprisingly, many of the speculators refused to go through with the contracts already made, and the entire economy of the country was threatened. Finally, the central governing body, the States of Holland, stepped in, in April 1637, and suspended all contracts for the sale of tulips. A decree authorized the growers to sell off the bulbs involved in the abrogated contracts, for whatever they could get, and then go after the owners for the difference between what they had bid and what the goods actually fetched in the market. This worked about as well as it usually does, with some of the buyers paying off the contracts at 2 or 3 per cent of their value, and the rest refusing to pay anything and taking their chances with the courts.

Tulip mania was certainly not the first example of wild speculation leading to financial ruin in human history. If we could probe deeply enough, we would probably find evidence that *Australopithecus* dealt off bits of the haunch of a venison he had yet to catch, and that Neanderthalers flogged seats around the fire to each other at ever-rising prices until someone foreclosed on the cave. Still, Tulip Mania is important because it combines the same elements – a nice mixture of larceny, optimism, and a sturdy belief in the something-for-nothing school of finance – that bob up in so many of these stories and provide the fodder for bankruptcy.

The speculative fever that spawned Tulip Mania proved to be portable. When the Americans got their own country, they immediately began to speculate on land, currency, bonds, and stocks, then called "scrip," short for "subscription stock." One of the most notorious speculators was also one of the nation's early bankrupts, William Duer, whose ruin caused the Panic of 1792. Duer had joined the patriot side early in the Revolutionary War and worked closely with Washington and his circle. At war's end, when the new government was setting up temporary quarters in New York City, it was Duer who found a house for Washington and arranged the lease. He was also a friend of Alexander Hamilton, first secretary of the treasury of the new nation. He married a relative of Hamilton's, and Washington gave the bride away.[4] Hamilton named him his assistant secretary in 1790, and Duer used the post to advance his own private speculations and those of a group of friends and allies. He shook down contractors who wanted to sell to the government and used treasury funds to finance some of his own speculations.[5] His inside information on the government's financial dealings helped to make them all very rich, especially after he formed a cabal with a group of other investors to gamble on the government's public-debt issues.

To handle this debt, Hamilton created the Bank of the United States, which would guarantee the national credit. It was capitalized at $10 million, made up of 25,000 shares with a par value of $400 each; the treasury would subscribe a fifth of these, and the general public the rest. By the time the bank was launched, Duer had left the public payroll, because of increasing complaints about his activities, although he still maintained close personal ties with Hamilton. He was thus an early and enthusiastic purchaser of the Bank of the United States stock, which was soon selling at seven times the issue price.[6] Duer and his clique began to purchase their shares on margin, paying a small portion down and borrowing the rest. Other banks were soon incorporated, and speculation in their stocks, buoyed by the usual stew of rumour, guesses, and planted news reports, blossomed.

Then, in March 1792, the market went through one of its periodic "corrections," and stock prices fell – temporarily. Duer had borrowed so heavily, and at such high rates, that he could not meet his interest payments, because, as soon as the share prices dipped, his creditors pulled back. At the same time – for disaster never strikes in a solitary state – the comptroller of the treasury, having gone over the books for the period when Duer was assistant secretary, presented him with a bill for $250,000 for money that had disappeared during his tenure. That did it. On March 23, Duer was marched off to debtor's prison. (One of his creditors rushed to the prison and confronted Duer with a brace of duelling pistols, giving him a choice between paying off his note, for $1,500, or shooting it out. Somehow, Duer paid.)

Duer's arrest immediately set off a panic among speculators in New York and Philadelphia, where the new federal government had re-established itself. Gold was shipped out of the country in fear of financial collapse, and money for new ventures dried up. On March 24, another twenty-five bankruptcies were reported, with many more to come. In all, about $5 million, a huge sum in those days, was lost by speculators. Hamilton, who already had enough on his plate (the husband of his mistress was blackmailing him and had to be paid off; these public service jobs are never the piece of cake that outsiders think they are), stepped in to clear up the mess. By instructing the treasury to support the share prices, he stopped the panic, and, by midsummer, the markets had recovered.

Duer had not. He was still in jail, although he was able to conduct his various speculations from there and eat his meals at a local tavern, where he met his business colleagues. He did well in these transactions, but was never able to clear his name or the debt, and died in prison on May 7, 1799.

Many of the great speculations, and consequent collapses, that marked the United States's coming of age had to do with railway scams, which I have described in some detail elsewhere,[7] but there were also similar scandalous crashes in canal, real-estate, and municipal bonds. Pennsylvania, the richest state, drew in huge investments from over-seas, especially England, backed by the state itself, and when, in 1842, Pennsylvania went into insolvency and repudiated its own bonds, Sidney Smith, the English clergyman, writer, and wit, who was himself badly stung by the repudiation, unburdened himself in a letter to the *London Morning Chronicle* that began:

> I never meet a Pennsylvanian at a London dinner without feel-ing a disposition to seize and divide him; to allot his beaver to one sufferer and his coat to another; to appropriate his pocket handkerchief to the orphan and to comfort the widow with his silver watch, Broadway rings, and the London guide which he always carries in his pocket.[8]

Smith contended that a man from Pennsylvania "has no more right to eat with honest men than a leper has to eat with clean men" and went on:

> Picture to yourself a Pennsylvanian receiving foreigners in his own country, walking over the public works with them, and

showing them the Larcenous Lake, Swindling Swamp, Crafty Canal, and Rogue's Railways, and other dishonest works. This swamp we gained (says the patriotic borrower) by the repudiated loans of 1828. Our canal robbery was in 1830; we pocketed your good people's money for the railroad only last year.[9]

Smith ended, as a clergyman might, by exhorting the Pennsylvanians to pay back the money and thus wash themselves clean of sin:

And now, drab-coloured men of Pennsylvania, there is yet a moment left. . . . Start up from that trance of dishonesty into which you are plunged: don't think of the flesh which walls about your life, but of that *sin* [emphasis in original] which has hurled you from the heaven of character, which hangs over you like a pestilence, and makes good men sad and ruffians dance and sing.[10]

It was a noble try, but, like so many attempts to equate debt with sin, didn't bring in a dime, and the depression of 1870 saw a number of states repudiate their debts, transferring the bankruptcies from the governments to the individuals and corporations who had bought the paper.[11]

While the Americans have always shown a talent for bang-up bankruptcies, perhaps the most startling pratfall in history was performed by the English poet and novelist, Sir Walter Scott. Diplomat Henry Cockburn wrote in his memoirs:

The opening of the year 1826 will ever be sad to those who remember the thunderbolt which fell on Edinburgh in the utterly unexpected bankruptcy of Scott, implying the ruin of Constable the bookseller, and of Ballantyne the printer. If an earthquake had swallowed half the town, it would not have produced greater astonishment, sorrow and dismay.[12]

By profession, Scott was a lawyer, who earned a considerable annual stipend in a patronage job as clerk of the Court of Sessions in Edinburgh. As his romantic poems, based on the legends of his native land, began to sell, he acquired a secret interest in, first, the publishing firm, Archibald Constable & Company, which brought out his books, and later, James Ballantyne & Company, the company that printed them. The conventional history of his downfall[13] is that the carelessness, extravagance, and bad judgement of his publishers caused the firm to collapse in 1826, and that Scott was caught in the rubble. Then, the story goes, he spent the rest of his life slaving to pay off the firm's and his own debts. This is the version told by his official biographer, John Lockhart, who just happened to be Scott's son-in-law.

More recent scholarly research suggests a rather different story. Eric Quayle, author of *The Ruin of Sir Walter Scott*,[14] obtained documents, long buried in the publisher's vaults, which show that Scott had been the controlling partner in the firm from 1809 onwards and used his position ruthlessly to acquire the funds to build his palatial home, Abbotsford, outside Edinburgh, where he entertained the high and mighty, including and especially King George IV, in a style which neither he, nor certainly his publisher, could afford.

As controlling partner, he allotted himself advances for books years before he wrote them, and then had to scribble furiously to keep up with the contracts. He also bullied his partners into printing the works of his friends, many of them dreadful, most of them unsaleable, and insisted on Ballantyne publishing *The Edinburgh Annual Register*, a magazine that said kind things about Scott and his circle, promoted his political views (which were that God had arranged for the rich to be rich and the poor poor, and that any attempt to rearrange this "natural order" amounted to treason), and lost money at a steady, draining rate, year after year.

Scott also set up an arrangement under which he bled the printing firm dry. When he got control, he instituted a process under which either partner, himself or James Ballantyne, could advance cash to the firm and collect heavy interest on it. In a single year, he made interest of £1,000 on a loan of £3,000 to the company. As an author, he collected from the royalties, from the publishing, from the printing contracts, and, until he used up all his cash buying land at inflated prices, from interest charges to his own company. He also induced both firms, the publisher and the printer, to borrow money at high rates of interest, to advance to him, so that he could go on with his building projects at Abbotsford.

As Eric Quayle notes, "It was the craving to supply funds to buy land and build his magnificent fairy castle on the banks of the Tweed that caused him to churn out novel after novel at such indecent speed."[15] It also caused him to plunge the companies into ruin.

In fact, he, not his printer or publisher, was responsible for the debts of £116,838 11 3d[16] that finally brought down not only Archibald Constable & Company and James Ballantyne & Company, but Hurst, Robinson & Company, the London firm that distributed his works in England. In turn, Hurst, Robinson's failure brought down scores of smaller concerns. The firms' bankruptcies quickly bankrupted Scott as well, because he owed so much to the companies, and the creditors insisted that he pay up. In what he called "a last cast for freedom," Scott sought personal protection (it was then called "sequestration") from his creditors and made a proposal to them. If they would hold off seizing his assets, he would write his way out of debt:

> I will be their vassal for life, and dig in the mine of my imagination to find diamonds (or what may sell for such) to make good my engagements, not to enrich myself. And this from no reluctance to be called insolvent, which I probably am, but because I will not put out of the power of my creditors the resources, mental or literary, which yet remain to me.[17]

Only one creditor refused to hold off. A London bill-broking firm, Abud & Company, that had bought £2,000 worth of Scott's notes, insisted on being paid, or it would petition Scott into bankruptcy.

"They are Jews, I suppose," Scott wrote. "The devil baste them for fools with a pork griskin." [18] (A griskin was a loin of pork; this clearly was, and was intended to be, a racist slur.)

Sir William Forbes, a leading Edinburgh banker and longtime friend of Scott's, paid off Abud, while telling Scott that the firm had changed its mind and dropped its claim. This nicety of feeling towards Scott, who showed none whatsoever towards the people he had ruined, was based on his towering reputation. The Earl of Dudley exclaimed, "Scott ruined! The Author of *Waverly* ruined! Good God, let every man to whom he has given months of delight give him sixpence, and he will rise tomorrow morning richer than Rothschild!" [19]

The outpouring of sympathy that followed the public exposure of Scott's insolvency led to the setting up of a trust fund – something that would become familiar to our own day – to look after his debts, while he kept hold of most of his personal property. His beloved Abbotsford was already safe; he was enough of a lawyer to have seen to that years earlier. It was part of the marriage portion he settled on his daughter-in-law at the time of his son's marriage. While he lived in Abbotsford, and ruled it, the property actually belonged to his son (since his son, under then-current law, owned everything in his wife's name). This rather neat dodge angered the Bank of Scotland, who wanted the trustees to launch a lawsuit to demolish the marriage settlement, but they were persuaded to withdraw this demand because, after all, the trust would soon be paying them off with the proceeds from a new novel, *Woodstock*, and Scott's *Life of Napoleon*.

It didn't work out that way. Scott may have been his creditors' vassal, but he was a well-paid vassal. He made no attempt to live on the £1,600 annual stipend the trustees allowed him (a large but not extravagant salary for the day), and he spent about twice that annually, borrowing, with the trustees' permission, against works to be written some time in the future. (He managed to collect in advance for as many as four books on which he had done no work whatsoever; I have asked McClelland & Stewart for a similar arrangement, but ours is a cruel and untrusting time, and it declined the honour.) He continued to entertain lavishly, lived in Abbotsford, and still kept a butler, although some of the other domestic staff were let go. He certainly worked hard – he had always worked hard – but, in fact, when he died on September 21, 1832, he owed more than he had when the bankruptcy occurred. In the end, thanks in part to a life-insurance policy, and the sale of his collected works and the biography of Napoleon, his creditors and those of the Ballantyne printing and publishing firms received two shillings and ninepence in the pound (or 14.5 cents on the dollar).[20]

His partners were not so lucky. Archibald Constable lost his home, furniture, pictures, library, horses, and personal possessions of every kind, which were sold at auction to pay off part of his debts. He moved, with his wife and eight children, into a set of furnished rooms. James Ballantyne, who had recently bought a new house, lost it, along with a collection of *objets d'art* and antiques, although he was allowed to hold on to his furniture. His younger brother, Sandy, was also ruined, although he managed to hold back £500 by selling a Stradivarius violin, his most prized possession.

Scott found out about this £500 from James and promptly wrote to Sandy to beseech him to lend it to him. Which he did (it was never repaid).

It remained only for his son-in-law, in his *Memoirs of the Life of Sir Walter Scott, Bart* by J. G. Lockhart, seven volumes, 1837-8, to wipe out all his extravagances and vilify his erstwhile friends and colleagues, Archibald Constable and the Ballantynes,[21] but the nub of Scott's bankruptcy, as Eric Quayle writes, was that "his financial success, which at times must have dazzled even his own extravagant dreams, could never quite keep pace with the rate at which he squandered the money his writing brought him."[22]

There was another lesson here, still applicable, and that is that Scott moved with swift cunning to salvage all he could from the wreckage and fared far better than the men who were associated with him, and who behaved with less cunning and more honour.

At least Scott wasn't an out-and-out crook, which is more than can be said about another well-connected Briton, Whitaker Wright, a mining promoter. Towards the end of the last century, he managed to launch, and later bankrupt, no fewer than forty-two companies which were supposed to be mining gold in Australia, through a galaxy of companies with names like the London and Global Finance Corporation, Lakeview Consols, and the Wealth of Nations.[23] In point of fact, they were mining the money of the credulous in England, who were lured in by Wright's reputation, which, like his companies, was based mostly on wind and water.

Wright had enough social connections to wangle an acquaintance with the Prince of Wales, who condescended to come to lunch on Wright's yacht one sunny day in 1895. This proved that Wright was all right, and allowed him to move his stocks. All the best people invested, including Lord Dufferin, governor general of Canada from 1872 to 1878, who accepted a post as chairman of the London and Global Finance Corporation. The Duke of Connaught, who was the Prince of Wales's brother, Lord Loch, former governor of Victoria, and Prime Minister Arthur Balfour were among the other swells who bought stocks and took leading positions in his interlinked firms. While the money rolled into his companies, Wright rolled it out again, buying himself a palatial home from William Ewart Gladstone, building another – at a cost of $2,500,000 – and spending the rest on yachts and lavish entertainments. The home he built, in Surrey, contained a billiard room constructed beneath a lake, with a glass ceiling through which the players could watch the fish above.[24] They should have been suckers; in point of fact, they were carp. Dufferin's biographer, his nephew, Harold Nicholson, greatly admired Wright and waxed ecstatic about his country house, where, he wrote, "Mr. Wright had revived the luxuries and the enterprise of the Roman Emperors." Then, there is this bit:

> He moved mountains, he transplanted orchards, he made valleys blossom where not the slightest declivity had existed

before. He possessed a private observatory, a private theatre, a private velodrome, a private hospital.[25]

He also possessed the nerve of a canal horse, since all of this was done on the never-never, with other people's money. When the Boer War broke out, stocks slumped, and Wright was called on to pay for some of the shares he had purchased with borrowed funds. That was when it was discovered that the $111 million in capital shown on his various company books was in fact about $10 million, and the whole string of firms went into bankruptcy. Wright was charged, convicted of fraud, and about to be sentenced when he committed suicide.

According to Curtis D. MacDougall, a student of frauds, "Dufferin and Loch already were dead from shame."[26] Well, there is something we don't hit on much in our day; nobody succumbs from shame any more. Actually, according to Nicholson, Dufferin perished rather more prosaically, from "gastric inflammation,"[27] but it's the thought that counts. Certainly, Nicholson wrote, "He knew that the whole business had encased him gradually, and that his honour had been compromised. . . . He returned to Clandeboye broken in fortune, in reputation, and in health."[28]

Ivar Kreuger, the Swedish entrepreneur, who rose to glory in the heady days just before the Great Depression, was another whose bankruptcy stunned the world around him. He began as an engineer, worked for a time in Chicago and New York, then returned to Sweden to take over two match factories owned by his father and uncle. He created a match monopoly and was quickly dubbed the "Match King" by a fawning press. As the profits rolled in, he invested them in other companies, which grew and multiplied. And multiplied. He was one of the first to adopt the techniques of the modern conglomerate, using one firm to buy the shares of others and paying off the purchase price with the cash flow of the new company. He was so successful at this that he was able to build up a worldwide empire of more than four hundred companies, into which investors poured nearly $1 billion.

Essentially, however, he was running a pyramid scheme, using the new money advanced by stockholders to pay off debts as they came due, and then repeating the performance. When he couldn't come up with the cash, he forged government bonds and borrowed against them; his safety-deposit box in Stockholm turned out to contain $140 million in fake Italian-government securities, which he had pledged as collateral against various loans. He had forged the names of the appropriate government ministers himself.[29]

He also invented something called "XYZ" contracts, in which the investor put up the money without knowing what Kreuger intended to do with it. His prestige was such that a Boston investment firm, Lee, Higginson, bought $150 million worth of the securities of Kreuger & Toll Inc. and took his word for the fact that it was best if they didn't know exactly what he wanted the money for.[30]

When the stock markets began to collapse in the fall of 1929, some of Kreuger's shareholders were able to force an audit, which disclosed the fact that his empire was essentially insolvent. Kreuger fled to Paris, purchased a brace of pistols and a box of cartridges, and blew his brains out. Even then, no one realized he had been running a swindle; the newspapers reverberated with his praise, and the *New Statesmen* described him as "a very Puritan of finance."[31] But he was no puritan, financial or otherwise; indeed, one of the reasons he often needed cash in a hurry was to pay off various blackmailers who had got onto the fact that he had an active and unorthodox sex life. It was only after Price Waterhouse, the British accounting firm, had been called in to look at the books that the general public was told that Krueger had written more than $250 million into his books that didn't exist. His entire empire was built on fraud. The shock was so great that people refused to believe it, and, for years after the thousands of bankruptcies caused by Kreuger's collapse, rumours circulated that old Ivar was still alive somewhere and living on the proceeds.

Our native modesty has always kept Canadians from boasting about our own record in this line, but no account of the link between rascality and bankruptcy can avoid the awesome career of Francis Hincks. Born in County Cork, Ireland, he emigrated to York (later Toronto) in 1830 and became the cashier, and later manager, of the Bank of the People. With the backing of his business friends, he went into politics and became prime minister of the united Province of Canada, which was a nice post from which to manipulate the stock of railroad companies, whose major financing came from the government. He was a land speculator, a con man (who pushed through a swindle on City of Toronto bonds with the help of the city's mayor), and the cheerful recipient of bribes.[32] He received a payoff of £50,400 in the stock of the Grand Trunk Railway for helping to sell the company's charter to an English firm. When this came to light, through a series of speeches made by George Brown, then a Liberal MP, and the Conservatives lost power, Hincks was sent off to the West Indies, as governor of Barbados and the Windward Islands. His appointment came from Lord Elgin, who had also received a substantial bribe from the Grand Trunk.

Hincks returned, cleansed, in 1869, the same year he received his knighthood, and became Sir John A. Macdonald's minister of finance, a post he used to sell off fishing rights for personal gain and to raise more money for railway speculation. It was Hincks who arranged the Canadian Pacific Railway contract that led to the Pacific Scandal when its notorious payoff clauses came to light.

The defeat of the Macdonald government on this issue allowed Hincks more leisure time, so he put together two shaky banks, the City Bank and the Royal Canadian, into one really shaky bank, the Consolidated, of which he became president, and which proceeded to spend a lot of money it didn't have. By the time it came crashing down, in August 1880, taking with it the fortunes of a great many investors, he had sold off all but fifty of his own shares at a substantial profit.

This bankruptcy ended more happily for its principal than most. Hincks was charged with filing false annual returns to the authorities, under a law that he himself had framed while in government. The bank's books were balanced by neglecting to show that $622,000 of the firm's assets were, in fact, advances from other banks, and therefore debts, not assets. Hincks was convicted by a jury, to the astonishment of all the right-thinking people, who naturally assumed he would, and should, get off. The minimum sentence for his crime was two years in prison, but it was never carried out. After all, you don't chuck people of Hincks's stature in the clink for one tiny wee crime. Or, as Adam Shortt wrote in his *History of Canadian Banking and Currency, 1600-1800*, "The public were amply satisfied with the fact that a striking warning had been given to presidents and directors of corporations."[33]

Hincks was restored to virtue. The most influential financial newspaper of the day, the *Monetary Times*, concluded that he must have been temporarily insane when he committed his many crimes, and Hincks passed into our history books as an able and upright man, except for these occasional spells when he was happened to be a crook.[34]

Nothing changes, nothing ever will. From the time of the collapse of the Consolidated Bank in 1880 to the demise of the Principal Group in 1987, Canadian business history was punctured periodically by bankruptcies brought about by the same rich mixture of enthusiasm, avarice, and credulity, aided and abetted by a legal system that changed very little over that period. The Home Bank débâcle of 1921, the Windfall Mines disaster of 1964, the Osler Inc. collapse of 1987, and hundreds of others are all tributes to an unacknowledged, but undoubted, national affinity for noisome bankruptcies.

Out of this rich feast, we can pluck as typical the demise of Atlantic Acceptance Corporation Ltd. in 1965.

Atlantic Acceptance was founded in 1953 by a Hamilton, Ontario, accountant, C. Powell Morgan, who was tired of working for other people and wanted to run his own firm. He was, at least when he started, so conservative that he didn't give up his accountancy job at International Silver until 1958, five years after Atlantic Acceptance was launched. It was a consumer-finance company, which borrowed money from others – investors, banks, other companies – at low rates and loaned it out to people who wanted to buy cars, T V sets, refrigerators, washing machines – at higher rates.

There was obviously some risk in the business, which is why the consumer-loan companies charged higher interest rates, but, at that time, when the banks were much too stodgy to touch such business, it represented a large and growing market, where money could be made. But, Morgan, once his company began to enjoy a modest success, began to take greater and greater risks, in return for greater and greater profits.

He turned the company into a public one, selling shares to the credulous through the Canadian Stock Exchange; created a trio of subsidiary firms, Commodore Sales Acceptance, Commodore Factors Ltd., and Adelaide Acceptance Ltd., through which money was channelled and laundered on its way through Atlantic's books; and he paid himself "management fees" on the complex transactions that ate up most of the profits. Not his profits – he did very well – but the profits of the shareholders who thought they owned and controlled Atlantic Acceptance.

Between 1958 and 1965, Atlantic expanded rapidly, lending money on more and more dubious transactions, at higher and higher rates, and borrowing in turn to cover the outflow. It became a classic pyramid scheme, where increasing funds had to be found each month to cover the money flowing out. The company plunged into various stock scams, using the trio of firms as the main operating companies for Atlantic. They all sold stocks of large reputation and little merit to the great unwashed. This trio in turn was connected to a galaxy of private companies, with names like Dallas Holdings, Aurora Leasing Corporation, and Valley Farm and Enterprises, in a paper empire so convoluted it is doubtful if anyone, including Morgan, fully understood it.

In a typical play, Dallas Holdings, a stock-trading company, borrowed $850,000 from three other Morgan companies, who had in turn borrowed it from Commodore Sales Acceptance, all of whom paid fees and kickbacks to Morgan and two of his partners, who owned Dallas.

This might have worked if Dallas had been any good at stock-trading, but it wasn't. It invested mainly in shares of the other companies in the group and went bankrupt, adding to everyone's woes. Morgan paid himself kickbacks on every transaction.

The usual public paeans of praise to Morgan and his financial genius reverberated throughout Canada's business press, as Atlantic Acceptance grew to be the fourth-largest finance company in the country, but the end came with startling swiftness. The Toronto-Dominion Bank, Atlantic's main lender, had given the company a standing overdraft limit of $3.7 million, to which Morgan paid very little heed. In May 1965, he had driven this to $8.8 million, and the bank threatened to call its note. The next month, it hit $9.5 million, and the bank phoned with a final warning. Morgan rushed off to New York to raise short-term money, as he had done a number of times before to stave off catastrophe, and he was still there, scrambling around the markets, when, on June 15, Royal Securities Corporation Ltd., a Toronto investment house, presented an Atlantic cheque for $5 million, and the TD Bank bounced it.

Overnight, the Montreal Trust Company Ltd., as trustees, stepped in to manage Atlantic's affairs until, as they say, "the situation could be clarified." Montreal Trust soon found that there was a slight discrepancy between the value of the company's assets as carried on the books and their real value. The discrepancy came to $52 million. The company was insolvent.

The bankruptcy brought down a score of companies associated with Atlantic, wiped out $150 million in loans advanced to the various firms by such blue-chip companies as U.S. Steel, the Ford Foundation, the Royal Bank, Royal Trust, Campbell Soup, and, in a nice touch, Moody's Investors Services, the company that assesses other companies on the basis of their financial soundness. It was finding, too late, that Atlantic was not really sound.

British Mortgage and Trust Corporation, which was owed $12 million, nearly followed Atlantic into the dumpster, and the Ontario government had to inject $3 million into the trust company after a run began, with nervous depositors lining up to take out the cash while they could. Then Victoria and Grey (now part of National Trust) stepped in and bought out British Mortgage, stopping the bank run after $22.2 million had been withdrawn.

But it was the shareholders of Atlantic who took the hardest knock. The shares went from $20.00 in early June 1965 to $1.65 on July 13, when trading was suspended. Shareholders' equity, the difference between a company's assets and liabilities, was estimated at about $10 million on the day that the $5-million cheque bounced. A month later, it was zero.

A royal commission was assembled to make the right reassuring noises, but Morgan never appeared before it. He fell ill quite suddenly, in April 1966, while the commission was getting under way, and died that October. The commission castigated Morgan as a blot and aberration on an otherwise smoothly flowing financial system. Mr. Justice S. H. S. Hughes wrote:

> Morgan, and Morgan alone, drove Atlantic forward to catastrophe and, like all the well-known swindlers of history, he did so with a fatalistic and cynical disregard of those principles of fair and honest dealing which have been generally accepted and adhered to for generations in both the civilized and savage world.[35]

I don't know much about how stock scams work in the "savage" world, but anyone who believes that the principles of fair and honest dealing are generally adhered to in the "civilized" world should come up to my place; I have some shares for sale in the Lion's Gate Bridge. The commission also made a number of recommendations which can be examined, through the layers of dust, on the third floor of the Toronto Reference Library. The report takes up four volumes and more than four thousand pages, which might be summarized this way: "You remember those guys in Amsterdam back in 1634? Well, they and their kind are still at it."

CHAPTER FOUR

Oh, What a Relief It Is

"Chapter 11 is not just a shield for corporate debtors; it is a magic sword. By dominating the courts, creditors and shareholders, companies in Chapter 11 are able to accomplish whatever agendas they choose. Chapter 11 has provided corporate debtors with a powerful means to bust unions, pick the pockets of suppliers and lenders and elude responsibility to those who have been injured and killed by their products – all at very little risk to the jobs of their top executives."
– Laurence H. Kallen, *Multinational Monitor*, 1993

$

We had come a long way from the days of debtor's prison to the notion that the bankrupt, unless he was an out-and-out crook, was more to be pitied than censured. Still, going broke was fraught with financial danger to corporations that plunged too deeply into the swamp. To make the world safer for deadbeats, and to open the doors to the bold new world of global corporations, mergers and acquisitions, and leveraged buyouts, something more was needed. Wild gambles like the $20-billion-dollar buyout of RJR Nabisco in 1988 could not take place if there was a chance that the debts piled up along the way would destroy the corporation as soon as you grabbed it. What the corporate predators needed was an escape hatch. In America it was called Chapter 11.

By 1970, both Canada and the United States were using bankruptcy laws that were frayed and worn. The Canadian amendments made in 1966 were mostly technical changes in a law passed in 1949, and erected, as we have already seen, on a scrap-heap centuries old. The American Bankruptcy Act of 1898 was amended by the Chandler Act of 1939, in an age of comparative innocence. By 1970, the business world had reinvented itself in both countries; it was as if we had in place a highway-traffic act that required the driver to ensure that his horse was properly fed. As with everything in law, there were a number of little reasons, and one big reason, for this molasses-like approach to reform. One of the little ones had to do with the difficulty of getting a complicated, arcane law changed; another was the fact that there was no partisan zip to inspire the enormous legislative effort that such change would require. No government was going to be elected, or defeated, on the contents of subsection b(iii) of paragraph two. Just about any change that might please one group of voters would displease another; it was easier to go on drifting.

But the big reason, in both countries, that reform was so slow in coming was that those in the banking community, the chief creditors, were perfectly content with the way things were. Under the prevailing law, the banks got theirs, no matter what. If the bank loaned a business or an individual money on the basis of named security, and got nervous about that security, all it had to do was call the loan and send in the receivers. There is no need to put the debtor into bankruptcy to do this. Once the loan is in doubt, the lender can appoint a receiver to look after its interests; if this requires liquidation, so be it. ("When there is a general security agreement," says Uwe Manski, "I regard that as a cloud over the assets, but the business continues. When the lender decides to realize on those assets, the cloud descends.") If somebody else threatened to call a loan from an insolvent debtor, the bank could step in first and scoop the secured asset. If the debtor wanted to file a voluntary proposal to seek protection from his lenders, the bank could step in first and scoop the secured asset. If some third party petitioned the poor slob into bankruptcy, the bank could . . ., etc.

The way to avoid such *force majeur* is to make a voluntary proposal, to jump before you are pushed, but that was blocked. Frank Bennett notes in his text on the law:

> Therefore, in practice the debtor must generally make arrangements with its secured creditors before lodging the proposal. If not, secured creditors may appoint receivers and repossess equipment and inventory, leaving the debtor few resources to continue the operations. [1]

The same rules, generally, applied in both Canada and the United States. The secured lender could step around whatever protection was raised by the act of filing for bankruptcy and realize on the asset. If you missed on a mortgage payment, the bank went into court and foreclosed, getting an order that said that it, not you, now owned the property. If a corporation missed payment on a bond secured by its head office, it could lose that head office.

In the case of unsecured loans, the creditor was not in nearly so strong a position, because there was a stay of proceedings against unsecured creditors. None could get paid until they all got paid. This was only fair, because it placed all the unsecureds in the same position. Without such a provision, the first one to rush to court might grab all the assets, and others, with equally valid claims, would be out of luck. Therefore, all creditors with provable claims had to line up in court for the shareout, which would be equally divided according to the amount owed. But banks were seldom unsecured creditors in the good old days; they were not so much in the business, as they now seem to be, of lending on a smile and a handshake.

In short, the law was tilted very much in favour of the creditor, especially in the area where it mattered, secured lending, and life was sweet, if you were a bank.

Two things happened to change this. The first was that the banks, as a class, got themselves a bad name for the way they threw their weight around. They would dole out the money, and then, the moment things began to look a little tricky for the debtor, they would send the receivers galloping in, grab the assets, sell them, and get out. Sometimes they went in too quickly, and sometimes they were just plain wrong about the shakiness of the business, and sometimes their receivers sold the assets out for much less than might have been obtained in an orderly, planned disposition. This tended to make the insolvent debtor a little cranky, and a rich body of cited law built up on cases in which an over-hasty bank found itself nailed in court for its precipitate action.

The second change was that the banks, trust companies, savings and loan associations, and credit unions got into the unsecured lending business in a big way. They began spinning out credit cards, for one thing. Credit-card costs are not secured loans, but instead of getting nervous when you don't clear the debt at month's end, when it is technically due, the bank or trust company (or, now, auto company, department store, or whatever) just giggles and tacks on an interest charge. They don't want the money back; they want you to pile up as much as possible in interest charges before the regrettable day comes when you pay it off. If you start to spend more than your credit limit, they beef up the credit limit. How's that for creating unsecured loans?

For another thing, the lenders became heavily embroiled in the commercial-paper business – less politely, the IOU business – in which a large corporation borrows a dollop of cash on a note redeemable in sixty days, or six months, or whatever, backed by nothing more than the promise to repay.

For a fourth, the lending institutions kept inventing new ways to lend money, and charged fees for having thought up the new ways. Mortgages were bundled into packages and sold in blocks. Bonds carrying high interest charges to make up for the fact that the real security behind them was as transparent as a politician's promise were floated out onto the market. Debt, that dour spinster of earlier years, was suddenly a party girl and welcomed everywhere. It was a different world, and the rules that regulated the old world simply made no sense. In particular, the mushrooming credit industry, which included the banks, wanted a wider safety net beneath their increasingly dangerous loans.

The Americans got off the mark on July 24, 1970, when Congress established a "Commission on Bankruptcy Laws of the United States" to study the issues and report back. Faster than a speeding bullet – that is to say, only three years later – the commission, made up of legislators, judges, and academics, filed its study, recommending a wholesale rewriting of the law. Nobody cared. By 1973, the Congress, and the American nation, were going through the convulsions of the Watergate Scandal, and nothing was done about the report.

There were hearings over the next three years and two running battles that took up most of the time, and attention, of the legislators. The first was an almost-endless debate about whether the rules governing consumer bankruptcies were too harsh or too lenient. Were ordinary borrowers being persuaded to forsake thrift? (yes) or being punished for simply following the enticements of the credit-card firms? (yes). This was vote-worthy stuff, and what the corporations were up to was not.

Then there was a nasty battle between and among the judges. In the United States, the men and women who sorted out bankruptcies were called "referees" up until 1973; then they became full-fledged judges, and the federal-court judges didn't like it much. They wanted the bankruptcy judges to be subordinate to them; the bankruptcy judges demurred. While this battle was raging, the National Bankruptcy Conference, a lobby of bankruptcy practitioners, made up mostly of lawyers and academics, was working on its own version of the new law; it was this version, in the main, that was finally passed[2] and signed into law on November 6, 1978, by President Jimmy Carter. It came into force in 1979.

The congressional commission had concentrated on personal bankruptcy and had paid almost no attention to business reorganization, because it was not a major issue. In 1974, only 163 publicly traded companies filed for bankruptcy, and in 1975, a recession year, 189. The way out for large corporations at the time was through government. It was about this time that a number of large corporations began to apply for public bailouts for their private ills, led by Penn Central Railway, Lockheed Aircraft Corporation, and Chrysler Corporation.

Under Lee Iacocca, Chrysler managed to wring $1.5 billion in loan guarantees out of the federal government, as well as millions by way of concessions from its own unions and suppliers. It did this by threatening to go into bankruptcy and leave the blame for all the lost jobs at the feet of Congress.[3] Iacocca claimed that two million Americans would be "severely impacted" if his company collapsed.[4] At the same time, the 452 banks involved were pressured into accepting about thirty cents on the dollar for $4.75 billion in loans. Between them, Congress and the banks bailed out the company so that it could avoid bankruptcy in 1978, while the new law was struggling into life.

From the point of view of the legislators, the problem was how to make the bankruptcy process less damaging, to prevent a recurrence of this sort of blackmail. From the point of view of the corporations, the problem was that the process then in place ensured detailed public scrutiny of the companies. Lee Iacocca himself made the point: "We should have a program to help big business in trouble without them having to go before the bar of the press."[5] That is precisely what big business got in the unexamined portions of the bill that slid through Congress.

The consumer portions of the bill were fiddled with, and then a giant loophole was driven through the process when the bill allowed the states to continue to determine what share of the debtor's assets could be held out of the wreckage; as in Canada, there is no national standard applicable (see Chapter Ten). The judges' issue was eventually sorted out by making the bankruptcy courts subordinate to the federal district courts – in theory – but in fact giving them almost complete control over issues which are, technically, "referred to" them by the district courts.

The matters that created all the fuss and fury amounted to very little; the changes that passed with almost no debate or examination were something else again. They tilted the balance between debtors and creditors heavily in favour of the debtors, especially in the case where the debtor was a large corporation. There were five main instruments for this upheaval, all of them affecting the section of the law dealing with corporate bankruptcies. This section had been known as Chapter XI; under the new act, it became Chapter 11, and it is the current law.

The first key change lay in the intent of the law, which is designed to keep the company going, or, if it has stopped, to get it going again.[6] The law has nothing to do with punishing anyone, or even inquiring too closely into what happened to cause the bankruptcy in the first place. Rascality, fraud, bad faith may all be involved; the law doesn't much care. Its purpose is to cleanse the bankrupt of its debts and send it out to borrow again.

The second key change, in line with this philosophy, provides an automatic stay on all claims against the corporation. The firm fills out a one-page petition with the clerk of the bankruptcy court in the district in which the company has its head office, requesting bankruptcy protection under Chapter 11. (Large corporations can shop around for the most favourable district in which to file, since they often have more than one home.) Applying for protection does not make a firm officially bankrupt; that only comes about if the process fails and protection is withdrawn. Bankruptcy protection is, and is meant to be, a simple operation. A court file is opened, the case is assigned to a bankruptcy judge, and the company becomes a "debtor." To make the action less unsavoury, the word "bankrupt" was deleted from the Bankruptcy Code.[7]

As soon as the petition is filed, the portcullis comes down; every claim, secured or unsecured, passes into limbo. The debtor cannot pay one creditor until it has come up with a "plan of reorganization" to pay them all. The only advantage a secured creditor has is that, in return for continued use of whatever collateral is involved – machinery, buildings, the inventory – there is usually some monthly payment towards the interest charges. These become part of the "costs of administration" of the bankruptcy case; but the secured creditor can no longer seize the assets and sell them as long as the stay lasts, no matter what it says on the mortgage bonds or leasing agreement. As Laurence Kallen, a bankruptcy lawyer, writes in his mammoth study of the law, *Corporate Welfare*, "The banks would have to sit and stew just like all the other creditors."[8]

A third key change allows the people running the corporation that got into trouble to keep on running it. Under the old law, whenever a public corporation sought protection under Chapter XI, a trustee was automatically appointed to prevent management from sacrificing the rights of the stockholders during the reorganization. Under Chapter 11, this oversight function was given to the Securities and Exchange Commission, but the SEC, in a new, deregulatory era, plays no role in bankruptcy cases. The companies run themselves. And if the shareholders don't like it, too bad. A judge can, and has, forbidden shareholders even to hold annual meetings during a bankruptcy.[9]

This is a fundamental issue in bankruptcy law everywhere. Once the managers have run the ship on the rocks, should they be removed from command? In Britain, the law is clear; they should be. It was their lousy navigation that caused the problem; get them out of the wheelhouse. Under British bankruptcy law, the moment a company applies for bankruptcy protection, or is petitioned into receivership, administrators take over the estate on behalf of the creditors and run the company. In the United States, before the 1978 reform, the court-appointed trustee might allow the old management to continue with day-to-day operations, or he might not; it depended on the circumstances of the bankruptcy.[10]

But the 1978 law did not provide for the automatic appointment of a trustee. Like everything else, that was a matter for the bankruptcy judge to determine. In the overwhelming majority of cases, no trustee is appointed in the case of a large corporation. Moreover, even if there is a trustee, the law made it clear that, unless there was evidence of theft, fraud, or other criminal behaviour, the old gang would run the firm in bankruptcy as they did before. Again, the purpose of the law is to rehabilitate the firm, to get it up and running again, and the people who know best how the company works are the men and women who work it. Accountants, receivers, others of that ilk might know how to add numbers, but they do not know how to fly airplanes, build cars, develop real estate, or make medicines. You could hardly expect them to improve the company's position; at best, they hope to preserve the status quo. Trustee-run firms are not likely to emerge from bankruptcy; they are more likely to proceed to liquidation. Therefore, under the reform, management will continue in place, under the supervision of the court.

In truth, this is a bit of a giggle. The court, which is to say, one judge, can no more run a large corporation from the bench than an accountant can from the counting house. The judge has none of the required expertise. How could he have? He becomes, inevitably, a rubber stamp for the decisions made by management, and he is constantly nudged from behind by the overwhelming purpose of the law, which is to get the company out from under the shadow of insolvency. This cannot be done by the judge constantly second-guessing managers.

The fourth key change was a deletion from the old law. The new Bankruptcy Code does not say, anywhere, that a debtor has to be insolvent in order to claim bankruptcy protection. You might think that no one would be crazy enough to go into bankruptcy if he or his company was still making money, but you would be wrong. This innocuous little elision transformed the law and rewarded large corporations at the expense of their creditors, suppliers, unions, and pension funds.

Finally, there was no time limit on the bankruptcy protection. Once in Chapter 11, a company could discharge its debts and re-emerge either by proposing a plan of reorganization acceptable to the creditors or by accepting a plan proposed by its creditors. The other side of this coin, of course, is that if the creditors reject the proposal, the protection ends, upon which the debtor becomes a bankrupt, and the liquidation process begins. The tendency is, therefore, to drag out the process, while trying to come up with an acceptable plan.

This had normally been accomplished within a year, but the new code says nothing about when it is to be done; the company can stay in the sheltering arms of the court for years. The law says that there shall be a meeting of creditors within forty days, but the only time limit after that says that only the debtor can make a proposal during a period of 120 days after filing. In practice, the bankruptcy judges extend this exclusionary period, and, in practice, judges will not accept plans which haven't either been proposed by, or espoused by, the debtor, unless the debtor has been a very naughty boy, indeed. If the judge thinks the debtor is not acting in good faith, he can establish a time limit, but it is not required by the law, and seldom happens in practice.[11]

Moreover, while the law says the debtor has to make a "disclosure statement," which is sent to the creditors to guide them when it comes to voting for or against the plan, there is nothing to say what has to be in the statement. Depending on the vigilance, or energy, of the judge, it may contain a detailed exposition of how the company got into difficulty and proposes to get out of it, or it may contain a load of fertilizer.

Once the company gets around to filing its plan, each class of creditors votes on it. The classes are created by lumping together those who have equal claims – first-mortgage bond holders are normally in a different class from second mortgagees, unsecured creditors form a single class, and so on. The shareholders, incidentally, are unsecured creditors, with very little power to affect the behaviour of the company they supposedly own. A majority of the creditors, representing two-thirds of the debts owed in each class, must approve the plan, but there are ways of whipping the reluctant ones into line. The process is called "cramming down." The judge may rule that any rejecting class is being treated fairly, even if it thinks it isn't. Therefore, its rejection of the plan is not valid, and it will be deemed to have accepted it after all. Double think, at its finest.

This Orwellian approach arises from the law's emphasis on rehabilitating the firm, no matter what, and on the faith the American system puts in the judges and lawyers. All over the United States, judges are running huge corporations, usually at the direction and behest of the same people who ran them before, and with the high-paid help of shoals of lawyers who represent all the creditors' committees – one for each class of lenders – required by the law. The lawyers are all paid for out of the cash flow of the corporation, which means that these advantages are, by and large, only available for large corporations with large cash flows. To avoid instant liquidation, there has to be enough money sliding through the till to pay all the lawyers, and the accountants, and the court costs, and something on account for secured creditors who have a grip on vital equipment. Once all this is covered, the company is home free. And the really nice thing, from the debtor's point of view, is that all these costs come out of the creditors' hides, since this is money that is no longer available to pay off the loans.

The new rules turned bankruptcy in the United States from a disgrace into a haven – for very large firms. Creditors are at a huge disadvantage. If they try to press a secured claim they are blocked by law; if they are presented with a plan of reorganization that offers them ten cents on the dollar, they can vote against it, but it may be crammed down on them, anyway. Besides, the company can stay in hiding for years, while interest charges pile up, and the creditors are whipsawed into accepting less and less of their original claim or into watching the whole thing be eaten up in costs of administration.

The net effect is that those firms that are large enough to wade through the process on their cash flows may do very well, but smaller firms are no better off than they were under the old system; they usually get shoved into liquidation. An academic study of seven years of the operation of the law showed that fewer than 12 per cent of the companies that go into Chapter 11 ever emerge. [12]

When corporate America's lawyers had had time to digest the new rules, there was a mad dash for the bankruptcy courts by giant companies with unsatisfactory balance sheets; they would use Chapter 11 to shed their debts. Chapter 11 filings jumped 53 per cent in the first year and another 93 per cent in the second, from 7,403 filings in 1980 to 22,057 filings in 1983.[13]

One of landmark cases involved Itel Corporation, a conglomerate that was in computers, railroad-car manufacturing, aircraft operation, insurance, and the leasing of shipping containers. By expanding too fast, and not keeping control of costs, the company managed to build a mountain of debt and, in 1979, losses of $443.3 million.

At that point, Itel dove into Chapter 11 protection in San Francisco and simply stopped paying interest on its $1.7 billion in loans. The tab for that came to $150 million annually, and because most of the debt was unsecured, the interest didn't even accumulate, it just evaporated. Itel paid $2 million a month to lawyers and accountants to keep the Chapter 11 kettle boiling, while shedding more than ten times that in interest charges alone. The longer it stayed in sanctuary, the more its creditors were losing, so, not surprisingly, they were willing to settle when the company finally came forward with a plan.

In the end, Itel spent two and a half years in Chapter 11 and wiped out $1.7 billion in debt by paying its creditors $587 million in cash, plus 975,000 shares of common stock and 1,650,000 shares in preferred stock. Not long after emerging from Chapter 11, Itel bought up two other companies for $835 million. Laurence Kallen writes, "Chapter 11 merely was a rest stop on the path to Itel's greater glory."[14]

It soon became clear that a company could prosper even if it didn't dive into bankruptcy, but was shoved there, as happened in February 1981 to Seatrain Lines, a giant shipbuilding company. Three creditors filed an involuntary bankruptcy case against Seatrain, led by Chase Manhattan Bank, to whom it owed $150 million. Seatrain had four thousand other, smaller creditors, and one really huge one, the U.S. government, which kept advancing money to keep the firm, and its jobs, afloat. In all, Uncle Sam guaranteed more than $500 million in loans to Seatrain. Two days after the filing, Chase Manhattan had to lend the company another $5 million to keep it going; a few days later, the government came up with another $18.2 million. Neither the government, nor Chase Manhattan, nor anyone else, could collect, and

Seatrain dragged on the Chapter 11 protection until 1983. Then it got rid of its secured creditors by giving them stock in the company, and transferred all the rest of its debts to the government, emerging well-nigh unscathed.[15]

Bankruptcy was becoming a way to slough off every sort of problem. When an Illinois newspaper, the Alton *Telegraph*, got nailed for $9.2 million in a libel case, because a reporter incorrectly named a businessman as a criminal, the paper fled into Chapter 11 to prevent the plaintiff's lawyers from seizing and selling it to pay the award. The *Telegraph* was profitable at the time, and, in opposing the Chapter 11 filing, the plaintiff argued that the law was not intended to allow a company to escape the results of its own blunders. However, the bankruptcy court judge held that the key to the new law was that it was to provide an "open" system. It didn't really matter why the company chose Chapter 11; it was entitled to court protection anyway. The newspaper remained in shelter until it was able to get the plaintiff to settle for a fraction of the original award.[16]

By the spring of 1982, Chapter 11 filings were pouring into the courts at the rate of five hundred per week. Some of them were eyebrow-raisers on a grand scale. One of these was Wickes Companies, a conglomerate that owned building-supply companies, furniture firms, supermarkets, pharmacies, clothing stores – twelve hundred retail outlets in all – and even a grain-and-beans company. Wickes went into Chapter 11 in April 1982, because the gaggle of forty-four banks from which it had borrowed $1.2 billion – nearly all of it unsecured – were getting a little testy about not being paid. One of the things that made the lenders sore was that Wickes had switched $135 million of the money it had borrowed out of accounts with banks where it owed money to other banks where it didn't owe money, so it couldn't be seized back. Not playing the game. In addition, once it went into Chapter 11, Wickes didn't have to pay any interest, a provision that saved the company more than $100 million a year on its unsecured debt.

You might also think that a company in bankruptcy would have trouble getting anyone to ship to it the goods it needed to stock its store – certainly that was the general perception in the past, and the major reason retailers tried to avoid bankruptcy – but it turned out not to be the case in fact. As mentioned earlier, because debts incurred during bankruptcy have priority in payment over those incurred beforehand, suppliers are actually more likely to get their money from a company in Chapter 11 than from one that is simply in trouble.

The conglomerate remained in shelter for two years, shed hundreds of millions in interest charges, and then re-emerged, after paying its creditors sixty cents on the dollar. About half of the company's workforce was laid off during the restructuring, and the company shareholders were badly battered as the share price tumbled. But management wound up better off than ever. The president of the firm, Sanford Sigoloff, awarded himself and other executives $18 million in bonuses for their fine work. His share, which had to be, and was, approved by the bankruptcy court, was $3.5 million. He also picked up a title, bestowed by the bankers; he was henceforth known as "Ming the Merciless."

American taxpayers, had they known about it, would have approved the title; Wickes was able to show $500 million in paper losses, and this was carried forward to be written off against future profits as the company became financially sound again. Sigoloff, reviewing the performance, said, "You can say we were good or you can say we were lucky. Take your pick."[17]

Or you could say the law was crazy.

Laurence Kallen, reviewing this case, argues:

> The whole bankruptcy system has been founded on shaky, unexamined premises. . . . Now that the Bankruptcy Code has been seized upon as a financial tool of megacorporations, with numerous cases affecting billions of dollars of other people's money, its unexamined premises have become an embarrassment. As a huge, hidden welfare program for megacorporations and their executives, it is a scandal.[18]

Another eyebrow-raiser was provided by Frank D. Lorenzo, the hardbitten, tightfisted corporate raider. On September 24, 1983, Continental Airlines, which had just been swallowed by Lorenzo's Texas Air Corporation, filed for Chapter 11 protection. The company had lost money in 1982, but there was no question of insolvency; it had cash of $58.2 million when it went into Chapter 11 and $230.2 million in receivables – money others owed to it. However, Lorenzo claimed that he would become insolvent in the future, because he had to pay high wages to his unionized employees. So, safe in bankruptcy, he fired all twelve thousand of them and then rehired them at about half their previous pay. Flight attendants earning $37,500 were offered $15,000 for longer hours. When the unions went on strike, Lorenzo claimed the work stoppage was illegal, because the unions had failed to abide by the contracts he had just thrown out the window.[19] Lorenzo made no bones of why he went for Chapter 11: "It wasn't a problem of cash or too great a debt load. Our sole problem was labour."[20]

Continental saved millions in interest charges, all of which were suspended by the filing, more millions on the cancelled labour contracts, and still more when the bankruptcy judge overseeing the case not only condoned the company's action, but prohibited the company's suppliers from refusing to sell to it on the grounds that they had no way of knowing if they would ever be paid. In the end, the Supreme Court backed the contract abrogation, Justice William Rehnquist writing that, since the "policy" of Chapter 11 was to "permit successful rehabilitation of debtors," trashing the union contracts was permissable if the process was "vital" to the purposes of Chapter 11.[21]

Continental wound up with fewer and cheaper workers, and Lorenzo walked away with $30.5 million for his stock, just before the company went bankrupt again in 1990.[22] It emerged in 1993, with backing from Air Canada, which now owns 55 per cent of the carrier.

In the meantime, Lorenzo used some of his profits, and a wheelbarrow full of junk bonds sold by Michael Milken, later a jailbird, to take over People Express Airlines Inc. of Newark and Eastern Airlines of Miami, which was already in deep trouble. Frank Borman, the chief executive officer of that company, had used the Continental case to browbeat Eastern's unions into accepting deep pay cuts – the alternative presented was that the airline would go into Chapter 11 and shed them entirely – and when Lorenzo took over, the already-poisoned atmosphere was made worse by his belligerence. He insisted that pilots, machinists, and flight attendants all take pay cuts – the company was losing money despite the earlier cuts – and, on March 4, 1989, all the unions walked out rather than comply. Five days later, Lorenzo plunged Eastern into bankruptcy protection and began arrangements to sell off the profitable pieces. He unloaded the East Coast Shuttle to Donald Trump for $365 million and tried to sell the rest to a group headed by Peter Ueberroth, the former baseball commissioner. The unions agreed to take pay cuts to help the sale. They would work, they said, for anyone but Lorenzo. The deal collapsed; the company's creditors, mostly banks, were wary of it and refused to approve the plan of reorganization.

Eastern had been badly run even before Lorenzo took over; he merely made matters worse. One of the company's brilliant ploys while in bankruptcy was to offer frequent-flyer miles to funeral directors who used Eastern to transport bodies, prompting some to suggest that the airline should strike a new motto: "People are dying to fly Eastern."

There were serious safety concerns as well, which pre-dated Lorenzo's arrival, but did not cease when he took the helm. The company pleaded guilty and paid $3.5 million in fines for a practice called "pencil whipping," in which supervisors wrote up aircraft maintenance logs to show work that had not, in fact, been done.[23] Lorenzo's antics, and the clear evidence that the unions would not go back to work for him, finally got through to the friendly bankruptcy-court judge, Burton R. Lifland, who appointed a trustee to administer the airline in April 1990, while Lorenzo walked away. By this time, Eastern had lost another $1.2 billion.[24]

The trustee, Martin R. Shugrue, Jr., the former vice-chairman of Pan American World Airways Inc., gave himself a pay hike in

December 1990 and thoughtfully made it retroactive to the day he took over. He went from $425,000 to $600,000 annually. Judge Lifland approved. Shugrue then installed a colleague of his, Jack E. Robinson III, as president of one of Eastern's subsidiaries, Bar Harbour Airways Inc. and expanded that commuter line. The creditors objected to this, but Judge Lifland overruled them. Robinson ran Bar Harbour into bankruptcy in January 1991.[25]

Eastern staggered on, losing more money, until October 1991, when Shugrue accepted the demand of unsecured creditors that it be reclassified as a Chapter 7 bankruptcy. Chapter 7 of the Bankruptcy Code covers liquidation; in Chapter 7 there is no attempt to keep the company going – instead, it is wound up as quickly and cheaply as possible.

You must not think that this was a total disaster for everyone – only for those who worked for, loaned to, supplied, or otherwise dealt with Eastern. The firm of Weil, Gotshal & Manges, one of Lorenzo's lawfirms, billed the estate $22 million; Shugrue's own firm got $7 million, and, in all, lawyers, accountants, and consultants scooped $86 million out of Eastern's fast-emptying till, while the unsecured creditors wound up with what one of them described, in a poignant, one-word epitaph, as "zilch."[26] They lost $2.25 billion.

Upon which Lorenzo applied for a charter to open a new airline, which he was going to call Friendship Airlines, until he was persuaded that this wouldn't work, given his record, so he changed it to AXT. The unions laid a complaint before the transportation department in Washington, charging that Lorenzo was unfit to run an airline, and Lorenzo was refused the charter.[27]

Lorenzo had sailed through two and a half bankruptcies, if we give him only half points for the second Continental failure, getting richer all the time, while thousands of his employees saw their wages cut and then their jobs disappear.

In Chapter 11 terms, no doubt the world was unfolding as it should. Things would soon get much worse for creditors, and much better for giant corporations.

CHAPTER FIVE

Canada Lurches Towards Chapter 11

"We *condition* people to borrow. If you have that kind of a system, you need an escape valve. In the old days, you could be drawn and quartered, but that doesn't add anything to the economy. We want a rehabilitative process." – Bankruptcy lawyer Harvey Miller, 1991[1]

$

Meanwhile, back in Canada, we were going through something of the same evolution, but in a much more stately – and, in the end, slightly less damaging – manner. Here, as in the United States, the process began in 1970 and led to innumerable committees, commissions, legislative proposals – seven, in all – and, at last, a new law. The process is briefly described in Chapter Two, along with some of the provisions of that law. For our purposes here, we need only to look at the way Chapter 27, 40-41 Elizabeth II, An Act to amend the Bankruptcy Act, compares to the U.S. version on the crucial issue of corporate insolvency. The very first paragraph of the act changed its name from the Bankruptcy Act to An Act Respecting Bankruptcy and Insolvency (BIA).

Remember, BIA is not a new law; it is a series of amendments to the old law, the 1949 law, as fiddled around with in 1966. The attempts to bring forth a brand-new piece of legislation were frustrated by the infighting that took place over the years as the various lobby groups, representing creditors, debtors, wage-earners, wage-payers, and practitioners, squabbled. The end result, however, like so many things Canadian, moved in an American direction, but did not go all the way.

In part, this was because we have a different judicial approach and, in part, because Canadian practice varies from that in both the United States and the United Kingdom. Uwe Manski, president of the Canadian Insolvency Practitioners' Association, explains, "American law is lawyer-driven; it is very adversarial; ours is much more driven by the need to sort out the mess, not to declare a winner."[2] Furthermore, we have never had a bankruptcy court in the American sense. In most provinces, bankruptcies are handled by the regular courts. In Ontario and British Columbia, a number of judges of the senior court circuit specialize in commercial law ("the commercial list"), and a handful of these become experts in bankruptcy law. The key cases are directed to these judges, but there is nothing in law to say they must be.

Moreover, the BIA does not have a Chapter 11 for companies only, or even a Chapter XI. Our law says that an insolvent person is someone who owes at least one thousand dollars to a creditor or creditors and has committed an act of bankruptcy. The subject may be a person or a corporation. The law dealing exclusively with large corporations is not contained in the BIA at all; it is the Companies' Creditors Arrangement Act, the CCAA. That is the law that is referred to as "Canada's Chapter 11." Or, by its critics, as "Chapter 11 without rules." It was hastily adopted from English insolvency practice during the Great Depression to help stricken companies survive.

If we look at the combination of the BIA and the CCAA under the five headings we used above in connection with American reform, we find some similarities and some major differences.

1. The Canadian law, like the American one, makes recovery from bankruptcy the primary goal of the act. The CCAA says this in so many

words; it is "an Act to facilitate compromises and arrangements between companies and their creditors."[3] The BIA weaves this goal through the dense, almost-impenetrable clauses of the law itself. Bruce Leonard, a Toronto lawyer, told *Canadian Lawyer* magazine that he doubted "Parliament can be credited with having much idea at all what it was doing when it passed the act."[4] This is probably true, but the experts who actually wrestled with the law over the decades did have a clear intent to make it easier for a stricken company to reorganize, short of bankruptcy. Derrick Tay, a prominent Canadian legal authority, described the new law as "the move from liquidation to rehabilitation."[5]

2. There is an automatic stay against both secured and unsecured creditors, just as with the American law, but as we shall see, it is not nearly so sweeping or durable. In Canada, the debtor files a notice of intention to file a proposal with the official receiver[6] and is automatically protected for thirty days, unless the debtor is not acting in good faith or "will not be likely to be able to make a viable proposal before the expiration of the period in question."[7]

This is one of those murky areas of law. In one Ontario case, creditors have been able to get the stay killed and the proposal terminated, followed by liquidation. In a parallel Quebec case, Nationair, the troubled regional airline, was given a thirty-day stay and three extensions, when it was clear that it could never come up with an acceptable proposal.[8] The Nationair case seems more in line with what the law meant, and a stay is considered to be normal part of the process.

3. In Canada, as in the United States, management of the company normally continues in place. The act doesn't spell this out, it is simply the usual practice. A trustee is appointed, with a number of duties, such as contacting the creditors, providing a cash flow from the insolvent person or company, reporting on the state of the debtor to the first meeting of creditors – which he is also responsible for calling – bird-dogging the proposal through the court, and reporting on it to the official receiver.[9] But the trustee does not try to oversee the firm's internal

workings, only the reorganization or, if that cannot be accomplished, the liquidation. In day-to-day matters, the company continues under the same management, except where there has been a gross violation.

4. Unlike the United States, we demand that our debtors be broke, at least on paper, before seeking protection. The nub of the amendments are the sections under which a person or company under financial seige can file a voluntary proposal; this triggers the protective stay. But proposals may only be made by: "(a) an insolvent person; (b) a receiver . . . but only in relation to an insolvent person; (c) a liquidator of an insolvent person's property; (d) a bankrupt; and (e) a trustee of the estate of a bankrupt."[10] Similarly, under the CCAA, only a "debtor company" can apply for protection, and "debtor company means any company that: (a) is bankrupt or insolvent; (b) has committed an act of bankruptcy"[11]; or has been petitioned into bankruptcy.

5. Finally, the protection extended by the law is hedged with deadlines, again, in direct contrast to American practice. The trustee named when the proposal is filed must produce a cash-flow statement within ten days, to start with, along with a statement as to its "reasonableness." The cash flow is the amount of money passing through the till, minus expenses. Even a company deeply in debt may have a lot of cash coming in; the problem is that more is flowing out, because it has to pay interest on borrowed funds. The cash-flow statement is an attempt to show how much money, if any, there is to work with. One trustee told me, "You make a wild guess. The company produces the numbers, you look at them, compare them to last year, and sign something that says you have no reason to doubt their reasonableness. You would be crazy to go further than that."

Many of the trustees argue that ten days is entirely too short a time span in which to grasp the complexities of a large corporation's affairs. The problem is exacerbated by the fact that the law doesn't specify what period of the company's operations is to be covered by this estimate. Is it three months – the time you would expect to pass before a proposal is approved by creditors? A year? Forever? Obviously, the longer the period, the more it costs to prepare. Uwe Manski comments, "I remember one trustee saying, 'I had to charge $30,000, because we did a three-year cash flow,' and I said, 'Why three years?' and he said, 'Well, in order to pay [the creditors] what we could pay them it would take three years to sort everything out.'"[12] However, there is no provision for an extension of the ten-day time limit to prepare the cash-flow statement, whether it covers a month or three years; the trustee has to make the best guess possible, and that is that.

Then, the debtor must be ready with a proposal within thirty days, in which he states how much he can or will pay, and, within twenty-one days after that, there must be a first meeting of creditors to consider the proposal. The court can extend the time for the meeting, in increments of forty-five days, to a maximum of five months, so that the maximum period of protection against creditors is seven months (ten days, thirty days, twenty-one days, plus five months).[13] This is the opposite of the American approach and came about in reaction to the deliberate stalling visible under Chapter 11 cases across the border.

There are, however, a number of other debtor-friendly items in the new law. For one thing, a corporation can repudiate commercial leases that it considers to be too high by paying a penalty of six months' rent, if it can show that such a shedding is necessary to get the company on its feet again.[14] Corporate leases are often for very lengthy periods – up to twenty-five years – so this is a huge advantage, which, in effect, transfers some of the pain of insolvency over to the landlord, who, presumably, had nothing to do with the problem. This relief is now being used by bankruptcy trustees to bludgeon landlords, as Uwe Manski explained in an interview. "Trustees are negotiating their way out of the leases for less than the six months. They tell the landlord that if he insists on the six months, he's not going to get anything. We're just going to take the goods, close the place, and be out of there in a couple of days. He might make a decision to accept a one-month penalty, and that will help the restructuring."

The net effect is to put the landlord in a worse position even than other unsecured creditors, and, while not many of us want to shed tears for landlords, this does raise a question of equity. Why should landlords, and investors in the development companies that become landlords, be singled out for discriminatory treatment?

Another club handed to the debtor lies in the fact that it is he who can determine which secured creditors are lumped into which classes for purposes of voting on the proposal.[15] (The unsecured creditors, as we have already seen, form a separate class.) This gives the insolvent a weapon like the "cram down" available to his American cousin; if one group of creditors appears to be likely to balk at the meagre fare offered, they can be stuck in with other, friendly types and voted into acquiesence. If the perceived inequity is gross enough, the offended class of creditors can apply to the courts to have the classifications overturned,[16] but this will prove to be an expensive, and time-consuming, business. One bankruptcy lawyer told me, "Walk through the court door in any major case, and you'd better have $50,000 to spend; and then you might lose." As well, if a single creditor represents enough of the debt to be able to block acceptance of the proposal, he can insist on equity, whether the others wish it or not; the law works directly against the smaller creditors. What is just about this?

On the other hand, suppliers are given a powerful new right under the act, which puts them in a much better position than their American counterparts. In the past, unpaid suppliers were simply unsecured creditors and were often dragged in at the end of the pay-out line. But, under the BIA, a supplier has the right to repossess goods shipped to the insolvent company, provided the right is exercised within ten days of receiving notice of the bankruptcy filing. The right only applies to goods shipped in the thirty days previous to the filing, so it would not prevent a company stocking up, waiting thirty days, and then ducking into protection.

However, any company that doesn't fancy its chances under the BIA can simply apply for protection, instead, under the CCAA. This law says, in an astonishingly brief eight pages, that, where a debtor company has "secured or unsecured bonds," either the company, or a creditor, or a trustee in bankruptcy can go to court and have the court approve an arrangement which will allow the company to continue, provided that a majority of the creditors, representing three-quarters of the debts, sanctions the deal in a recorded vote. And, if it does, the arrangements are binding on all the creditors, whether they approve or not. [17] This is the same sanctuary provided by Chapter 11 (except that we require a three-quarters vote, where they require two-thirds) and is another example of how we are moving closer to the Americans; secured and unsecured creditors alike are stayed. And, like Chapter 11, the protection has no time limit; it is in place, once the court approves, "until such time as the court may proscribe or until any further order." [18]

Under Chapter 11, interest on secured debts continues to pile up, while that on unsecured loans disappears; under the CCAA both kinds of interest are maintained and, in the unlikely event that there is money enough to pay them, they will be paid. In the far more normal course, they will be written off for pennies on the dollar.

Again, while the secured creditor, under the BIA, can be held off for only thirty days to start with, and seven months if every possible extension is granted, once that time lapses, he can realize on his security, although he is required to give ten days' notice before doing so; under the CCAA, he can only slink off into the night, muttering, "Curses, foiled again."

Uwe Manski notes, "The Canadian system has been superior because of the fact that you can't take away the secured creditor's right to realize on his security. He can just say, 'Well, no, I'm going to call this in.'"

That advantage disappears if the debtor can afford the legal and accounting bills required to shelter under the CCAA. The argument behind the vast vagueness of the CCAA, and its debtor-friendly atmosphere, is that a company may have been plunged into financial trouble by one drastic mistake in an otherwise blameless career; give it a chance to wipe clear the debt created by that blunder and it will rise and shine once more. The alternative is to send it into liquidation and send most of its employees onto the unemployment rolls. That is true, and there have been cases under the CCAA in which an ailing company has been successfully nursed back to health, where a harsher regime might have led to liquidation. Algoma Steel Corp. Ltd. of Sault Ste. Marie, Ontario, was such a case.

Algoma, the Soo's largest employer, ran into trouble shortly after it was taken over by Dofasco Inc. of Hamilton, Ontario, in 1988 and lost $702 million in 1990, largely because of a steelworkers strike.[19] The company went into CCAA protection in February 1991, owing $800 million, and spent fourteen months working out a rescue plan. The problem was as much political as financial, with six thousand jobs at stake, and the solution involved a hefty injection of politics. The Ontario government put up a loan guarantee of $110 million, Dofasco wrote off its investment of $600 million, and most of the debt and all interest owed were converted into "distressed preferred shares," which are non-voting shares, but on which the dividends, if any, escape taxes. Control of the company, once Dofasco was out, passed to the employees themselves, and they paid for their ownership by taking a $2.89-per-hour cut in wages, and the loss of a week's vacation pay. Salaried employees also had wage cuts of 14.5 per cent.[20] In addition, the union agreed to slashing twenty-four hundred workers from the payroll, through attrition and early retirement. One of the first things the workers did, after docking their own pay, was to remove the time clocks.

The creditors, and the workers, are sharing the pain and the risks, which include the fact that the union insists on obtaining iron ore for its steel from a low-grade mine in Wawa, Ontario, which is unionized.[21] With its debtload gone, and markets recovering, Algoma posted a profit in the third quarter of 1993 of $4.9 million. The comparable figure a year earlier had been a loss of $27.9 million. Algoma shares, in turn, traded at $20.75 on January 17, 1994; they had been as low as $1.50.[22] The company's future is far from rosy, in part because of American protectionism, blocking the firm's products from the U.S. market in the name of free trade, but at least the Algoma experiment has to be viewed as a brave try to make the CCAA do something other than funnel money to lawyers and accountants.

The other side of this coin is that a corporate management which has piled up debts through bad judgement, arrogance, and business blunders can slough off the debts – provided there is enough money to remain under the court's protection – and transfer much of the pain to its creditors.

The law has been used, with varying degrees of equity, in a number of recent Canadian financial adventures:

• Grafton–Fraser Inc., a large men's clothing retailer, shed $25 million in debt in six months of protection in 1992. Grafton–Fraser owned three chains, Jack Fraser, Grafton & Co., and George Richards. In the process, the company closed 103 of its 221 stores, fired 700 employees, and wound up with majority ownership in the hands of Cadillac Fairview Inc., the American-owned developer.[23]

• Creditors owed more than $400 million were held at bay by Westar Mining Ltd. for three months, only to have the British Columbia coal company continue to bleed money until it finally staggered into liquidation in 1993. All the directors and company officers quit, to avoid personal liability for the wage claims of the 2,000 employees. Secured debts of $370 million gobbled up all the available money, and the directors were afraid they would be stuck with the unpaid wage claims, so they downed briefcases and walked away. Edwin Phillips, the former chairman, said that fraud and negligence were one thing, "but punishing a director with levies in the millions of dollars for failing in his efforts to save a company from bankruptcy" was both "unjust in the extreme" and "counter-productive."[24] True, but not much comfort to the workers.

• Peoples Jewellers Ltd. dodged into protection when it began to sink under the weight of debts it took on while acquiring Zale Corp. of Dallas, Texas. CCAA protection did not work; the company went into bankruptcy in July 1993, when its restructuring plan was voted down.[25]

• Bargain Harold's Discount Ltd. got into difficulty when it spent millions trying to change the company's computerized merchandise-control system into a replica of that used by the giant Canadian Tire Corp. Ltd. Not coincidentally, the company was being run by Dean

Muncaster, former chairman of Canadian Tire. The new computer system, which cost $15 million, was not properly managed and had the retailer ordering supplies it didn't need for its 160 stores and predicting profits it was not going to make – what a court judgment would later call "erroneous gross market assumptions."[26] On October 2, 1991, there was a 1991 profit of $500,000, which was remeasured to become a loss of $3 million on October 3, $2.2 million on October 8, $4 million on November 14, $8 million on December 6, and a grand minus of $20 million on February 19, 1992. There was, let us say, a certain inexactitude in the process. Adding to the problem was the fact that Bargain Harold's had been bought in 1990 by Muncaster and a group of fellow investors for $100 million, almost all of it unsecured debt, and it could not meet the payments.

The company applied for CCAA protection in February 1992, owing $130 million. However, the court, for a wonder, refused the application and turned the company over to a receiver for liquidation. The court's ground for the decision was that the company didn't really have a restructuring plan, beyond closing stores and laying off employees, and it didn't need CCAA protection for that. The net result was a loss of 1,600 full-time and 2,360 part-time jobs.[27]

As so often happens, the bankruptcy drew in others. Dominion Smallwares Ltd., the largest unsecured creditor, was owed $2.5 million by the retailer, which it could not collect, so it in turn scuttled under CCAA protection. In all, unsecured creditors, many of them suppliers of goods to the discount chain, saw $51 million go up in smoke. The CCAA was virtually useless in this case, but perhaps no other law would have worked, either.

The CCAA case with which I am most familiar is that of Olympia & York Developments Ltd. of Toronto, the remarkable creation of the remarkable Reichmann brothers, Albert, Paul, and Ralph.[28] They came to Canada from Morocco in the fifties, after a long, torturous flight from their native Hungary during the Second World War, and went into the tile business in Toronto. As the business prospered, they built a new warehouse – so efficiently that other companies asked them to build for them. Before long, they had blossomed into a development company, first in Canada and then in the United States. They bought up eight huge office buildings in Manhattan, when New York was at its nadir, and gained a worldwide reputation, as well as a fortune, when the deal paid off with the city's recovery. Then they got into a lot of businesses about which they knew very little – oil, gas, paper, food, and liquor – at just about the same time they embarked on their largest-ever development at Canary Wharf, in London, England.

In 1987, O&Y took over this project from a colourful Texas developer, G. Ware Travelstead, when Travelstead ran out of money. In the next four years they pumped $3.1 billion into a development built at the wrong place at the wrong time. It was the assumption of the family strategist, Paul Reichmann, executive vice-president of O&Y, that London's financial district would remove itself to Canary Wharf, on the Isle of Dogs, three miles east of downtown London, and there would establish the financial centre of the European Community. Reichmann assumed this would have to come about, because the City of London had passed a bylaw prohibiting further development within the "Square Mile," the financial centre of the British capital.

It was not to be. First, the City amended its bylaw, wiping out much of the pressure to expand elsewhere. Then, the European Community chose Frankfurt for its financial capital. And then the world went into a recession that plunged real-estate values – and business leases – into the nether depths.

On May 14, 1992, O&Y, which had been stalling its clamouring creditors for months, could stall no more. It filed for bankruptcy protection for twenty-nine of its subsidiary companies under Chapter 11 in New York and under the CCAA in Toronto. Soon after, the company applied for administration in London. Those actions blocked every attempt by banks and other creditors, who had extended more than $16 billion U.S. to the giant conglomerate, to collect. O&Y remained in court sanctuary until February 5, 1993, while its debts were reorganized, renegotiated, and written off. Since the Canadian system is not so blind, or forgiving, as the American one, the Reichmanns lost control of their companies, eventually. (In England, they lost control at once.) Their creditors now own what was O&Y property.

But the Reichmanns escaped almost unscathed. They lost the paper fortunes built up within the family empire, but held onto the real money that they had paid themselves over the years. On February 8, 1993, three days after a Toronto court approved the restructuring plan submitted under the CCAA, Paul Reichmann announced a new family partnership, Reichmann Partners International, which was soon involved in a $1-billion development deal in Mexico City.

The O&Y debt had been transferred to the shareholders in the banks who put up the money and bondholders who believed the hype about the Reichmann genius. The banks responded by cutting back on business loans, especially in real-estate areas, jacking up bank charges – or inventing new items to charge on – and laying off staff. The Canadian Imperial Bank of Commerce, the largest Canadian lending bank to the Reichmanns, laid off twenty-five hundred employees, not one of whom had advised management to shovel out more money to O&Y.

One of the disturbing facets of the O&Y restructuring was the way it dealt with the fact that some of the companies within the empire were still making money and others were not, and all were pooled together. This doesn't sound like much of an issue, but in the world of finance, it is. O&Y set up separate companies for most of its buildings, and these separate firms would issue bonds backed by the property. Thus, if you invested in the bonds issued by First Canadian Place in Toronto, your loan was backed by the building itself, which was, for most of its life under O&Y, a moneymaker.

However, money from the profitable buildings was being used to finance the débâcle on Canary Wharf. The investors might not have cared; it was the Canadian property that covered their loans. But when the company sought CCAA protection, the court, in a number of cases, declared that companies that were solvent were insolvent; the stream of cash was pooled. This meant that bondholders whose funds were covered by profitable buildings were in the same position as those who had invested in far-more-dubious properties. Unfortunately, there was no way the investors could have known that, no way of allowing for it by, for example, exacting a higher rate of interest from O&Y to cover the higher risk.

The rules were made up by the courts as the case went along. The only power given to the court in the actual law is in section 11, which states, "The court . . . may, on notice to any other person or without notice as it may see fit," make an order staying all proceedings against the company. That's it. The court does not have the right to make up new rules, it just does so.

And the rules being made up under the CCAA are, in some instances, even more bizarre than those under Chapter 11. In one case, the court ordered that suppliers had to continue to ship goods to the bankrupt company, even though they had not been paid for goods already shipped and with no guarantee that they would be paid for the new goods. This is a clear contradiction to the provisions of the BIA, and Toronto insolvency lawyer Rick Orzy asks, "If, in the BIA, the only time this century Parliament ever looked at this type of issue in a meaningful way, it decided that the creditor was entitled to be assured payment for new shipments, it is hard to see the basis for making an order that allows a supplier's rights to be ignored."[29]

In another case, under the court order granted Majestic Electronics, suppliers were actually commanded to "continue to pay volume rebates and advertising" to that firm while it was in CCAA protection.[30] Even more astonishingly, creditors were prevented from demanding payment for letters of credit issued by the firm, and the issuing banks were enjoined from honouring such letters of credit, if they were presented for payment.[31] One way a company can protect itself from the insolvency of another firm with which it has dealings, and about which it has doubts, is to demand letters of credit, which are normally as cashable as a traveller's cheque. Indeed, such letters became common as a way to avoid the traps judges were building in CCAA cases. It is a matter of international treaty that "LCs," as they are called, shall not be invalidated, so the Majestic ruling not only attacked the company's more prudent lenders, it put the Canadian banks in default of their international obligations.

In a third case, the court effectively ordered a creditor to continue to supply money to Pacific National Leasing, which was already in CCAA protection, and they did, and they lost it. In a fourth case, the judge ordered an insurance company to keep up its fidelity insurance on a company in receivership, although the CCAA provides no basis whatsoever for such an order. Fidelity insurance is the sort of insurance that covers bonded carriers; there is no way to measure the risk in such coverage on a company which is insolvent. The insurer is faced with either cancelling the policy, and being found in contempt of court, or keeping it up and, in effect, providing insurance for free for an insolvent client. No legislature ever pronounced that this is what is wanted or needed in insolvency cases. Here we have judges making up public policy under the CCAA in exactly the same way American judges create law.

In the case of Bramalea Limited, the giant development firm owned by the Edper Group, the stay extended by the court covered "any person who is, directly or indirectly, obligated for the obligations of an Applicant."[32] This meant that any creditor who had been wily enough, or nervous enough, to demand the backing of a guarantor for his loans (such as the parent companies in the Edper Group) was out of luck. The court said, with no justification in the CCAA or any other written law, that this, too, was blocked.

This is all done to keep the companies going. That is a good thing, in principle, but to keep an insolvent company going long after it ought to be liquidated is both unfair and perverse, and simply transfers the costs, and the job losses, to creditors, who were not the ones who caused the problem.

The woolly vagueness of the CCAA provides a loophole through which billions of dollars are driven every year. As in the Chapter 11 cases, the judges tend to become advocates for the debtor, to such an extent that many bankruptcy practitioners are alarmed and outraged, although they are unwilling and unable to make their views known, except under the cloak of anonymity, for fear of inviting a contempt-of-court citation.

One lawyer who has acted in a number of bankruptcies in Montreal told me, "They are writing orders under the CCAA for which there is no basis in law whatsoever. I have had cases where it was perfectly clear that the judge would always decide everything in favour of saving the company. And if they couldn't do it in open court, they would call you into their chambers and beat up on you. I had one of these meetings in which, every time the judge referred to the insolvent company, he would say 'we.' Kind of hard to go up against that."

One western judge is famous for scheduling meetings with lawyers for late in the afternoon, forgetting to give notice to legal counsel for the creditors, neglecting to have a court reporter present for a verbatim account of the proceedings, and then writing up court orders that benefit the debtor corporation. As one lawyer who has seen a number of these orders argues, "You get notice of what happened in chambers, and you can fight it, but you are up against a presumption that is very hard to overturn, once the document has been issued."

Another bankruptcy lawyer complains that "debtors' lawyers go to the judges weeks and sometimes months before they file, and they start making friends with the judges on these points. Not every judge will do this, but some will. They almost make deals with the judges. I've got to the point where I send a letter to the other side that says, 'Every time you go before a judge I want to be there,' and of course they never honour it, but my letter is on file. They even draw up draft orders and show them to the judges, and I know for a fact that one judge said to a company's lawyer, 'Come and see me at four o'clock to do our filing and don't tell anybody else, and by the time they hear about it, it will be tomorrow, and we'll deal with them then.'"

Not the way they teach it at Osgoode Hall. To make a bad situation worse, it is the smaller creditors who get blindsided. In a CCAA restructuring, you will remember, the deal must be accepted by creditors representing three-quarters of the amount outstanding in each class.

Thus, any creditor who represents 25 per cent or more of the debt can exercise a veto. Again, an insolvency lawyer explained to me how this works.

"We represented suppliers to a major clothing-store chain that went into CCAA. When it came time to make an arrangement, the landlords who owned the properties where the stores were located got a much better deal than we did.

"The chain had simply walked away from all its leases. Now, normally they couldn't do that, because the leases would survive the bankruptcy, and, after they came out of the restructuring, the landlord could go after them for the money still owing. However, the judge ruled that walking away from the leases amounted to effective termination, and the money owing was unsecured debt. So, we went to the judge and said, 'This isn't fair. You made an order that the landlords were unsecured creditors, so they are in the same class as we are. You can't give them a better deal than us.' But the lawyer representing the landlords stood up and said, 'If you don't give us a better deal, we'll kill it.' That was his total legal argument, and, since they represented a large portion of the money owing, they could have done it.

"The way the judge got around this was really outrageous. He said that, when he made his order that the landlords were unsecured creditors, he shouldn't have done so. There were twenty lawyers present when he said this, but no court reporter. Then he ruled that they were in a different class than we were, because a landlord has the right to distrain – he can seize the goods in the stores for money owing on the leases. So, because at one time they had this right, they were different from us, which was totally ludicrous, because he was the one who killed the leases. He said they didn't have these rights, but he was going to give them to them anyway. These judges have ceased to be judges and are dealbrokers instead."

The CCAA process apes the basic weakness of Chapter 11, in that it transfers most of the pain away from those who caused it and leaves everything to the direction of the courts – which seems to mean to the direction of the companies. The lawyers and trustees who like it praise its "flexibility"; since it leaves so much unsaid, there is more room to manoeuvre. Peter P. Farkas, a financial consultant and bankruptcy trustee, has described it as "the same as Chapter 11 proceedings in the U.S., but without rules."[33] It is precisely this aspect that brings down the wrath of its critics. Rick Orzy says, "It's heaven for debtors, because obviously they can do very well if they can get the right judge."

Judge-shopping has become as important a principle in bankruptcy law as anything the legislators have bothered to enact, and this, again, is an imitation of the worst parts of American practice.

Rick Orzy's solution is simple. "If there are seventy-five things wrong with the BIA, what we ought to do is to abolish the CCAA and fix up those seventy-five things."

The Mulroney government contemplated abolishing the CCAA. However, by the time the lobbyists, led by the bankruptcy lawyers for whom CCAA work is manna from heaven, had finished their pleading, the best the legislators could come up with was the provision to look at the law again in 1995.[34]

I regard the failure to scrap the CCCA as ominous, although many of the busiest bankruptcy practitioners do not. Uwe Manski says, "I used to think the CCAA was a very bad piece of legislation. But I think its flexibility has shown it to be useful. And I don't believe we are going to end up with a Canadian Chapter 11." However, in my view, taken together, the CCAA and the reformed BIA have moved us in the direction of American practice. And the record shows that American practice stinks.

Moreover, there is no provision under the CCAA, as there is under the BIA, to keep track of statistics, and none are kept. Thus, we have no idea what the operation of this law is costing us, which means we have no measure of by far the most important sector of bankruptcy in Canada. In 1992, the year the O&Y restructuring was taking place, the Office of the Superintendent of Bankruptcies reported that the total liabilities in bankruptcies in Canada came to $7.4 billion.[35] But the O&Y liabilities under the CCAA came to more than $18 billion,[36] and there were other bankruptcies going through the courts involving more than a billion each, such as Bramalea. By far the largest sector of our bankruptcies, and losses, goes unreported. How we can have a rational national policy in these circumstances remains one of those eternal mysteries, like how they put the gooey stuff inside the Cara-milk bar.

We face two sets of damages from the way our bankruptcy system operates; one has to do with the cost and inequity created when companies plunge into insolvency through cupidity, stupidity, or plain bad luck; the other with bankruptcies brought about because the protection afforded is a positive boon to the corporation involved. I propose, in the next two chapters, to deal with the most prevalent of the former cases in recent North American experience, the collapse of the savings and loan associations in the United States and their Canadian equivalents. Then the focus will shift to two cases where insolvency has been made into a positive perversion of justice.

CHAPTER SIX

The S&Ls

"Greed has been severely underestimated and denigrated. There is nothing wrong with avarice as a motive, as long as it doesn't lead to anti-social conduct." – Conrad Black, 1988 [1]

$

There is probably no clearer story of the way in which fraud and bankruptcy are interlinked than the tangled tale of the savings and loans associations of the United States. The collapse of these once-proud companies led not only to hundreds of corporate bankruptcies, but thousands of personal bankruptcies, as well. The S&Ls raise a number of issues that we must confront if we are ever to deal with problems of debtors' and creditors' rights. Chief among these are: How much regulation is enough? and How far should the state go to protect individuals from their own greed and stupidity? As we will see, the same motives and methods that brought down the S&Ls are actively in play in Canada today and keep popping up in such débâcles as the demise of Greymac Trust, the Osler collapse, and the bellyflop performed before a horrified audience by Standard Trustco.

The name most people associate with the S&Ls is that of Charles Keating, the Arizona executive who wound up in jail as a result of his less-than-perfect financial dealings. But he was only one of a star-studded cast, some of whom now wear numbers across their chests, and others of whom are still – or again – at large. Many of these men were not financiers at all, but real-estate developers, who were turned into bankers by the magic wand of Ronald Reagan, the good fairy of free enterprise and the foe of regulation. Developers, until Reagan's time, were always running short of capital, just when they had some-thing really good – a mall, a hotel, a housing development, or a busi-ness complex – lined up in their sights. What they needed, and what deregulation provided for them, was their very own piggy-banks. Well, not their very own, in the sense that they put the money in – oth-ers would take care of that – but they would take it out, whenever they wanted to. All they had to do was to buy an S&L.

In the bad old days, there was very little point, for a financial high-flyer, in owning an S&L, even if the law would allow you to do so, which, if you were a developer, it would not. These companies were formed for the very restricted purpose of financing houses. The first savings and loan, the Oxford Provident Building and Loan Soci-ety, was formed on the same basis as a credit union, in 1831, in Frank-ford, Pennsylvania, now part of Philadelphia. At the time, about the only way to own your own house, if you weren't rich, was to borrow from someone who was, but the thirty-seven men who started Oxford Provident worked it out that, if they each chipped in, one of them would be able to buy a house with their joint savings, and then another, and another. They contributed five dollars each to start with, and deposited an additional three dollars a month. Comly Rich, the village lamplighter, drew the lucky straw on April 11, 1831, and borrowed $500 to buy a house on Orchard Street.[2] The institu-tion charged no interest, and paid none; the purpose was to buy houses, not to make money.

Other S&Ls sprang up over the years, and the institutions became more sophisticated, but the underlying principles remained the same.

They gathered deposits by paying people interest and loaned the money out to other neighbours at a slightly higher rate than they themselves paid. The difference, once costs came out, was profit, which was ploughed back into the capital base to allow more lending. Some of the companies were called "mutuals," because, like Oxford Provident, they were owned by the depositors. Others were owned by shareholders and, together with the credit unions they closely resembled, were called "thrifts." Since S&Ls made up by far the most important sector of the thrifts, the two words are used interchangeably.

However they were set up, these institutions were locally controlled, and they served the community. In the Frank Capra film *It's a Wonderful Life*, Jimmy Stewart played the perfect manager of a local thrift, who, what with one thing and another, was contemplating suicide. Then, with the intervention of an angel, something we could all use these days, he was given a series of visions of his town in a world in which he had not been born, had not been handing out needed loans to worthy locals. The town without Jimmy, he learned, was a very grim place indeed. Upon which, Stewart cheesed the suicide, went home to Donna Reed, and loaned happily ever after.

In point of fact, the S&Ls were never the dream institutions of Frank Capra's 1946 film; they tended to be used mainly on behalf of the community élite. Still, they were community institutions, with modest rates and modest aims. They were prohibited by law from engaging in risky loans, including most commercial loans, and the rate of interest they could pay depositors was also controlled and always low.

When the Great Depression struck, hundreds of S&Ls all over the United States failed, along with the banks, and for the same reason: panicky depositors rushed in to try to collect their money before it vanished down the spout of general insolvency. To try to halt the run on deposits, the Hoover administration established the Federal Home Loan Bank System in July 1932 to provide a reserve, and some federal oversight, for the S&Ls, which were, and are, mostly state-chartered. The Federal Home Loan Bank was set up "to encourage thrift and economical home ownership" by stepping in when one of the thrifts faltered and keeping an eye on the system, generally, through a Bank Board, charged with "supervising and regulating savings institutions which specialize in the financing of residential real estate."[3] The Bank Board was the S&L equivalent of the Federal Reserve Banks, who keep a generally genial eye on the commercial banking system. The money for bailouts was, and still is, provided by assessments on twelve Regional Federal Home Loan Banks, who collect in turn from the S&Ls. Or, to put it another way, the regulator is paid by the regulatees. (Just as, in Canada, the inspector general of banks is paid by the banks.)

The gap was filled by President Franklin Roosevelt's National Housing Act of 1934. This created the Federal Savings and Loan Insurance Corporation (FSLIC), which guaranteed deposits up to $5,000 in the S&Ls. Now, you had some sort of supervision and, more importantly, insurance for the individual depositors, to prevent future runs on the institutions. Every account was covered, up to $5,000; if the bank went under, the depositors would be paid back by the FSLIC, out of its own funds, and, if necessary, out of the national wallet. The Federal Deposit Insurance Corporation (FDIC) formed in 1933 in the teeth of the entrenched opposition of the American Bankers Association, which pronounced it "unsound, unscientific, unjust and dangerous,"[4] brought the same protection to commercial bank deposits, at the same level, $5,000 per account.

As the economy came back to life, the S&Ls expanded, following what came to be called the "three-six-three" rule: pay depositors 3 per cent, charge borrowers 6 per cent, and be on the golf course by three in the afternoon. It was a nice life for the people who owned and ran S&Ls, but not one that would assuage greed.

It was not until inflation changed all the rules in the seventies that the thrifts began to suffer. If you deposited $1,000 in an S&L which paid you 7.5 per cent, and inflation was running at 10 per cent, you were worse off, in current dollars, at the end of year than when you made the deposit. That was one problem. Another was that the interest the S&Ls could pay was limited by law to 7.5 per cent under

Regulation Q, while the amount they could charge for mortgages was, generally, 6 per cent.

In 1980, during the last throes of the Carter administration, the thrift lobbyists got to work and persuaded Congress to pass the Depository Institutions Deregulation and Monetary Control Act of 1980, also known as Diddymac, which, among other things, dismantled Regulation Q over time. However, while the controls on interest that could be paid were gradually lifted, those on the mortgage rates that could be charged were not – that would have been politically unpopular. This meant that many of the thrifts found themselves taking in money on which they had to pay 10 or 12 per cent, because they couldn't get deposits for less than that, and lending it out again at 6 per cent. Not the way to riches, or even survival. In 1980, fifty S&Ls went into bankruptcy, and a tremor ran throughout the system.

It was about to get worse. While Diddymac was sliding through Congress, the California S&L lobby managed to attach to it an increase in the amount of deposits to be covered by insurance. This had started at $5,000, rose to $25,000 in the mid-seventies, and now stood at $40,000. It was upped to $100,000 (the same amount was applied to the commercial FDIC banks), through a clause slipped into the bill late at night, during a negotiating session dealing with the House and Senate versions of the law, and passed without public discussion.[5] Moreover, the way the wording read, it was the deposit, not the depositor, that was covered; a single person, by using various account combinations, could gain coverage for up to $999,999 in deposits. This still didn't solve the S&Ls' difficulty with having to pay more interest than they could collect, but it did ensure that the rich would not be discommoded if the S&Ls collapsed.

Finally, Diddymac lumped all the various banking institutions – S&Ls, commercial banks, credit unions – into one general category, "depository institutions," allowed them all to have interest-bearing chequing accounts, and blurred many of the other regulatory distinctions between them. They could operate outside of their own states, for example, both for lending and investing.

While the law was being gutted, the U.S. League of Savings and Loans Associations, the lobbying arm of the S&Ls, asked for, and got, two rule changes that would quickly make them richer, and shakier, investments. The first reduced the amount of capital an S&L was required to keep on hand from 5 to 3 per cent of its average deposits; the bank needed only $3 million in capital to lend $100 million. The second change was to drop the rule limiting "brokered deposits," which were deposits gathered in by brokerage houses, who sold them to clients in the form of investment certificates. A client who wanted to invest $1 million risk-free could buy ten certificates at $99,999 from, say, Drexel Burnham Lambert, the junk-bond brokers (who would later wind up in bankruptcy). The broker would find the best interest rates and deposit the funds, taking off a commission. The money would be covered by insurance. Of course, to make enough interest to profit in a rising market, the S&Ls that took in the money would have to engage in high-pay, and therefore high-risk, ventures, but not to worry, every dime of the deposits was insured.

And then, with the glad cry – "Deregulate!" – Ronald Reagan swept into Washington in early 1981 and began throwing *all* the rules out the window. The process was orchestrated by lobbyists for the S&Ls and the banks, working in tandem to produce one of the sharpest instruments for looting, skulduggery, and the assuaging of greed ever invented, the Garn–St Germain Depository Institutions Act of 1982. It was named for its sponsors, Fernand St Germain, a representative from Rhode Island who made a fortune borrowing at advantageous rates from banks and investing it in condominium projects aided by tax breaks, and Senator Jake Garn of Utah, chairman of the Senate Banking Committee. This act expanded the types of investments the S&Ls could make, to include almost every high-risk venture known. At the same time, it wiped out all rules governing the ratio between what an S&L could lend a developer and the appraised value of the project.

Martin Mayer, in his book *The Greatest Bank Robbery*, called this "probably the single most damaging provision in the law."[6] A property was worth whatever the lender said it was worth; the s&l could put up as much as a developer wanted on it, and there was nothing to prevent the s&ls from being the developer, under new rules that relaxed conflict-of-interest regulations into non-existence. The only hurdle that remained was that some needle-nose trying to protect the value of the federal deposit insurance might make a fuss, but that was taken care of by the best change of all under Reagan, an attitudinal change in Washington. We didn't want bureaucrats poking in everywhere, we didn't want inspectors cluttering up the premises, we didn't want, in a word, regulation.

When he was signing the Garn–St Germain bill into law in the rose garden outside the White House on October 12, 1982, President Reagan, wearing his genial smile, nodded at the assembled s&l executives, politicians, and lobbyists and said, "I think we've hit the jackpot on this one."[7] They smiled and nodded back; they knew who would be raking in the jackpot.

Developers like Donald Ray Dixon of Dallas could see at once what the spirit of deregulation meant in practice. You could buy the shares in an s&l, get it to loan you the money to do whatever it was you wanted to do, pay high interest rates to depositors to make sure the funds kept flowing in, and transfer the risk over to the federal government, via deposit insurance. If, by chance, the high-risk ventures into which you had plunged the depositors' cash turned out to be turkeys, you could lend them more money to keep up the payments and jack up interest rates even higher to keep the money flowing. You would never have a problem getting deposits, because, after all, the money was risk-free. Reagan, the ultraconservative, had created socialism for the suckers. Why not take advantage?

Dixon bought control of Vernon Savings and Loan in Vernon, Texas, the hard-scrabble town where he was born, just south of the Oklahoma border, and quickly turned it into a money-churning machine that expanded on an explosive mixture of fraud, flamboyance, and prostitution. One of the more interesting items that came to light, when Vernon Savings finally collapsed in rubble, revealed that during Don Ray's run, the bank spent $10 million on "prostitutes and parties."[8] An all-service bank.

Dixon bought Vernon Savings and Loan on July 10, 1981,[9] through a holding company of his own, Dondi Investments. It was a community-based, conservative, prosperous little outfit. Dixon would fix all that. He began to use the S&L to bankroll his own ventures, which were high-risk, high-profit, and, as it turned out, quite often highly crooked. Every time Vernon S&L floated a loan, there was a kickback, to Don Ray or to one of his cronies, or to the S&L, as a fee. The fees created paper profits, and these were used to justify the payment of huge dividends to Dondi Investments. The real money, put in the vaults by depositors, was siphoned out by fraudulent accounting. One of the fastest ways to create profits, real and paper, was to flip properties back and forth between buyers, at ever-higher prices. Journalist and author James O'Shea quotes a federal regulator describing a visit to Dallas, where this was going on:

> I went down there and this Texan showed me this piece of land and told me how this guy had sold it to that guy and that guy had sold it again, until it had been sold about six times, and I said, "My God. That's terrible," and he said, "Only if you're sixth."[10]

Among its other investments, Vernon Savings and Loan bought six aircraft, fleets of cars, oceans of booze, and a beach house in Del Ray, California, for Don Ray and his second wife, Donna. Then it bought a few boatloads of antiques to stick in the beach house and in a much larger mansion, also in California, which had a garage that would hold thirteen cars, including two Rolls-Royces, also owned by the S&L, and used by Don Ray. Hey, it saved on taxi fare. The wine racks in this place, which was decorated by Donna Dixon, who happened to have a decorating business, cost $38,000.

We are talking class. Don Ray thought he might want to invest in a French restaurant to help tone up Vernon, so he and a bunch of the boys jetted over to France and ate and drank themselves into a stupor, as research for the project. The bank's directors were not in a position to complain; he flew them from Vernon down to California, to show them some properties he was thinking of buying, and flew hookers along to take their minds off all the money that was being spent on things unknown to Jimmy Stewart. Under Don Ray's relentless huckstering, Vernon Savings went from a poky little Texas S&L with $78 million in deposits to $1.3 billion – a seventeen-fold increase – in four years.[11]

The beauty of the system worked by Dixon, and dozens of others, was that the actual project the S&L invested its money in didn't have to make any sense at all, because there was no longer anything in law to keep the loan from including enough money to keep the interest paid for two or three years, by which time, rising real-estate prices would wipe out the debt, interest, and kickbacks. This is how it worked.

A developer would decide to buy a block of vacant land outside Dallas and put a few hundred condominiums on it. He would work out that it would cost, let's say, $10 million. He would want another $2 million for himself, for being so brilliant as to see the possibilities – $12 million. He would need two or three years' interest set aside in a special account to keep the loans up to date. Call it another $2.5 million. We're up to $14.5 million. For financing the deal, the S&L would want a fee of 5 per cent. Another $2.1 million. Now all we need is an appraiser to go out and look at the land and come back with a report that says this thing will be worth $16.1 million some day. No sooner said than done. When the development is built, all these costs will be transferred into the unit costs of the condos, out of which all the kickbacks, interest, and original investment have to be paid.

The developer might be the S&L itself, or Don Ray, or a chum – or the S&L, through Don Ray, might cut a deal in which it, as part of its payoff, would collect half the profits from the scheme, if any. In the meantime, the fees would be put through as a profit, and a nice dividend declared. And if, as turned out to be the case in a distressing number of these investments, the whole thing sank because the condos fell down or the market collapsed, well, the feds had to cover the loss.

It was our old friend, the pyramid scheme again, and the minute real-estate prices began to droop, it would come crashing down. In the meantime, everybody had fun.

Then there was the "daisy chain," which is what the bank examiners who eventually got summoned to sort out some of these messes called it. An S&L that had a loan on its books from a developer who couldn't pay the money back, due to the fact that the buildings had fallen down, or some other unforeseen calamity had occurred, would get another S&L to lend the developer enough money to pay off the note – plus, of course, the usual fees, so that everyone could show a profit. Then the first S&L would take another lousy loan off the second S&L's books to return the favour. When these loans in turn went sour, new S&Ls would join in, forming an unending chain that showed profits at every link, on paper, while the whole mess sank slowly into the mire.

It kept the examiners, poor lambs, at bay. There were two sets of examiners who were supposed to be looking at these things, the state examiners and the federal ones attached to the Federal Home Loan Bank Board and its regional Home Banks. The state examiners were not much of a problem, since the states where most of the really wild activity took place – Arizona, Texas, and California – tended to take the broad and generous view of these matters. Thus, we had examiners borrowing money from some of the institutions they were supposed to oversee, being flown hither and yon to conventions and parties by the S&Ls, and, in general, behaving in a non-hostile fashion.

L. Linton Bowman, the Texas savings and loan commissioner, became acquainted, during his remorseless probing into Vernon S&L, with a Vernon employee who rejoiced in the name of Joy Love, and who was not a banker. He jetted off to California with the savings and loan executives – and companions – went pheasant hunting with the gang in Kansas, and did it all, as he later explained, because he felt he had an obligation to go along and find out what they were up to.[12] An examiner's gotta do what an examiner's gotta do.

The feds were more of a problem. It should not have been that way, because the man who was made chairman of the Bank Board, the overseer of the federal interest, was Edwin J. Gray, who had been one of Ronald Reagan's Republican campaign stalwarts and a former employee of a California S&L. He was appointed, amidst the purring of the industry lobbyists, in 1982, and nobody expected any lip from him. His heart was certainly in the right place, but, unfortunately for him, Gray took his job seriously, and that soon brought him into conflict with Donald Regan, Reagan's right-hand man, secretary of the treasury, and chairman of the Depository Institutions Deregulation Committee (DIDIC), which was specifically entrusted with removing the brakes from the system. Regan moved to Washington from a position atop Merrill Lynch & Co., the Wall Street brokerage firm that had made millions out of brokered funds. Gray, soon after he took over the Bank Board post, began to worry about these funds, which he could see did not make a whole lot of sense from where he sat, however fine they might appear to Merrill Lynch (which had thoughtfully hired Gray's predecessor, Richard Pratt).

Regan quickly sized Gray up as "not a team player,"[13] and the new Bank Board chairman was soon isolated, his staff cut, and his views ignored. As the S&Ls slewed into deeper debt, Gray thrashed around in increasing impotence. He was caught in one of Washington's perfect catch-22s. As the slump in energy prices hit the Southwest, and money dried up for the wondrous real-estate ventures the S&Ls had invested in, the S&Ls began to show losses that even the creative accounting of their staffs could no longer hide. But if the regulators, finally, closed a thrift, the federal insurance became due and payable to the depositors, because they certainly weren't going to get it out of the long-emptied S&L vaults. Unfortunately, there wasn't enough in the FSLIC account to cover the losses.

Gray tried to meet this by imposing a 1-per-cent fee on the deposits of all the S&Ls, who screamed bloody murder. Most of the high-steppers, and crooks, were operating in a handful of states, and the honest, prudent, well-run thrifts objected to paying for the sins of the Dixons and Keatings of their world. One of the many unfair brutalities of this whole business was that many states kept their s&ls under control, only to find themselves saddled with the debts incurred in runaway states like Texas, California, and Arkansas. As of February 1, 1989, there were 114 insolvent s&ls in the state of Texas, and none in Delaware, Hawaii, Idaho, Maine, Massachusetts, Nevada, New Hampshire, Rhode Island, Vermont, or West Virginia.[14] The House Banking Committee, taking its cue from the industry lobby, the U.S. League of Savings and Loans Associations, killed Gray's proposal; there would be no 1-per-cent levy, no money in the till, and, therefore, no way to shut down the ailing thrifts.

However, it was becoming obvious to everyone that something would have to be done, so a bill was drafted, which took years working its way through the Washington labyrinth. Its purpose was to fatten up the FSLIC kitty, so the Bank Board could afford to seize insolvent institutions, pay off the depositors, and shut them down. In the meantime, they just kept rolling along, piling up debts.

A typical case was that of Empire Savings and Loan of Mesquite, Texas, which ballooned $40 million in assets to $320 million in less than a year, propelled largely by land-flip sales, brokered funds, and fraudulent bookkeeping. In one of these deals, later detailed in court, a piece of land went from $1 million to $7 million, through multiple sales in a single day, and the last sale was used to justify a loan of $7 million, out of which everybody got handsome fees.[15] Empire was involved in the building of a huge array of condominiums along Interstate Highway I-30, outside Dallas, which were so shoddily constructed that they could neither be sold nor repaired and had to be bulldozed down. When the firm's collapse forced the Bank Board to step in and shut down Empire on March 14, 1984, the FSLIC had to pay out $300 million to cover insured deposits. And that was one S&L out of three thousand.

On the heels of the Empire collapse, Gray fired the supervisor of the regional Home Loan Bank in Dallas and tried to hire more examiners to gain some control over the thundering thrifts. But the Office of

Management and Budget in Washington had imposed a hiring freeze and blocked him. At the very time when the S&Ls most needed overseeing, examinations were cut back.

Some of the stunts that would later come to light were mindboggling. When he began to run into money problems, Dwane Christensen, the proprietor of North American S&L, forged bank certificates of deposit and put them in the vault. These then became assets, on the basis of which he proceeded to go out and spend the money his depositors had given him to care for.[16] In the case of American Savings and Loan Association of Stockton, California, when the management guaranteed to state examiners that they had "looked at" the appraisals on loans to ensure the properties were worth the amounts borrowed, what they meant was that they had seen the bookshelves that held the documents, not the appraisals themselves, many of which were false or inflated.[17] This is not really difficult fraud to track down, but there was no adequate staff to do the tracking.

However, even the bliss of ignorance had to come to an end, and, as the bad assets loaded onto the S&L books turned riper and riper, the institutions began to fail. By 1985, 329 thrifts had failed, about 10 per cent of the industry, and the deposit-insurance fund was itself threatened with bankruptcy.[18] It would take about $20 billion to provide the money to allow the Bank Board to close down and clean up the ailing industry, and the fight over the next three years was waged over this money. There seems little doubt that, if it had been forthcoming in 1985, the subsequent débâcle would have been avoided. By the time a reluctant Congress provided $10.8 billion, in 1989, it was much too late; S&Ls were keeling over and conking out at a rate that the deposit-insurance money could never fund, and the whole bill was dumped into the hands of the taxpayer.

To repeat, the regulators could not acknowledge that the S&Ls were bankrupt, because if they did, the FSLIC would have to pay off the depositors, and there was not enough money for that. So the insolvencies were ignored, the companies remained in business, and their debts continued to multiply. They were called "zombie thrifts."[19] The book-cooking stunts they used to keep going were dubbed "gua-camole accounting."[20]

It was, from beginning to end, a matter of politics, the ideology of deregulation, and lobbying. The more active S&Ls, like Don Ray Dixon's and Charles Keating's, spread money around Washington to frustrate and delay any action. Vernon S&L bought a yacht, *High Spirits*, which floated up and down the Potomac, full of booze, bankers, and bimbos for the politicians. Dixon and other S&L owners began to ladle money into the political action committees of congressmen and got, in return, protection by Congress against Ed Gray and his minions.

There was nothing subtle about this process. Charles Keating, who contributed more than $2 million to five friendly senators, later told a press conference, "One question, among the many raised in recent weeks, had to do with whether my financial support in any way influenced several political figures to take up my cause. I want to say in the most forceful way I can: I certainly hope so."[21]

Keating needed all the help he could get. He had launched himself in Phoenix, Arizona, with a company called American Continental Corporation (ACC). The company bought, along with other things, Lincoln Savings and Loan in Irvine, California, a suburb of Los Angeles. Among the other stunts he pulled, Keating sold junk bonds issued by ACC in the lobbies of branches of Lincoln Savings. Many of the purchasers were elderly Californians who thought they were buying government-insured certificates. They were, in fact, unsecured subordinated notes, so odoriferous that *Grant's Interest Rate Observer* called them "the worst securities available."[22]

The $1,000 bonds were sold by "bait and switch" tactics. Elderly patrons who came into Lincoln to buy insured certificates that had been advertised in the newspaper would be persuaded instead to buy the junk bonds, which carried even higher interest rates. The old folks thought they were insured. The bank staff got extra bonuses for selling them. In the end, twenty-three hundred Californians bought this paper, which became worthless when ACC went bankrupt in 1989. In the meantime, Martin Mayer notes, Keating and members of his family took $34 million out of ACC,[23] while the junk-bond holders lost $288.7 million.[24]

Keating's victimization of the elderly probably did more than any other single factor to rouse public wrath when these matters came to light, and his whole strategy for a period of about four years was to keep them from coming to light. For that, he needed the help of the politicians, to sit on the heads of the regulators. So, he and other S&L operators went out and bought themselves some more protection.

The law placed a limit of $1,000 on individual contributions to political action committees of politicians, which spawned a small new industry of lobbyists, faking phoney receipts in their expense accounts, on the one hand, to get the money to bribe the politicians and, on the other, rounding up the names of all their staffs, and their relatives, to provide the putative donors through which the bribe money was passed. Common Cause, the Washington public-interest group, was able to document $11.7 million in contributions from the political action committees of S&Ls to congressmen of both Republican and Democratic parties.[25]

By and large, Don Ray Dixon bribed members of the House of Representatives and left senators to Charles Keating, who donated $850,000 to Allan Cranston, the ranking Democrat on the Senate Banking Committee. (They were not alone; hundreds of S&L operators were involved.) And it paid off, in two ways. First, the S&L lobbyists were given a platform on which to stand and bash Ed Gray and all regulators, and second, the direct intervention of powerful politicians hampered any attempts to bring the institutions under control. Every time Gray and the Bank Board threatened to take action, up would pop a congressman or senator to complain about government interference with free enterprise.

Thus it was that, when the Federal Home Loan Bank of San Francisco accused Keating of unsafe and unsound banking practices, the "Keating Five" senators – Allan Cranston, Dennis DeConcini, John Glenn, and Donald Riegle, all Democrats, and John McCain, a

Republican – all of whom had received cash from Keating's slush funds, set up a meeting with federal regulators and spent more than two hours grilling them on their treatment of Keating and Lincoln, his personal S&L. The word went out to lay off Lincoln, with the result that, when it eventually crashed, it cost the taxpayer $2.5 billion.[26] Keating blamed government interference.

Gray gave way to the pressures put on him, in most cases, even going so far as to remove a Bank Board employee who had offended one of the complainers. Scott Schultz had been appointed conservator by the Bank Board, to operate a California thrift that had collapsed; his job was to try to rescue what he could from the wreckage. One of the institution's major debtors was Craig Hall, a Dallas S&L owner and real-estate investor, and Schultz proposed to foreclose on Hall's properties to get some money back for the California thrift.

Through a mutual friend, Hall got himself a meeting with Jim Wright, a powerful Texas Democrat, and House Majority Leader, who had received a heavy freight of cash from the S&Ls. Wright then set up a meeting with Ed Gray in Washington, which turned into a litany of complaints about the chairman and his staff interfering with the thrifts. Soon after this, Wright phoned Gray to talk to him in detail about Hall's case, and, within days of this, Wright blocked further consideration of the bill to recapitalize the FSLIC fund.

Gray took the point – make nice or forget about the rescue money – and pulled Schultz out of Dallas, replacing him with a man who was given strict instructions to find a way to renegotiate Hall's notes. Even caving in, though, didn't do Gray much good; Wright and his cronies wanted his hide and eventually got it.

Gray's appointment came up for renewal in July 1987, but he did not ask to be reappointed – not that he would have been. He went back to San Diego, deep in debt and somewhat embittered. He was replaced by Danny Wall, who had been chief of staff on the Senate Banking Committee for six years. He knew how the game was played, and he would not make the same mistakes that Gray did. One of the first things the Bank Board did under his new direction was to fire Harry

Joe Selby, the man Ed Gray had put in charge of thrift regulation in Dallas. Selby had the nerve to issue a cease-and-desist order against Vernon s&l, requiring the thrift to adopt new and stricter lending practices and to stop renewing loans for its insolvent borrowers. Wright, at a meeting with Ed Gray, demanded that he fire Selby. Gray never did, but Wall made right the deficiency.

Wall also had many a kind word for Charles Keating, whom he called "a very active and very entrepreneurial man for at least the last thirteen years that I've known him."[27] Wall's brief, friendly tenure – he was forced to resign when the details of Keating's various malefactions came out – prepared the way for the final débâcle, as 517 thrifts went under before the end of 1988.[28]

Even then, the money to finance the rescue of the s&ls was not forthcoming. Jim Wright kept the recapitalization bill from coming to the floor of the House, and Congress adjourned without considering it. In this way, the developing crisis was kept out of the way during the 1988 election, which was just as well; after all, the Republican candidate had a son, Neil, who was connected with Silverado Savings and Loan of Denver, Colorado, which was drifting onto the rocks, and which kept afloat by a combination of trick accounting and political clout. Silverado officers, according to documents produced before a later congressional hearing, boasted that when Bank Board examiners tried to crack down on the institution in 1987, they "had been run out of town."[29] Neil Bush, as a director of Silverado, both approved and sought loans from developers with whom he had personal deals. In one case, he obtained $100,000 from a business partner, who in turn borrowed $100 million from Silverado, a loan which Bush voted to approve. Bush never paid the $100,000 back, because, as he later told a congressional hearing, "The loan was never meant to be repaid unless there was a success."[30] Wonderful; in accord with s&l principles, he had worked out a risk-free deal. Not the sort of stuff to lay before the voters.

When the recapitalization bill re-emerged in the new Congress, early in 1989, it had been through more facelifts than Phyllis Diller; the bill eventually provided $10.8 billion to the fund, but, by that time, $10.8 billion was woefully inadequate. The FSLIC itself became insolvent; it had liabilities of $100 billion more than its assets. It was dismantled.

On February 6, 1989, newly anointed President George Bush proposed to take over the failing thrifts at a projected cost of $50 billion, or nearly five times the money appropriated by Congress. To cover this, the government would issue bonds; the thrift industry would repay the principal on these bonds, over time, and the taxpayer would pick up the interest. This was the first of a series of steps that seemed to lead the government, the S&Ls, and the taxpayer ever deeper into the swamp. By early summer, it was clear that $50 billion wouldn't begin to cover the insured deposits in dying thrifts and, on August 9, President Bush signed a bill to provide $166 billion over ten years to close or merge ailing institutions.

The same bill created the Resolution Trust Corporation (RTC) to look after the rescue work. The RTC would dispose of the sinking thrifts by subsidizing their sale, or would close them down. There was also a "conservator-ship" program, still in place, under which the RTC assigns a managing agent and credit specialist to every fainting S&L, to see if the poor dear can't be brought around. The Federal Home Loan Bank system was also discarded and replaced by the Office of Thrift Supervision, or OTS (you can't have a federal establishment without initials), which is charged with identifying financially troubled institutions and calling in the RTC when necessary.

To the astonishment of all, putting bureaucrats in to run institutions that were already in trouble did not work too well; the required skills are not the same. The RTC inherited billions of dollars worth of crummy real estate and really didn't know what to do with it, beyond holding on and hoping for happier times, as the debts kept piling up. The sound of S&Ls hitting the pavement drowned out the voices of the president and his advisers, who were maintaining, from time to time, that the end of the problem was now in sight and that the total cost would be in the neighbourhood of $50 billion, $100 billion,

$300 billion, $500 billion, $600 billion, and now, writes James Ring Adams, author of *The Big Fix*, "According to the best current estimates, the total cost of the savings and loan disaster could well exceed $1.5 trillion."[31]

This is an advance over the $10.8 billion proposed in 1989, but Lord knows if it is accurate. The cost will be horrendous, that much is clear, even without any reckoning of the thousands and thousands of bankruptcies, personal and corporate, that followed the collapses. One of the fallouts of the failures occurred when most of the developers who couldn't pay back their loans dived into Chapter 11 bankruptcy protection, which made the task of getting anything out of them anywhere from very difficult to utterly impossible.

Congress became a trifle annoyed when the public sat up and began to take note that it had been handed an unsolicited future tax bill of, at the very least, several hundred billion dollars in the name of deregulation, and there were lots of hearings to see where the blame could be shifted. The Senate Ethics Committee looked into the activities of the Keating Five and found very little to complain about. One highlight of the hearings came when Edwin Gray came back to Washington and insisted on reading into the record a newspaper column written by former senator William Proxmire, which had a lot of harsh things to say about the S&L lobbyists and their contributions to the politicians. It ended, "These contributions to members of committees with jurisdiction over the contributors' industry are bribes, pure and simple."[32]

The senators listened in stony-faced silence and voted to issue a mild wristslap to Senator Allan Cranston, who had taken $850,000 from Keating. That was it.

Over on the House side, the Ethics Committee refused to consider Jim Wright's wirepulling for the S&L owners, which was, the committee said, "not inconsistent with congressional standards."[33] Congressmen had that right, and that was precisely the trouble. Wright, in fact, was forced to resign on quite another matter; he had used royalties from a self-serving book to circumvent campaign finance limits.[34]

The legal authorities were not quite so kind. Don Ray Dixon was eventually convicted on twenty-four counts of misuse of funds and sentenced to five years in jail in April 1991.[35] He went personally bankrupt. Vernon S&L's insolvency cost the taxpayer more than $1 billion. It was renamed Monfort Savings and Loan, after the Vernon, Texas, street where it is located. Cleansed of its debts, it was sold for $315 million to a new group of investors, lured in by generous tax concessions, and is back in business again.

Charles Keating was convicted of eighteen securities frauds, fined $250,000, and sentenced to ten years in jail.[36] He was also ordered to pay $2.1 billion in damages to the people he had defrauded.[37] There is about as much chance of this money being paid as there is of the ACC junk bonds coming to life again.

As more and more information came rolling out, more and more charges were laid. In over one-third of the thrift failures, there was evidence of criminal activity.[38] Associated Press carried a roundup showing that, as of August 1, 1990, there were 328 defendants indicted in S&L cases, of whom 231 had been convicted and 5 acquitted. The average jail term was 1.9 years, and AP noted, parenthetically, that "the average jail term for a bank robber is 9.4 years."[39]

The S&L calamity was unlike the earlier tales of crooks-who-go-broke in a couple of key ways. The first concerns the magnitude of the disaster. There has never been, since the Great Depression, so costly a series of financial collapses. We do not know, at this writing, what the final toll will be, but we do know that it will be in the hundreds of billions of dollars and that the drain on the public purse will continue for decades. This is a different level of magnitude from most bankruptcies, and most bankruptcies are cleaned up, one way or another, within a couple of years.

It's as if the ordinary financial failure – say, the collapse of Ivar Kreuger, the Match King – were a storm. On that scale, the S&Ls were a hurricane that altered the financial landscape out of all recognition.

However, at least in the S&L case, a few of the villains were bunged off to jail, and a few of their friends and comforters showed signs of embarrassment, and the general public was, and still is, mad as hell about the whole thing. In the evolution of bankruptcy, we were about to improve on that, by removing both shame and punishment from the equation.

Before we go on to that next step, we might stop to ponder what the guardians of our collective wisdom learned from the débâcle. That there is too much regulation, so help me God. Michael Bliss, in an unfriendly review of Martin Mayer's book, commented, wrongly, that "only about a fifth of the losses, perhaps fewer, can be blamed on thievery or obviously unacceptable business practice." He goes on to say, "Intelligent regulatory decontrol could have prevented most of the mess."

Then there is this: "The tragedy of the American thrifts is that incompetent political regulators dug the channels that led an industry into a whirlpool of destruction. And because politicians did not have the courage to go the rest of the way, and truly privatize the industry, the bailout is financed mostly by innocent taxpayers."[40]

Well, it's an argument. If there had been no federal insurance on deposits, the S & Ls would have crashed much sooner, and much more cheaply. This is an argument I will come back to in the next chapter. However, that does not begin to address the problem of the wholesale looting that took place in so many of these institutions. Bliss – and he is not alone – seems to think that a ratio of only one crook to every five operators in the financial business is nothing much to worry about. The real number, as we have already seen, is closer to one in three, but let it go. If only every fifth operator carries a gat in his hip pocket and a packet of fake bonds in his briefcase, the argument runs, then what we should do is to establish a program of "intelligent regulatory decontrol," and then refuse to help the depositors who get sucked in by the thugs.

Mayer agrees, on at least one point. "Deposit insurance has proved to be the crack cocaine of American finance," he writes.[41] But he puts the disaster in much broader terms:

In the light of this bonfire, we must ask whether our great professions are still capable of self-regulation, of giving honest service, and of accepting fiduciary duties in an age when all costs and benefits are reduced to monetary measurements and all conduct that is not specifically prohibited has become permissable. Watching the obedient dance of our officials and politicians when their patrons pipe a tune, unrebuked by a public that attends this show as it might any other, we must ask whether this generation of Americans remains capable of self-government.[42]

This is the issue that comes up, in every nation, whenever we look at financial dealings, of which bankruptcies are the most obvious symptom. One solution to the "crack cocaine" of deposit insurance is, obviously, to drop the stuff. Let the buyer beware. A depositor who is not going to be covered by insurance will pay much more attention to what is going on. He will keep an eye on things, and, as soon as the institution's officers start to play around with the piggy-bank, they will move their money elsewhere.

This argument supposes that the general public is, or can be, informed as to what is going on, and, to put it at its mildest, that is not the case, in either Canada or the United States. Which brings to a consideration of our own version of the S&L débâcle.

CHAPTER SEVEN

S&Ls, Maple Leaf Division

"Q: Did anyone ever ask you what will happen to their money if the
institution runs into difficulty or goes out of business?
A: I would have told them that, you know, that the investment is a safe
investment. . . . So, you know, it was never looked at from the point of
view that the institutions should ever go out of business."
– from the testimony of a salesperson in the inquiry into the collapse
of Principal Group [1]

$

There is a regrettable tendency on the part of many Canadians to congratulate ourselves on a society superior to that maintained by the
slobs to the south of us. They may be rich, but they are wicked; we are
the virtuous poor, who, according to rumour, will one day own the
kingdom of heaven (while the meek inherit the earth). Alas, it is not so;
in the roguery game, the Canadian branch-plant operation is, and
always has been, active. While we have not had the particular disaster
of the S&Ls, that is only because we have no such things; we have had

119

to make do with fainting trust companies and drooping banks, instead.

Look on the works of Leonard Rosenberg, a rotund and robust little businessman from Hamilton, Ontario, currently a guest of Her Majesty for five years, who brought down three trust companies and a bank and gave the financial regulators a scare that made them rigorous in their examinations for a good, long time. Ten minutes, at least.

After almost completing a business-administration degree at the University of Buffalo in 1961, Rosenberg got a job, at $35 a week, working for the Lincoln Collection Agency in Hamilton.[2] He banged on doors, shouted at people, and did quite well. Rosenberg is not a sensitive man. However, the money stunk; it would never bring him the Rolls-Royce, the chauffeur, the other accoutrements of wealth that he desired, so he went to work for Berfried Enterprises, as a mortgage broker, and, five years later, set up shop in Toronto on his own. He did rather better. "I cleared about a million dollars a year," he told me, "and netted a few hundred thousand after taxes."

In 1975, through one of the Toronto lawyers he used in the mortgage business, he met Branco Weiss, a Swiss businessman, who became, for handsome fees, his backstage moneyman. A year later, Weiss put up the capital for the takeover of a tiny Hamilton company called Greymac Mortgage, through a holding company, Greymac Credit. Then Greymac Mortgage bought up a Mississauga, Ontario, trust company, Macdonald–Cartier Trust, to which Rosenberg was steered by one of his business buddies, Bill Player, and turned it into Greymac Trust. This transaction was financed by a loan of $7 million from the Canadian Commercial Bank, run by another buddy, G. Howard Eaton. The bank got a $7-million deposit in Greymac Trust as part of its security for this loan.

This arrangement was typical of the way our financiers get to use other people's money to back the projects from which they scoop the returns (a very detailed book on the subject, by Terence Corcoran and Laura Reid, is called *Public Money, Private Greed*[3]). Greymac Mortgage was a deposit-taking institution. In effect, money from its depositors flowed out to buy another company, which would be owned by Rosenberg and his pals, and, if anything went wrong, federal deposit insurance would pick up the tab. The Ottawa mandarins were not pleased. Rosenberg didn't care; he ended up with a trust company which could really suck in the money. Now he had a federally chartered deposit-taking institution, in Greymac Mortgage, and a provincial one, in Greymac Trust. He spat on his hands and got to work.

When Rosenberg started on this, federal deposit insurance was limited to $20,000; by the time he had finished, and because of his activities, it was tripled to $60,000, to cover the money of all the suckers he had sheared.

By active advertising, attractive rates, and ceaseless activity, Rosenberg increased the deposit base of Greymac Trust from $61 million to $241 million, or 294 per cent, and its loans from $73 million to $216 million, or 277 per cent.

Like the S&L operators, Rosenberg charged fees for putting together deals, showed those fees as profits, and used the profits to expand the equity base of the trust company. Here's how that works: Trust companies, like banks, are restricted to lending a multiple of their equity base, which is the money put up by shareholders, plus profits. The leverage ranges from fifteen to thirty times equity. If your bank or trust company has $1 million in equity, and is at the top end of the scale, it can lend $30 million; if it has $100 million, $3 billion, and so forth. The money is created out of thin air; but there is a limit to it, the limit imposed by the base. Increase that base by a little, and you increase the institution's capacity to manufacture money by a lot – by whatever the multiple happens to be. Leverage, with a college degree.

In one deal, Greymac Trust loaned $55 million to Daon Developments of Vancouver, which needed $50 million. Rosenberg then charged a $5-million fee. The Vancouver developer got a loan of $50 million, Rosenberg created an instant profit of $5 million, and that allowed him to lend another $110 million (the multiple in his case was twenty-two).

Together with Bill Player, who operated through a holding

company called Kilderkin Investments Limited, and Andrew Markle, who controlled Seaway Trust of Port Colborne, Ontario, Rosenberg became involved in a whole series of complex deals that caused money to blossom and bloom like a fruit tree. And then came the Cadillac Fairview flip.

In the summer of 1982, Rosenberg heard that Cadillac Fairview, then the largest Canadian developer, was willing to sell a block of 10,931 Toronto apartments, which it had appraised at $250 million. Like his brothers below the border, he had worked out a more "spacious" way to set the values of buildings against which he could borrow money from his own trust company. This depended on the "earning capacity" of the property. To make it work, Rosenberg was going to give the earning capacity a goose.

Provincial rent controls meant that the Cadillac Fairview properties could not make much money, but, if they were sold, the new rents could be based on the sale price. On August 24, 1982, Rosenberg signed an agreement to purchase the complexes in a bloc, for $270 million, and issued a letter of credit for $10 million to ensure that he would go through with the arrangement on November 5. That was real money, out of his trust company. At the time, there were first mortgages totalling $110 million on the properties, and Cadillac Fairview agreed to take back second mortgages of $113 million. That left Rosenberg $47 million short. He got his Swiss partner, Branco Weiss, to guarantee $40 million of this, by writing a letter to that effect.

He still didn't have enough to swing the deal, and, anyway, he had a problem with Greymac Mortgage. The federal regulators were making nasty noises, still, about the way he had bought it and the way he was running it. So, Rosenberg told me, he invited Bill Player up to his island in Georgian Bay and took him out fishing. "We were trolling and I said to him, 'How would you like to buy the Cadillac Fairview buildings and Greymac Mortgage?' He said, 'How much?' I said, '$350 million,' and he said, 'My God!' He knew it was a terrific deal."

You and I, being naïve, might not see it as such a terrific deal. At the time, Greymac Mortgage had a book value of $15 million, and Cadillac

Fairview had priced its own complex at $250 million and was now selling it for $270 million. That makes, under the old math, $265 million, and it makes $350 million seem a trifle steep. But you and I will never be rich; we lack the vast view, which tells us that there is no harm in paying too much for something, provided you aren't going to do the paying. Working that out was the next step.

Player signed an agreement to buy Greymac Mortgage for $37.5 million and the Cadillac Fairview block for $312.5 million, making up the $350 million. He didn't have it, any more than Rosenberg did, and it couldn't all be financed through Greymac, which didn't have that much to lend. So Rosenberg borrowed $40.3 million and bought another trust company, Crown Trust, of Winnipeg. He paid $62 a share, or three times the price at which it was then trading, for Crown Trust. He would get it back.

Now he had two trust companies, Greymac and Crown. Still not enough to swing the deal, so he cut in Andrew Markle and Seaway Trust. On November 5, 1982, Greymac and Crown advanced $76 million against third mortgages on the Cadillac properties, and Seaway advanced another $76 million, for a total of $152 million. The same day, Player would pay $350 million on his two deals, which he didn't have. The mortgages could not be justified, and the trust companies could not lend that much of their depositors' money on a single transaction. So, along came a group of fifty numbered companies, and along came a mysterious Saudi Arabian, Adeeb Hassan Qutub, who had rounded up a group of fifty investors to take on the transaction and pay $500 million for the properties Player was buying for $312.5 million.

We had a double flip. The bloc went from Cadillac Fairview to Rosenberg for $270 million and, in the blink of an eye, to Player for $312.5 million and, in another blink, to persons unknown offshore for $500 million. The $500 million so wondrously created (alas, it never materialized) allowed the mortgage liability of the bloc to be raised to $375 million, 75 per cent of the value which had now been established by the Arab deal. The Arabs would not put up the whole $500 million, you understand; just a down payment of $125 million.

On the way past, Seaway Trust took a fee of 12.5 per cent of the $125 million, or just under $16 million; that left $109 million to be paid, but that didn't materialize either. Instead, there was a slip of paper showing that $109 million had been placed on deposit in a bank in Grand Cayman, in the West Indies. This didn't do much to reduce the money owed by the Arab consortium, but it showed that their hearts were in the right place, and so was their money – out of harm's way.

The fact that there were fifty deals involved, instead of one, got around that nonsense about not being able to put so much of the trust companies' funds into a single transaction.

The only real money in this whole scam was the $152 million which the depositors in Greymac, Crown, and Seaway had plunked down on November 5, and out of that, Rosenberg wrote himself a cheque for $42.5 million. That represented his profit, the difference between the $270 million he paid and the $312.3 million he charged, for the Cadillac Fairview bloc. As he told me, "Not bad for a day's work." He sent $20 million to his Swiss partner, Weiss, for writing a letter, which was never used, stating that, if necessary, he (Weiss) would put up $40 million. Or, to put it another way, if people think you have $40 million, you can charge $20 million for offering to lend it out, if needed, while the rest of the human race is scratching around for chicken feed in the real world. Another $15 million went into Crown Trust.

Now you had all these apartments, with first, second, and third mortgages on them, which had to be paid, and which were very much higher on November 6 than they had been on November 5, so, of course, the rents had to go up – by 79 per cent over three years. An apartment renting for $400.00 in 1983 would rent for $715.50 in 1986. I asked Rosenberg if he had thought about the tenants' role in financing his little double flip, and he replied, "Well, if I wasn't doing it to them, somebody else would be. It's a harsh, cruel world out there and you don't see anybody holding tag days for landlords."

It's a harsher, crueller world for people who make about $400 a week than it is for those who can slide $42.5 million out of the till of their own trust companies, actually, and the tenants, when they found out about this deal, stood on their hind legs and screamed. The Ontario government of William Davis took a quick count and came up with this result: Rosenberg, Player, and Markle, three votes; the tenants, maybe thirty thousand votes, counting two-plus people for each apartment.

While the votes were still being added, the federal regulators weighed in, and what they had to say was not good. The Cadillac Fairview flip was only part of a vaster scheme he had in mind, to create his own bank. As Rosenberg told me, it would be "a world-sized bank. The banks do a lousy job, and I was going to compete, so they took me out of the game."

He and his partners proposed to merge the three trust companies, Greymac, Crown, and Seaway, with First City Trust Company of Vancouver, owned by the Belzberg family, and add on Fidelity Trust of Edmonton, owned by Peter Pocklington, Canada's answer to Ayn Rand. Then he would stir in the Canadian Commercial Bank (CCB) of Edmonton, in which he and his associates already owned a 27-per-cent share. (Every one of these institutions would later end up on the trash heap.) The partners were not allowed, by law, to own that much, but they did anyway. You can own all of a trust company, but only 10 per cent of a bank. The bank, of course, can own all of a trust company. The reason for this arrangement is to prevent the lessening of competition. I know it doesn't make sense; I'm just telling you how it is. In any event, the inspector general of banks, William Kennett, not one of the most vigorous regulators we have ever had, was finally provoked enough by Rosenberg's refusal to abide by the rules that he got in touch with the Ontario officials, who, by this time, had finished their headcount.

An investigation was launched by the province of Ontario forthwith, headed by Jim Morrison of the accounting firm of Touche Ross. A good deal of the digging on this investigation was done by Jack Biddell, a Toronto accountant with the temper, and persistence, of a fox terrier and a low regard for high-steppers and fancy dealers. (Rosenberg, among his other quirks, had his chauffeur drive the Rolls about halfway to work, and then he jogged the rest, in an attempt to control his weight. For some reason, this really ticked Biddell off.) By January 1983, Biddell had dissected the Rosenberg empire with a scalpel and concluded that the trust companies, their associated mortgage companies, and the money of the depositors in both were in grave danger. Biddell told Robert Hammond, the federal superintendent of insurance, and head of the Canada Deposit Insurance Corporation (CDIC), to have his wallet ready. He told William Kennett, the inspector general of banks, to have his smelling salts ready. And he recommended to the Ontario government that they seize the firms before any more money wandered off.

On January 7, 1983, provincial officials seized Greymac, Crown, and Seaway trusts, while federal officials grabbed Greymac Mortgage and Seaway Mortgage. There were months of fuss and fury, and everybody sued everybody else, but the companies were gone, and the CDIC had to pay off the depositors, to the tune of $709 million.[4] This was not a bankruptcy, but a seizure, a belly up by other means. The total losses of the three trust companies, which included deposits not covered by insurance, the wiping out of share values, and previous losses, came to $1.5 billion;[5] much of this was borne by ordinary investors and creditors.

The three main actors, Rosenberg, Player, and Markle, were terribly, terribly hurt that so many people seemed to think that this whole complex series of transactions was just a way to get their hands on $152 million of their depositors' money, but in the end – after Player and Rosenberg had both made a dash for freedom into the United States – they were hauled up on criminal charges of fraud. Bill Player got fifteen years (he pleaded not guilty), Andrew Markle and Leonard Rosenberg each got five years. It took ten years to get Rosenberg into a Toronto courtroom, where he pleaded guilty to thirteen counts on June 28, 1993.[6] He had been living in the Coconut Grove area of Miami.

What came to be called "The Trust Companies Affair" had repercussions on the Canadian Commercial Bank, which, you will recall, put up the $7 million that started Rosenberg on his way and which had now gone glimmering. This was just one of a whole string of injudicious dealings in this bank, which had started up in 1976, in the midst of a real-estate and energy boom. One of its major clangers was the purchase of a minority interest in a California bank called Westlands, which turned out to be a moneypit, because it had so many bad loans. G. Howard Eaton, who ran the bank, moved to Los Angeles, which seemed a funny place from which to run a Canadian bank. William Kennett, the inspector general of banks, called him in to explain his actions and then told him to move back to Canada, two years later, for sure.[7]

Then, when the Trust Companies Affair broke, and it turned out that Rosenberg et al. owned or controlled, quite illegally, nearly a third of the CCB, Eaton was forced to resign. Mr. Justice Willard Z. Estey, who wrote the inevitable government report on this one, noted, "The immediate impact on the bank was a loss of confidence and a run on deposits, driving the bank to the Bank of Canada for liquidity support."[8]

To keep going, the CCB indulged in some interesting accounting practices, such as accruing interest on loans when the payments weren't met, which was one of the favourite tricks of the S&Ls, as well. The money had not come in; whether it would ever come in was a matter of conjecture, but it showed up on books as income. The bank's auditors passed on the books, without a murmur, and the inspector general said, in effect, that if it was good enough for the auditors, it was good enough for him. At the time, the inspector general had a total of eight inspectors to scrutinize the activities of fourteen Canadian and more than fifty foreign banks,[9] but instead of clamouring for more staff, he tended to rely on the banks' auditors.

The CCB now moved into a twilight zone, a period in which everyone, especially the government spokespeople, pretended it was not moribund, while, on the side, putting in an order for flowers, a hearse, and shovels. When Eaton was forced out of the bank, Gerald Bouey, governor of the Bank of Canada, telephoned the *Globe and Mail* to insist that the CCB was a "solvent and profitable bank,"[10] information that came to him, presumably, via tea leaves or the Ouija board. The *Globe* duly ran the information, with raised eyebrows. Every few days, one of the opposition members would rare up in the House of Commons with a rude question and be reassured that all was okay. Three "everything's okay" statements from cabinet ministers equal one "head for the hills!" but this was not grasped at once, although a general sense of unease led to the withdrawal, over the next few months, of $1.3 billion in deposits,[11] which made the bank's position that much worse.

On March 25, 1985, a government press release set out to prove that everything was especially okay now, because the six largest chartered banks, the governments of Canada and Alberta, and the Canada Deposit Insurance Corporation, collectively referred to as "the support group," had weighed in with a rescue plan. The banks, collectively, and each of the governments, put up $60 million each, a total of $180 million, and the CDIC put up $75 million. This infusion of $255 million would look after all the soft loans out there, and William Kennett, the inspector general, gave the banks a letter to assure them that, with their help, the CCB "will . . . be solvent."[12] He had tea leaves, too. He had never done an inspection to determine whether the assets against which the CCB had issued loans were still worth the figures shown on the books.

Not that the banks doubted him, of course, but they wanted their own look at the loan portfolio. Accordingly, George Hitchman, the retired deputy chairman of the Bank of Nova Scotia, began a study of the CCB's loans on July 2, 1985, and, by August 1, had concluded, "It is clear that the CCB is insolvent."[13]

Bit of a shock to Bouey, Kennett, and anyone who had contemplated whipping their deposits out of the bank, but had left them in on the basis of the official reassurances. In a six-month period in 1985, the Bank of Canada advanced $1,272.2 million to the CCB,[14] pumping in cash at one end of the boat while it leaked out at the other. Finally, it became obvious to all that the bank could not survive, that no other bank would marry it and pay off the mortgage, and that there was not going to be another rescue package. The CCB was put out of its misery on September 1, 1985.[15]

At the same time the CCB was spiralling into the ground, so was another western bank, Northland, which was centred in Calgary. Like the CCB, it was born in the energy and real-estate boom in western Canada, loaned on shaky assets, and then, when these loans became non-performing, indulged in some very dodgy number-crunching. Mr. Justice Estey described the accounting methods used in the CCB and Northland cases as "imaginative," "energetic," "bizarre," and "risky" at various places in his report. The fainting loans were placed in a "workout" category and then improved by "the projected success of the workouts and anticipated improved economic conditions generally." That is the description of Mr. Justice Estey; I would call it financial faith healing. Believe, my son – or, in this case, my auditor – and the ill will be made well. The auditors believed, and the inspector general believed them, and Northland staggered on. In fact, it extended more loans, in hopes of getting some good ones to cover the bad ones.

Mr. Justice Estey, in his only flight of fanciful writing in 641 pages of prose, wrote, "The financial statements became gold fillings covering cavities in the assets and in the earnings of the bank."[16] By 1983, Northland was insolvent, but whistling past the graveyard, while the inspector general was otherwise occupied.

Then came the collapse of the CCB in March 1985. This led to a rapid withdrawal of deposits from Northland, which was seen, correctly, to be in the same condition. Again, the Bank of Canada stepped in, with a total of $517.5 million in advances.[17] Despite this, the inspector general's office allowed the bank to make a private debenture issue of $16 million and told the underwriters that "the OIGB [the Office of the Inspector General of Banks] was aware of nothing which would make it imprudent to proceed with the issue."[18] What is more, the governor of the Bank of Canada, Gerald Bouey, rejected a proposal from the bank to take a large write-off of its loans, which would certainly have spooked the market by more accurately reflecting what had happened.

Finally, the OIGB bestirred itself enough to look into Northland's bizarre banking practices, and, reeling, tried to get the National Bank to merge with Northland to save it. National Bank inspectors took one look at Northland's smelly loan portfolio and backed hastily away. A curator was appointed in September 1985, and the bank was liquidated in early 1986.[19]

The eventual price tag picked up by the federal government for the two banks was more than $1 billion.[20] The six chartered banks who had put in $60 million lost it. However, uninsured depositors in the banks were reimbursed, at a price of $875 million. These were mostly people who had more than the $60,000 maximum for CDIC insurance, and, in Ottawa, opposition MPs made quite a fuss about this bailing out of the fatcats. But Governor Bouey argued that "the causes of the present situation already existed at the time the official assurances were given,"[21] which was the crucial point. Without these assurances, from himself and others, the depositors would certainly have hauled out their money long since. It would not have been right to punish them for being dumb enough to take the word of cabinet ministers, given in the House of Commons. Actually, I guess that was pretty dumb, when you come to think of it, but the Mulroney government saw it in a different light and forked out the $875 million.

In March 1986, William Kennett, the inspector general of banks, retired at the age of fifty-three, saying that he was "in need of a rest."[22] I'll bet.

The liquidators for the CCB and Northland brought lawsuits against the former directors and officers of both banks and against their auditors, Ernst & Young International and Peat Marwick Thorne. In 1990, the defendants settled for $82.5 million in the CCB case and $43.2 million in the Northland case.[23]

In all these cases, involving three trust companies and two banks, we saw carefree loan practices, followed by creative accounting when the loans went sour, and a "What, Me Worry?" attitude on the part of the regulators. The parallel to events below the border is advanced another step in the next item offered for your consideration.

In the collapse of the Principal Group of Calgary, Alberta, in August 1987, there was the same maze of interlinked companies that marked, and obscured, so many S&L dealings; the same tendency on the part of confused elders to buy certificates they thought were government insured, but which were not; the same phenomenal growth followed by the same abrupt collapse; the same creation of paper profits, when things got rough; the same daisy chain of interlinked payments between and among connected companies; the same attempt by overworked regulators to bring the rascals to heel; the same political interference that kept them from doing their jobs; and the same fraud and deception.

No call girls, though, and no kickbacks to politicians in return for protection. This, after all, is Canada. Donald Cormie, the principal of Principal Group, always bristled with moral rectitude, even when he was skinning the rubes, and he always seemed perfectly sincere about it.

Cormie is one of those people who, like Alice's Humpty Dumpty, can make words mean what he wants them to mean; this is a terrific advantage when you are shilling shares or certificates of deposit. The $25-million, two-year Code Inquiry Report into his dealings provides, in its thousands of pages, one of those shining moments that tell us all we need to know. Cormie is on the stand, being grilled about an annual "review" released in 1985, which did not, to put the kindest possible interpretation on it, reflect what was actually going on. The company did not put out an annual *report* in 1985, because it would have had to follow accepted accounting procedures, whereas the review gave the number crunchers a trifle more scope. So much scope in fact, that a loss of $27.5 million somehow came out as a profit of $607,000.[24] (In 1992, Cormie would plead guilty to misleading advertising and deceptive marketing practices.[25]) Commission counsel was trying to find out whether Cormie thought the review's glowing picture of Principal's condition was candid, and we got the following exchange:

Q: Well, in the context of this article, you adopt this as a candid statement?

A: I don't understand what your word "candid statement" means.

Q: Do you not know what "candour" is?

A: It depends on the circumstances you're using it. What are you using it for?

Then, there is this:

Q: Can we try "true"? Can we try "true"? Is it a true statement?

A: Well, it depends on what it's being used for.

Q: Okay, accurate.

A: It could be a piece of a wider statement. I'm accepting it for what it says. For you to ask me whether it's true or candid –

Q: How about accurate?

A: Well, even accurate. It depends on what it's used for. [26]

So "candid," "true," and "accurate" statements given out by financial companies reflecting on their own current position are to be defined by "what it's being used for," whether, for example, the information is being used to flog bonds, gull investors, hold off creditors, fool regulators, or even, God help us, impart information.

Cormie is not a reflective man; he is aggressive, abrupt, dominant, clever, and impatient, but not reflective, or he might have wondered, when it was all coming apart, how a man who started a company dedicated to the principle of thrift could wind up in the centre of a bankrupt empire. His dad, a poultry commissioner for the Province of Alberta, brought him up to believe that you should save 10 per cent of what you earned, and Donald always did. One day in 1953, when he was at a football game with a friend, Ralph Forster, they got talking about this, and, according to Cormie's later testimony, out of this casual talk came the idea of founding a "department store of finance," based on thrift.[27] In 1954, Cormie, Forster, and three other Edmonton businessmen formed Bankers Investment Corporation, which later became First Investors Corporation (FIC), and which had as its mottoes: "Pay yourself first" and "10% of everything you earn is yours to keep."[28]

It was a pretty good time to start a financial company in the booming West, and, before long, a single company had become a whole stable of firms, covering the financial spectrum. In 1962, the FIC bought out Associated Investors of Canada (AIC), and both companies offered accumulation savings plans to the public. You put down a small amount every week or month and wound up with an interest-bearing savings certificate, which you could put into a Registered Retirement Savings Plan (RRSP). This was a fast-growing market. Principal Savings and Trust Company, established in 1965, provided trust and fiduciary services to the general public and, most importantly, sold RRSPs. Because the trust company was required to be a member of the CDIC, these RRSP deposits, and only these, were insured.

Principal Group Limited (PGL) was established a year later to provide management to others in the group and to sell promissory notes.[29] The group spread its wings and set up trust companies and financial companies in Alberta, Saskatchewan, British Columbia, New Brunswick, Nova Scotia, and Newfoundland. (Regulators in Ontario and Quebec kept it at bay.)

But they were all Donald Cormie. He ran them, controlled them, told them what to do. He had an effective 80.5-per-cent ownership interest in PGL through yet another company, Collective Securities Limited (CSL). His sons, James and John, held an interest in CSL, as did Ken Marlin, the executive vice-president of PGL, but, as William Code noted in his inquiry into the collapse, "Donald Cormie was the only individual familiar with and involved in every aspect of the operations of the Group."[30]

The honest thrift stage of the group lasted until 1978, when, with interest rates leaping like startled trout, Cormie and the boys went out to sell "single pay" certificates and automatic balanced concept

(ABC) plans – mutual funds – and promissory notes. There was a lot more money in mutual funds than in savings certificates, and there were, in the end, all sorts of mutual funds, from the rather staid collective mutual fund to the high-flying principal multiplier fund.

More money. As the money rolled in, the group expanded, sucking up all sorts of other companies, from breweries to development companies, and some of them made money and many of them lost it. By 1985, Principal Group had blossomed into an empire, embracing 130 companies, with $1 billion in assets,[31] and Cormie himself had a number of companies under his control that received payments and loans from the rest of the empire.[32] One company owned by his wife, but controlled by Cormie, received $360,000 in management fees from PGL in 1986 alone, by which time the group was in deep trouble.[33]

Cormie was the object of adoring newspaper and magazine articles and books, and wrote for a monthly newsletter produced by the group's marketing department. What the admirers were not to know for many years was that he was sucking money out of the group at the very time it was most needed, through a number of bizarre stunts. One of these was to pay his wife $275,000, ostensibly for chatting up the sales force. In fact, William Code found, "There is no evidence that Eivor Cormie did anything to earn the $275,000."[34] Then there was the $120,000 paid to his daughter, Allison, for a thirteen-month study of ancient weather cycles. This would help predict future economic cycles. Uh huh. Actually, no report was ever produced by Allison, and the payment to her was later declared "fraudulent and dishonest."[35]

The most successful, dangerous, and damaging scam the PGL companies got involved in was to sell pensioners and would-be pensioners certificates of deposit, usually within RRSPs, which looked as if they were covered by CDIC insurance, or were even safer than CDIC deposits, when they were not. In describing the way the seniors were sucked in, William Code gets so tired of using the words "dishonest and fraudulent" that, at one point, he reverses them, and they become "fraudulent and dishonest."[36] A few lines later, he is back to *d* and *f* again.

Would-be investors would read newspaper ads for certificates of deposit, backed with government insurance, and would trot off to one of the Principal Savings and Trust offices. There, they would be given a sales pitch, not for the advertised product, but for paper being sold by either Associated Investors of Canada or First Investors Corporation. The customer wound up thinking either that they were covered or that the certificates were even safer than the government-insured ones. This was exactly the same bait-and-switch tactic used by so many of the S&L salespeople and described in the last chapter.

In one survey conducted by the PGL internal audit department, it turned out that "41% of the respondents were not aware that FIC and AIC term certificates were not covered by CDIC."[37] If a customer was curious enough to ask directly about this matter, he got a line of gibberish to the effect that the certificates were "guaranteed," or "secure" or "safe."

When reports began to drift back to the regulators that this was going on, there were a number of phone calls to Principal Savings. An internal memo explained the danger of this:

> Certain authorities are making test calls to determine what explanations are being used. The severity of this problem must not be misunderstood by any member of the sales force. Misleading explanations can result in the Company's operations being suspended!!

You might think the solution would be not to make misleading explanations, but the PGL troops were told instead, "Do not attempt to explain 'Guarantee' over the phone." Instead, get the sucker to come in and tell him or her the following:

> If the client pursues the question of CDIC, respond that Investment Contract Companies like Canadian Life Insurance Companies do not have and do not require any outside insurance or guarantee. CDIC is only applicable to those institutions, such as banks and trust companies which face the risk of having an unexpected run on withdrawals.[38]

The sons of guns managed to make the government insurance look positively dangerous. In its place, the sales force was told to tell the customer that his certificate was "government guaranteed," because, under the provincial Investment Contracts Act, the company was required to place on reserve with a bank an amount of money equal to 104 per cent of the deposit. This was not the case, but most of the sales force thought it was, so the deliberate confusion and misrepresentation was compounded by the fact that the company lied to its own employees.[39]

The most glaring fact about the Principal Group was that it was unprincipled. In fact, the only assets behind the certificates were those of the two companies, the AIC and FIC, and the sales force had no information whatsoever on how these companies, whose assets were buried in the general accounts of the group, were doing. Thousands of people who thought they were insured found out otherwise only when it was much too late.

The Principal Group lost a good deal of money in real estate, and then lied to the customers about that, too. The company's 1985 annual review crowed, "Our success in moving out of real estate in advance of its subsequent collapse and moving into the stock and bond market at its low point are examples of how this strategic planning works for us and our clients." In fact, Principal got out of real estate and into mortgages on real estate; by the end of 1983, it had acquired huge amounts of foreclosed property, which was slowly dragging it down.

To cover its losses, the group became immersed in a whole series of complicated dealings between and among the companies that appeared to show profits, while in fact creating losses. The AIC and FIC even went into the development business, in violation of their licences, and managed to find new ways to lose money. One of their projects was the redevelopment of the Rimrock Inn in Banff. They got under way by digging a large hole. The inn was going to be turned into a five-star international resort worth $12 million, or $20 million, or $25 million, or $34.1 million – some hefty amount, anyway – and they tried to sell bits of it at the highest figure in Hong Kong. There were no takers, and, by the time the companies collapsed in mid-1987, $2.5 million had been spent. In return, "there was a big hole there."[40]

There were also complex dealings to benefit what were called the "upstairs companies," those owned or controlled by the Cormie family. They got service fees, placement fees, administrative fees, and "levies" that amounted to $54,530,886 between 1979 and 1986.[41] Then there were loans, totalling $10.8 million, to members of the Cormie family.[42]

The provincial regulators in Alberta began to get nervous about the FIC and AIC, the main companies that came under their purview, as early as 1973, when a "special report" indicated that the AIC had been "operating on the borderline" for some time, and the FIC had also "given rise to some problems, but not to as great an extent."[43]

Over the years, there were constant meetings, notations, letters, warnings, and expressions of concern. In 1981, the audit section of the provincial department of Consumer and Corporate Affairs found the two companies in violation of key requirements: they did not have sufficient unimpaired capital, nor did they have sufficient qualified assets on deposit. This led to a special report to the minister, but no concrete action. The next year, there were a number of meetings with company officers and more warnings. By this time, the regulators could see the companies were losing money, and a letter went out cautioning that "the ratio of liabilities to capital is so far out of line with other financial institutions that some kind of remedy must be considered."[44]

This was a bit like the cop saying, "Now that I've caught you speeding three times, please slow down." Like every other warning, this was ignored.

By late 1983, the province had hired its own appraisers to look at some of the properties the group was carrying on its books, and, to no one's surprise, they were worth less than the loans they supported. But it was not until March 2, 1984, that a memorandum was prepared by a senior provincial regulator that should have rung alarm bells all over Alberta. It was written by James Darwish, then superintendent of insurance ("contract" companies like the FIC and AIC came under his purview). It was addressed to Connie Osterman, then Alberta's Minister of Consumer and Corporate Affairs. Darwish had had a long, hard look at the FIC and said, among other things:

1. The company completely ignored guidelines sent to them setting out limitations on the size of investments. They proceeded to make huge investments without any regard whatsoever to the amount of capital they had and the discussions that were taking place between them and our department at the time.

2. They placed huge mortgages on undeveloped, speculative real estate.

3. They consistently pay higher interest rates in order to attract deposits than do other companies and therefore have to invest in more speculative types of mortgages and real estate in order to earn for themselves sufficient income to pay these high rates.

4. The present condition of their foreclosed real estate and mortgage portfolio is one of the worst, if not the worst, that the Audit Unit has examined.

5. The company continues to accrue interest on mortgages that haven't received a payment, in some cases, for over two years. [45]

The litany of doom went on to point out that "because of the high interest rates that the company offers, it attracts many thousands of Albertans as investors. . . . Should this company fail, the effect on the confidence in financial institutions in Alberta would be serious." On the crucial issue of its impaired capital, the FIC was in the red, to the tune of more than $5 million; it did not have enough in the vaults to justify the loans it was making. The appraisals it was using were not realistic, it was ignoring government directives and putting out false information. The memo described "a serious and emergency situation with regard to these companies," and Darwish wanted the government to force them to inject more capital at once, to bring them into conformity with the law.

Had Darwish's memo been made public, the doors of the group's trust companies would have clanged shut, not only in Alberta, but everywhere in Canada, and thousands of pensioners would have saved millions of dollars. Short of rushing up on the legislature roof and screaming "Fire!" the regulator had done about all he could to draw to the minister's attention the fact that things were going very badly in Donald Cormie's empire.

And what did Osterman do? She telephoned Darwish on April 30, 1984, to say that "[she] did not want any more recommendations from him. [She] did not regard the writing of such memoranda as part of his job, and [she] did not read the memorandum for content." Osterman then forced Darwish into retirement, as his reward for doing his duty.[46] She would later testify that she was hoping the economy would turn around and kiss Cormie's tottering group back to health. The effective result of Osterman's inaction was to suspend regulation of the two companies; they were no longer under any control. Not that the public was ever told this; so far as the public was concerned, the AIC and FIC were in fine shape and continued to receive provincial blessing. People went on trusting their funds to firms that the regulators knew were incompetent, insolvent, and untrustworthy.

It is now clear that both the FIC and AIC were technically insolvent as far back as 1983, that they kept going only by sucking in new money to meet current liabilities, and that the province ought to have yanked their licences, at the latest, in 1984.[47] But Principal Group staggered on, lying and selling CIDs by fraud, for three and a half more years, while the regulators fumed and fussed, and the Alberta government stared pointedly off in other directions. William Code, reporting on the situation, notes that "I am struck by both the inability and the unwillingness of the regulators to ensure that the companies observed appropriate financial safeguards."[48]

However, it would have been a bold regulator, seeing what happened to Darwish, who would dare to go after companies when the government had set out so clearly the penalty for being rude to them, even in a background memo: you got fired. Years later, in his report, Code found Osterman "in breach of her public duty," and ruled that her conduct was "neglectful, misguided or even reckless [although] her intentions were not in any way dishonest."[49]

I doubt if that came as much comfort to the thousands whose lives were devastated when the province finally got its act together and pulled the licences of the FIC and AIC on June 30, 1987. By that time, the companies were so far behind the required regulatory capital base that no amount of stalling could keep them going. The closings came four days after Principal Group sold two bonds worth $50 to a man named Scott Gyles, thus clearing the way for the parent company to duck into bankruptcy, under the Companies' Creditors Arrangement Act, on August 10, 1987. (Only corporations with bonds outstanding qualify for CCAA protection.)

The collapse left 67,000 investors, many of them elderly, with $450 million in certificates of deposit issued by the AIC and FIC. Another 6,000 had $135 million in cash in Principal Savings and Trust branches in six provinces. Most of this latter money was covered by the CDIC and was paid out quickly, but the certificate holders in the AIC and FIC were put through years of provincial inquiries, lawsuits, asset sales, and delays that are expected to stretch out another two or three years.[50] Another 11,000 investors held promissory notes worth $86 million. They will collect about half of that some time in the sweet by-and-by.[51] Barn doors were closed all over the country, as the provincial ombudsmen weighed in after the fact with stinging indictments of Cormie, Principal Group, and their own provincial regulators.

Stephen Owen, the B.C. ombudsman, pointed out that "Alberta government officials declined to act on clear evidence of the insolvency of AIC and FIC in 1984, and failed to advise B.C. regulators of this evidence."[52] However, he noted that the B.C. regulators were also slow in reacting to danger signals. The result was that 17,000 British Columbians lost $160 million, about 60 per cent of which will be recovered, over the years, from the sale of assets within the province. Alberta is committed to raising this to 75 per cent, as the major provincial authority responsible.[53]

The Saskatchewan ombudsman also investigated the activities of the Cormie companies, also found that the Alberta regulators had fallen down on the job, and that there had been a "total disregard of its regulatory obligations by the Government of Saskatchewan."[54]

In Nova Scotia, the ombudsman noted that the province relied on Alberta regulators, and in effect said that, if Principal was good enough for Alberta, it was good enough for Nova Scotia (this is known as the theory of "primary jurisdiction," providing adequate protection and ranks with the theory that storks bring babies, in terms of reliability). In Nova Scotia, the problem was compounded by the fact that there was never enough money for the registrar of securities to do his job, had he been so inclined.[55]

The theme song of our corporate lords and masters is that this nation is shackled by over-regulation. The Principal Group's history must be a source of great solace to these people; there was no effective regulation for them.

As for the pensioners who found themselves staring at worthless bits of paper, well, in due course, which is to say, over the years, they will get most of their money back, because the provinces recognize that they did such a lousy job. Those pensioners who are still alive, that is. More than a thousand of them have died since the collapse.[56]

Cormie moved to Arizona and went into the real-estate business. He managed to escape with a good deal of his money (the province paid $1.1 million towards his legal costs during the Alberta inquiry);[57] although his Alberta ranch was sold, he kept a house near Edmonton, another in Scottsdale, a suburb of Phoenix, a waterfront estate on Vancouver Island, and about $5 million in bank deposits outside Canada.[58] According to author Matthew Fisher, a little nest-egg of $4.2 million in cash went winging down to him just a few days before the Principal crash.[59] Walking-around money. He gives seminars to the locals on the need to save prudently and invest wisely. Various law-suits and charges against him and members of his family have been dragging on so long there is no way of knowing if or when they will ever come to trial.

I think Donald Cormie and Principal Group show us that we Cana-dians need not hang shyly back when Americans talk about their S&Ls. Even though our investors came out better than most of theirs, and our governments were not actually bribed into inactivity, our mess contained the same active ingredients as theirs: greed, stupidity, and regulatory numbness.

The case of Standard Trust Co. is a variation on the theme. Here the question was not fraudulent dealings, but the failure of timely disclosure.

The company was founded in 1963 by Steven Roman, the mining magnate, and owned by a holding company, Standard Trustco. A little less than half the stock was sold to the public, while Roman retained control. It grew to be the nation's ninth-largest trust company, and, like a number of other companies, got into trouble by imprudent, to say the least, loans on real estate. The most troublesome of these involved Owl Developments Ltd. of Edmonton, to which it loaned more than $100 million. Owl, in turn, was involved with a Winnipeg company, Berland Estates Ltd., a condominium development. Owl's president, John Barath, introduced Eric Stewart, the vice-president of mortgage production for Standard, to Victor Schultz, one of the prin-cipals in Berland, and, before the dust had settled, Standard Trust was lending Berland $2 million and Barath was pocketing a $35,000 fee.[60]

Berland Estates flopped, and Owl could not keep up its mortgage payments, so Standard wound up with a lot of real estate it didn't really know what to do with. There were other, similar deals, such as the one in Newfoundland, where Standard took over a strip mall, which it had financed, when the owners went bankrupt. To get rid of that one, Stan-dard auctioned it off to the highest bidder – who turned out to be one of the mortgagors who had gone bankrupt. Showing a breadth of mind and calibre of courage I have never been able to discern in any lender I approached, Standard turned around and loaned the man the money to buy back the strip mall at a knock-down rate. And then, of course, couldn't collect from him.[61]

By the spring of 1989, Standard was in serious trouble. The record now available shows that, by April, 8 per cent of its entire mortgage portfolio was in arrears, but you wouldn't know that from the information available then. In July, Standard Trustco Ltd. posted a record six-month profit of $7.8 million, up 24 per cent from the previous year. The moaning mortgages were taken care of by having the trust company simply accrue the missing interest. Instead of looking like money lost, or potentially lost, it was carried forward.

This affected a number of other players, including people who bought the company stock without the slightest hint that it might be in trouble, people who had money on deposit in the thirty-seven branches of the company, and the regulators, which included stock-market regulators and the Office of the Superintendent of Financial Institutions (OSFI). It was the OSFI that caught up to the fancy accounting. On September 12, 1989, Donald Macpherson, the deputy superintendent of the OSFI, wrote to Brian O'Malley, the chief executive of Standard, and told him to stop accruing interest on delinquent loans.

In April 1990, as part of its rescue of Owl Developments, Standard breached the regulatory rule that prohibits lending more than 1 per cent of its assets to a single lender, and, when that didn't work, wound up taking over the real estate. The company president, Juli Koor, would later admit that at least ten of the firm's loans were in breach of the regulations.[62]

On June 25, the OSFI, now alarmed, began an examination of Standard's books, and quickly discovered that its assets were overstated and that there was no adequate provision for loan losses. Again, the public was not given a sniff of this. Instead, the company reported a profit of $5 million and declared a quarterly dividend of twenty-five cents a share.

It was not until July 27 that the company announced that a special audit was being conducted. The stock, which had been selling for $17.75 in June, dropped to $16. The quarterly dividend was called off, on instructions from Michael Mackenzie, superintendent of the OSFI.

The results of the special audit were not released until November 9. They showed that Standard's non-performing loans totalled $215 million and the "profit" of $5 million, shown in June, was instead a loss of $50 million. The stock went into free fall.

Standard was required to present a "business plan" to the OSFI, showing how it intended to keep in business. This plan showed that it was losing money at a rate of $2.5 million a month, and the only way to keep its liquidity requirements in line with the law would be to sell securities and its good mortgage loans. Standard's leverage was twenty-five; under trust-company rules, the firm had to have $1 in capital for every $25 in deposits. Standard had $1.5 billion of the public's money, so it needed $60 million in capital. In short, it would have to sell its sound assets, making its continuation even more improbable. Again, the public was told nothing of this, although the company did issue a press release, saying that shareholders' equity had dwindled by $10 million to $27 million. The stock plummeted to $3.

Frantic attempts to sell the trust to Laurentide Bank or, indeed, to anybody with the necessary money, took up the next few months, and then, on April 5, 1991, Standard delivered its 1990 audited books to the OSFI. It had lost $102 million on the year. Again, the public was not informed, although, on April 9, the company announced that its loan-loss provision for 1990 would come to $117 million.

On April 16, the Ontario Securities Commission got into the act, accusing Standard directors of releasing misleading financial statements. The next day, the OSFI seized the trust, padlocking its branches and head office. Five days later, on April 23, creditors of Standard Trustco Ltd., the holding company, forced it into bankruptcy, and the usual swarm of lawyers and accountants descended.

The depositors were covered – at least those with less than $60,000, the limit of the Canada Deposit Insurance Corporation – but the stockholders were out of luck. On June 30, 1994, the *Globe and Mail* reported that the CDIC is suing the former directors, auditors, and the controlling shareholder of Standard Trust, the Roman Corporation, for $1.5 billion, in an attempt to get back the money it paid depositors. The Roman Corporation told the *Globe* "there are no grounds to the action." That lawsuit should last for a few years.

The OSFI defends the imposition of a cloak of silence over the fainting trust company with two arguments. The first is that its job is to protect the public, especially the depositing public. "We did everything we were required to do on that account," an OSFI spokesperson told me. The second is that, if the regulator went public with every breach of regulations that came to light, its job would become impossible. "No one would trust us with any information" is the way it was put to me. "There has to be a certain amount of trust in this business."

I think that's true, but I don't see how it squares with what is actually taking place in the financial community. If we are to assume that everyone in business, or even, to take Michael Bliss's optimistic ratio, one in five in business, is a crook, we will need armies of regulators to police them all.

What we are finding, in this exploration of bankruptcy, is that we are coming up against the fundamental dilemma of our time. If the standard of behaviour in the business world is that any conduct is permissible that does not actually inspire a criminal charge, and, if the threat of regulations that might lead to criminal charges is to be met by wiping out the regulations, we are in danger of creating not merely an economy, but a society, which is incapable of functioning.

The Canadian Bankers Association and the C. D. Howe Institute would meet the danger posed by deposit insurance by what is called "co-insurance,"[63] a euphemism for making the insurance deductible. Only 80 per cent of the money would be insured; the depositor would bite the bullet for the first 20 per cent (just as the car owner pays the first $500, or whatever, on deductible collision insurance). That is enough of an incentive, the banks argue, to ensure that prudent investors would look out for their interests more sharply than they do under a system where it literally doesn't matter if the lending institution to which they have entrusted their funds spends it on hookers.

The difficulty with this solution, which those nice people up at the banks and the C. D. Howe Institute probably missed when they were drawing this thing up, is that the day after such a change was made, money would begin to flow out of the trust companies and into the largest of the Canadian banks. The big banks aren't going to go bust, because the government can't afford to let that happen. So, why would anyone gamble with 20 per cent of his savings, when all he has to do is deposit it all with a big bank?

This is not so much a scheme to save deposit insurance as one to wipe out trust companies. And it is based on a false premise. In case after case, we have seen that the public hasn't the foggiest notion what goes on inside our financial institutions. As a *Toronto Star* editorial put it, "How can the C. D. Howe Institute tell ordinary depositors that they should be able to smell trouble brewing when it says that the expert regulators who get paid to monitor financial institutions 'have consistently failed?'"[64] The regulators don't know, until it is too late, and, even when they do know, they can't tell the rest of us. And why not? Because it would cause a run on the institution involved.

There's a catch-22 for you. You should yank your deposits at institutions that are on shaky ground, but we can't tell you which ones those are, because then you would yank your deposits.

It would be crazy, and irresponsible, to remove the insurance and allow hundreds of thousands of old-age pensioners, and other depositors, to be wiped out because they weren't shrewd enough to realize what only a handful of people can possibly know about the operations of any given institution. Cooking the books has become an honoured profession; the reasonable person beloved of economic texts cannot possibly keep up with the wily number crunchers of today. Remove the deposit insurance, or even co-insure it, and you will only ensure that the smallest rumour will start a run on any bank or trust company, no matter how well administered.

By the way, removing deposit insurance is what we are in the process of doing, without any formal decision. Prenor Trust, yet another company that got blindsided by an ambitious loans policy in a declining real-estate market, failed in January 1994 and was taken over by the CDIC. In June 1993, the CDIC board of directors issued an order that, in such cases, no interest would be paid on deposits after the takeover. This meant that 80,000 depositors, with $879.5 million on deposit with Prenor, lost their interest for at least the two months it took to return them their capital. People with RRSPs in Prenor (or any other failed trust company) also lose. That is because the CDIC liquidates the RRSP certificates by selling them to a bank, which transfers them into a daily-interest account. A friend of mine had about $7,000 in a Prenor RRSP which went from earning 11.25 per cent to earning 0.25 per cent. It had another two years to run, and she could not have cashed it, as a prudent investor, because it was in a five-year Guaranteed Investment Certificate. Tough nougies. She reinvested the money she got back from the receiver at 5 per cent; her contribution to Prenor's demise was several hundred dollars, despite the ads that tell us we are "fully insured" by the CDIC.

In short, we already have a form of co-insurance, without ever having decided to go that way. Tom Delaney, the nation's top expert on RRSPs, argues that, "The banker's lobby appeared to wield such power that the CDIC board effectively changed the law without Parliament's consent."[65]

The common factor in every one of the cases of abuse, in trust companies and in savings and loans, has been the same: a single investor, or a small group of investors, has bought control of a company that takes deposits from the public and used the institution as his own piggybank. This doesn't happen in the case of Canadian banks for one simple reason – no person or group is allowed to own more than 10 per cent of a chartered bank. The trust companies have fought off parallel legislation, because trust companies are very often much smaller than banks, and to apply such a rule might take many of them out of business. I think we have reached the point where we have to impose one of two constraints on the trusts. Either they submit to much greater outside regulation, or they submit to a 10-per-cent rule. Open up the books and close down the crooks, and we can probably save the deposit insurance for real emergencies.

CHAPTER EIGHT

Insulating Against the Injured

"By the last week of September, when Manville's Chapter 11 petition had dropped from the headlines, few people were aware that the bankruptcy filing was simply the latest episode in a fifty-year history of corporate malfeasance and inhumanity to man which is unparalleled in the annals of the private-enterprise system." – Paul Brodeur, *The New Yorker*, 1985 [1]

$

Bankruptcy, by the eighties, was not exactly respectable in Canada and the United States, but it wasn't really disgraceful any more, either. The next steps were to make it first a shield, and then a bludgeon, for the use of giant corporations, and this chapter and the next show how that was worked in two of the most stunning cases on record. These are American cases, and, if history is anything to go by, they represent the direction Canadians can expect to follow over the next few years.

On August 27, 1982, the *New York Times* carried a front-page story, whose contents ran like a galvanic shock through the North American financial community. The Manville Corporation, for decades one of the most successful, and profitable, enterprises in the world, was filing for bankruptcy protection under Chapter 11 of the U.S. Bankruptcy Code. It was the largest American industrial company ever to file for reorganization. The company was forced into this position, the article explained – and the explanation was echoed in a lead editorial, as well as in a full-page ad placed by the company in the same edition – due to circumstances entirely beyond its control. While it was still an immensely wealthy corporation, with a net worth of $1.1 billion, 1981 earnings of $60 million, assets worth $2 billion, and sales of $2.2 billion annually, it had been "completely overwhelmed," as John A. McKinney, its president and chief operating officer, explained,[2] by an avalanche of lawsuits launched by people who had been damaged, disabled, or killed by working with asbestos.

And who was to blame for this distressing turn of events? The government. Those rascals down in Washington, eschewing their responsibility by refusing to set up a compensation trust for injured workers, had forced a reluctant, and ignorant, firm into this defensive stance. McKinney, the *New York Times*, and the ad were all in agreement on that. As the editorial put it, "Not until a 1964 study by Irving Selikoff of the Mount Sinai Medical Center in New York did the danger of asbestos become fully apparent. Because lung diseases caused by asbestos took so long to develop, the first wave of epidemic has hit only recently."[3]

This was a comfortable and convenient echo of the material contained in the ad, headlined "DESPITE STRONG BUSINESS, LITIGATION FORCES MANVILLE TO FILE FOR REORGANI-ZATION."[4] The text consisted of a series of questions and answers exchanged between an unknown interrogator and McKinney himself, including the following:

Q: Your businesses are in good shape, but you filed under Chapter 11? Why?

A: We're overwhelmed by 16,500 lawsuits related to the health effects of asbestos, with many more projected. The federal government has refused to admit its responsibility to its shipyard workers. *Congress has failed to act to provide compensation for claimants* [emphasis in original].

Q: What are all these lawsuits really about?

A: It's a long story. *Not until 1964 was it known that excessive exposure to asbestos fiber released from asbestos-containing insulated products can sometimes cause certain lung diseases* [emphasis in original]. . . . In the absence of congressional action, the board of directors concluded there is no conceivable resolution to this burden, other than Chapter 11.

Having stumbled unwittingly into a swamp of court claims, the beleaguered company had turned to government to provide compensation for the injured. But the government refused; it would not even pay the claims of its own workers, struck down while applying insulation in shipyards, much less take on the burden for the thousands of Manville workers and independent contractors who had been stricken over the years. In those circumstances, who could blame the firm for ducking into the safety of Chapter 11? You would never know, reading any of this material, that the Manville Corporation, in its earlier incarnation as Johns–Manville Company Ltd., had known for decades that its product was killing people, and had fought for decades to conceal its knowledge and responsibility. You would never know that the battle for obfuscation, concealment, delaying, denying, and lying had been led by the company's legal department, of which McKinney himself was general counsel, or even that the *Times* had a library where it might have looked up some of this stuff before automatically bending its knee to a powerful corporation and championing its cause. "The need for order," thundered the editorial, "deserves Congress's urgent attention, before more victims die uncompensated, and other companies follow Manville into the bankruptcy courts." The newspaper carried eighteen articles on the subject in 1981 and had covered it for years. On October 7, 1964, just before the Selikoff study was released, the *Times* had a piece clearly linking cancer to asbestos.[5]

Among the other whoppers laid on a credulous public in the Q&A danced by McKinney and his unnamed partner was the claim that Manville had already disposed of "some 3,500" lawsuits and that, in "a significant number of cases" that had gone to trial, "juries have found that we were not at fault and acted responsibly in light of then existing medical knowledge." In fact, the company had settled 3,400 of the 3,500 cases, paying out $50 million in damages. It had also been hit with punitive damages in ten recent cases. Juries had found it to be very much at fault, and that it had not acted responsibly. Moreover, a New Jersey court had already specifically struck down, as the hogwash it was, the defence that the company didn't know of the danger until 1964. McKinney must have been aware of this, since the main reason given for seeking bankruptcy protection was the claim that future punitive damages would force the step if the company didn't dive for cover before it was forced there.[6]

The moral of Manville's Chapter 11, according to the world's finest newspaper, was that government inaction was causing untold harm. But the real moral, which might have been read in the newspaper's own files, is that Chapter 11 can provide a haven to a corporation whose behaviour over the decades has been despicable, can provide it with a means of ridding itself of responsibility for the lives it has destroyed, and can send it back out into the market, cleansed of debt and despair, to try again, while its victims get on with the business of hacking their lungs out and dying.

Asbestos has been used for thousands of years for its remarkable insulating qualities. The embalmed bodies of Egyptian pharaohs were wrapped in asbestos.[7] The name comes from the Greek word *asbestos*, meaning "inextinguishable." Roman slaves wove the mineral into cloth used for handling hot objects, and, even in that time, it was known to cause lung diseases;[8] Pliny the Younger (61–114 A.D.) commented on the "sickness of slaves" compelled to work with the material for any long period of time.[9] The very qualities that made asbestos so well suited for insulation also made it harmful to human beings. Its tiny, strong fibres resemble strands of silk; they are easily inhaled, and can become embedded in the lung. Phagocytes, the lung's protective cells, coat the fibre in an attempt to destroy it, and this process may cause scarring, damage to the lung, or fatal tumours, over time. This was not understood when the "miracle material" re-emerged after the Dark Ages. Marco Polo came across asbestos during one of his trans-Siberian trips, and the emperor Charlemagne convinced a guest at dinner that he was magic, by throwing a glove composed of asbestos onto the fire and then retrieving it unharmed.

Asbestos began to be manufactured in Europe in the sixteenth century and in North America after the discovery of a huge deposit in the province of Quebec, where the first mine opened near Thetford, in 1878.[10] The industry came to be dominated by a few huge corporations, all foreign-owned, led by the Johns–Manville Company Ltd. of New Jersey, which acquired control over the world's largest deposit at Asbestos, Quebec, in 1901. By the forties, 85 per cent of the world's asbestos fibre was being produced in a narrow corridor running north from the Vermont border, roughly northeast to Quebec City;[11] most of this was produced by Johns–Manville, which manufactured it into dozens of products and exported it all over the globe.

Propelled by the tax-breaks, legal favouritism, and huge quantities of cash our governments always feel compelled to shower down on private enterprise in the name of rugged individualism, Johns–Manville became obscenely wealthy, with profits running at 27 per cent per annum.[12] Canadian Johns–Manville Company Ltd. was so closely intertwined with government, in fact, that the provincial administration of Maurice Duplessis came down hard when the Asbestos workers struck for an increase of fifteen cents an hour in 1949. They were then making eighty-five cents, less than half the wage of their American counterparts. They also demanded better working conditions, including cleanup of the dust that hung over the place in a constant cloud.

The strike was declared to be illegal, and then, in a neat bit of Orwellian reasoning, the union was automatically decertified for taking part in an illegal strike.[13] Provincial police were called in, at the request of Johns–Manville, to "protect property" and did so by beating up pickets, getting drunk, and terrorizing the populace. *Le Devoir* reported, "Asbestos is a city occupied, terrorized. . . . [This action] literally means a lend-lease of the provincial police to Johns–Manville."[14] Catholic clergy became involved, on the side of the strikers, and in the end, the workers won recertification and ten cents an hour from a provincial arbitration board, after a bitter, ten-week struggle.

However, the arbitration board accepted, in the main, the company's argument that it was already doing a wonderful job on the industrial-health front. A company brochure trilled at the time, "More than $1,000,000 has already been spent at Asbestos to improve working conditions which have been recognized by health authorities as outstanding in the industry."[15]

The brochure also referred to the contamination as "nuisance dust,"[16] not as the killer the company already knew it to be.

Item: In 1887, a Viennese physician wrote that there was "no doubt" that inhaling asbestos dust was causing illness among workers.[17]

Item: In 1898, the Lady Inspectors of Factories in England wrote of the "easily demonstrated" injury to asbestos workers of prolonged exposure to the mineral.[18]

Item: That same year, Henry Ward Johns, who invented a new roofing material by combining asbestos, burlap, jute, and pith, died of "dust phthisis pneumonitis." Three years later, his firm was merged with the Manville Covering Company of Milwaukee.[19]

Item: In 1900, Dr. H. Montague Murray of Charing Cross Hospital in London, England, performed an autopsy on a thirty-three-year-old man who had worked in an asbestos factory and found spilicules of asbestos in his lungs.[20]

Item: In 1906, after fifty workers had died over a period of five years in an unventilated asbestos factory in France, a study concluded that people under the age of eighteen should not be allowed to work in dusty conditions, but did not finger asbestos itself.

Item: In 1917, in England, Dr. W. E. Cooke coined the name "asbestosis" for the disease that had killed a woman who had worked in an asbestos plant for thirteen years.

Item: That same year, in the United States, a study by the University of Pennsylvania revealed lung scarring among asbestos workers.

Item: In 1918, the U.S. Bureau of Statistics reported that asbestos workers were dying young and that insurance companies were refusing to issue policies covering these labourers because of "assumed health-injurious conditions" in the industry.

Item: In 1927, the first workers' compensation claim was accepted for asbestosis in the United States.

Item: In 1928 and 1929, the inspector of factories in Britain examined 363 asbestos textile workers, and found that 95 of them showed evidence of pulmonary fibrosis, scarring of the lungs. This resulted in a law requiring improved methods of exhaust ventilation and dust suppression in factories where asbestos was manufactured, the institution of periodic examinations for asbestos workers, and making asbestosis a compensable disease. [21]

Item: In 1930, in Canada, a study of 195 asbestos miners by a panel of doctors revealed that 38 of them had asbestosis. The study was not made public; instead, the *Canadian Medical Association Journal* ran an article in November 1930 which said that "no cases of specific disease have been reported in any asbestos workers in the Province of Quebec." [22]

Item: In 1948, Dr. Kenneth Smith, the medical director of Canadian Johns–Manville, conducted a survey of 708 workers in the Asbestos mine, and found that only 4 of them, all of whom had had less than four years' exposure to asbestos dust, had normal lungs. [23] Smith sent the survey results to the American headquarters of Johns–Manville, where they were buried for three decades.

Item: By January 1950, there were 146 articles documenting the disease in National Health and Welfare files in Ottawa and a clear link between exposure to asbestos and cancer, as well as asbestosis. National Health and Welfare's public posture was that there was no danger in the mineral, when properly used.

Item: In November 1950, there was a strategy meeting of officials from the Quebec Asbestos Manufacturers Association at Saranac Lake, New York, a research facility funded by the companies. In theory, this meeting was to prepare the way for a research paper on asbestos dust and lung cancer. In fact, as Dr. Ray Sentes of the University of Regina, who wrote his PH.D. thesis on the industry, discovered, the minutes of that meeting set out quite a different purpose: "To combat the adverse and often unwarranted pseudo facts that are put out by others." Regrettably, the study that was then funded did show a link between asbestos and cancer. No problem. "The phrase was removed from the study."[24]

For almost a century, then, it was obvious to anyone who cared to look that asbestos was a killer; since 1917 at the latest, asbestos manufacturers had before them exhaustive studies, reports, and files, compiled in England, France, Canada, and the United States, all pointing to the same set of facts that confirmed that working with asbestos over long periods of time caused lung diseases, which could be fatal; quite often, cancer resulted. The manufacturers responded by doing everything they could to prevent knowledge of the harm they were doing from coming to the attention of the public. They did this by hiring, and suborning, medical researchers, by persuading governments and medical publishers to distort or conceal facts, and by lying, especially to their own workers.

What frustrated this clear policy, in the end, was the very magnitude of the problem; the asbestos manufacturers were killing and injuring so many people that the documentation eventually reached the point where it could no longer be concealed. You had to give them good marks for trying, though. On April 24, 1933, which is to say, thirty-one years before the Manville Corporation was supposed to have known anything much about the dangers of the product, the Johns–Manville board of directors instructed its attorneys to settle eleven cases for $35,000 and a written assurance that the successful attorneys against them would not act in any other cases involving the company.[25] The memo containing this information did not come to light until 1979, during which time Johns–Manville managed to fight off most suits with claims of corporate ignorance.

The company was forced, by the increasing incidence of disease among its workers, to conduct periodic health inspections, but it adopted a deliberate policy of keeping the information from the workers until they became too ill to carry on. Dr. Ray Sentes dug up the minutes of a meeting between executives of Johns–Manville and the Union Asbestos and Rubber Corporation in 1942 that make this brutally clear:

> Vandiver Brown [J–M's corporate counsel] stated that Johns–Manville's physical examination program had, indeed, also produced findings of X-ray evidence of asbestos disease among workers exposed to asbestos and that it was Johns–Manville's policy not to do anything nor to tell the employees of the X-ray finding. Vandiver Brown went on to say that it was foolish of us to be concerned and that if Johns–Manville's workers were told, they would stop working and file claims against Johns–Manville, and that it was Johns–Manville's policy to let them work until they quit work because of asbestosis or died as a result of asbestosis-related disease.[26]

Much more convenient if they actually died, of course; then they couldn't either file for compensation or sue for damages. A memo written by Kenneth Smith repeated the point:

> It is felt that as long as the man feels well, is happy at home and at work, and his physical condition remains good, nothing should be said. When he becomes disabled and sick, then the diagnosis should be made and the claim submitted *by the company* [emphasis in original].[27]

If the company submitted the claim, it could conceal the fact that the disease had been detected years earlier, which might lead to a lot of rude questions, to say nothing of lawsuits, or, as Smith himself rather disingenuously put it, "If we told the workmen of East Brougham that they were affected by asbestosis, it would cost the company too much money."[28]

The asbestos industry showed great skill in damping down an excessive curiosity as to why its workers were keeling over in such large numbers in both Canada and the United States. In the United States, Occupational Health officials were precluded by law from informing workers that they were in danger, and so, even while studies showed an increasing death rate, this remained the government's, and the companies', own little secret.

In Canada, the Quebec Asbestos Manufacturers Association, with Johns–Manville as a leading member, created the Institute of Occupational and Environmental Health in Montreal, which it funded. Sounds like one of those goody-goody outfits, doesn't it? In fact, the institute was brought into being "to ensure that only those researchers approved by the mining companies would have access to records and data concerning Quebec's asbestos workers."[29] If the government wanted to know what was going on, it asked the industry, which said everything was fine, and the government tugged its forelock and said, Okay.

One study did get past the corporate guard, however. In 1976, a National Health and Welfare Working Group, which, for once, had no industry representatives or doctors among its members, looked at asbestosis and described it as a "slow, insidiously progressive pulmonary fibrosis," resulting from seven to ten years' exposure. The report said that irreversible lung cancer could be caused by asbestos, and that mesotheliomas, which were inevitably fatal, were "caused primarily by asbestos."[30]

This was rank heresy. The asbestos industry was still describing lung cancer as a "medical mystery" that only affected smokers and mesothelia as another "mystery."[31]

The discrepancy did not become a public embarrassment; somebody sat on the head of the National Health people, and the Canadian government's official position remained, and remains, that the material is safe if properly handled, and that it does more good than harm, taken all in all. The damaging National Health survey was kept quiet for fourteen years after the Selikoff study, referred to in the *New York Times* article quoted earlier, had been published.

It was not that Johns–Manville was ignorant of the damage it was doing until 1964 and then became responsible. It deliberately suppressed the information it had and continued to deny it even after the 1964 study. Just the same, that document did represent a watershed of sorts, because, after its publication, no company could go into court claiming ignorance of the effects of asbestos on human lungs.

Selikoff and two of his colleagues in a medical clinic had become interested in the high incidence of chest diseases among their clients who worked in an asbestos-manufacturing company that had plants in New York and New Jersey. The researchers attempted to enlist the aid of the company and the United States Public Health Service in establishing the cause of the illnesses, but could get neither funding nor cooperation. Then Selikoff went to the union representing the workers, which had already become concerned on the same subject. The union was more than happy to round up workers for study.

For a year, the researchers tracked the incidence of disease among asbestos installers and compared it to the general population. The results appeared in the 1964 paper, in which Selikoff made it clear that exposure to even the smallest amount of asbestos could lead to any of several types of lung cancer.[32] The death rate from lung cancer among asbestos workers was seven times the national rate, and for gastrointestinal cancer, three times. Of 392 men who had more than twenty years of exposure to asbestos, 339 – almost 87 per cent – had asbestosis.

This data was presented in a paper at the Conference on the Biological Effects of Asbestos sponsored by the Academy of Sciences at the Waldorf Astoria Hotel in New York City in October 1964. Upon which the industry slapped itself on the cheeks and said, "Oh, my goodness, why didn't somebody tell us this that before?" and agreed, for the first time, to start putting warning labels on their products, so that the people who worked with asbestos, day in and day out, might have at least a small indication of how dangerous it was.

In the wake of the New York revelations, Johns–Manville brought out the argument that no blame attached to the manufacturer, because the "state-of-the-art" information was that asbestos was safe. But by this time, a case was already working its way through the courts that would begin the process of caving in the company defence. It involved a short, slender, soft-spoken man of Cajun background named Claude J. Tomplait, who had worked for twenty years in and around Orange, Texas, installing asbestos. Tomplait had recently been diagnosed as having pulmonary fibrosis, and he asked Ward Stephenson, a lawyer in Orange who had handled a number of industrial-injury cases, to represent him in a claim for workers' compensation.

This was no simple matter. The asbestos companies had succeeded in having most state legislatures pass laws under which very limited compensation would be paid and which surrounded the process with thickets of paperwork. In Texas, for example, the worker had to file within three years of the onset of the injury, although asbestosis can take as long as forty years to manifest itself. Usually, the state boards found that the worker suffered from silicosis, or some other non-compensable disease, or that his injury came from smoking, not asbestos, and was therefore self-inflicted. In most cases, the worker had to give up his right to sue in return for compensation, and, even if he won, the most he could collect under Texas law was $14,305. This was not only the maximum under the compensation program, it was the most he could collect in a successful lawsuit under Texas law. If a jury awarded more than that, it had to be given back.

Stephenson, who knew all this, and had been bucking the system for years, filed on Tomplait's behalf on February 24, 1962. The Texas Industrial Accident Board denied the claim on the grounds that Tomplait's shortness of breath was caused by emphysema, not asbestos. Tomplait smoked. The insurance company report covering the case neglected to mention that the injured worker had scar tissue in his lungs.[33] Stephenson then filed suit against Travelers Insurance Company, then carrying coverage for the installation company where Tomplait worked. He asked for $14,035, the maximum allowable by law. Four years later, Travelers settled for $7,500.

However, in the meantime, Stephenson had launched a suit in federal court, in Beaumont, Texas, a tactic that would get him around the limitations of the Texas statute. He demanded $500,000 from eleven manufacturers, including Johns–Manville, who had made the stuff that was killing his client. By this time, the Selikoff paper had been made public, and Stephenson sued on the grounds that his client might have been spared if the company had printed a warning label on its products, advising installers of the potential danger.

After years of stonewalling, five of the companies were willing to settle, for $15,000 each. However, one firm, Fibreboard Paper Products, went to trial and won, on the grounds that it had no way of knowing that asbestos was dangerous at the time Tomplait contracted his illness, and that he couldn't prove it was *their* particular product, rather than that of some other asbestos manufacturer, that did the damage. Stephenson did not know of all the early studies that proved the companies' culpability, and, in any event, most of the courts who heard asbestos cases refused to allow board minutes, or other evidence of the firms' early knowledge, to be admitted.

By the time Tomplait had lost the Fibreboard case, Stephenson, who was himself in ill health – he was dying of cancer – had taken on another case, that of Clarence Borel, a co-worker of Tomplait's, and filed a $1-million complaint against the same eleven companies. Borel died on June 3, 1970, but his widow continued the suit, which the companies again defended on the "state-of-the-art" argument. Until 1964, they said, the had had no way of "reasonably foreseeing" that asbestos would kill an installer. Stephenson said this was like arguing, "I didn't know my pistol would kill a priest, because I had never shot one before, but I did know it would kill other things, because I had shot game with it."[34]

Stephenson produced a list of eighty-six articles on the dangers of asbestos, most of which had appeared before 1938, and read into the record the deposition of one of Johns–Manville's own expert witnesses, Dr. W. Clark Cooper, in which he admitted that it had been known for fifty years that asbestos could cause asbestosis.[35]

In 1971, the jury awarded Borel's widow $79,000, after being instructed by the judge that it could award nothing for pain and suffering, and the companies immediately appealed, on the grounds that the good asbestos did outweighed its harm, and that Borel had contributed to his own death by not wearing a mask – which, of course, there was no need to do if the stuff wasn't dangerous. Three years later, the appeal was denied, and the award upheld. Stephenson himself had just died of lung cancer, but a clerk in the appeal court had phoned him just before he died to leak the news that he had won. Borel's widow collected about $32,000 of the money, once legal costs were taken out.

The original Borel victory in 1971 set off a landslide of claims against the companies. John A. Karjala, a sixty-year-old insulator from Duluth, Minnesota, filed a suit which went to trial three years later against Johns–Manville. The company maintained, once again, that it had known nothing until 1964; the jury, once again, didn't believe it, and Karjala was awarded $200,000. Of course, it didn't do him any good; he died shortly after of malignant mesothelioma, a tumour associated with exposure to asbestos.[36] The judge in this case was Miles W. Lord, whom we will meet again. The company appealed, lost, and the case went into every law library in the land, where it was fashioned into a club with which to belabour Johns–Manville and other asbestos manufacturers.

New studies from New York's Mount Sinai were now showing that one out of every three asbestos insulators was dying of cancer; it was an epidemic. So, by this time, were the lawsuits. A class-action suit for $100 million was filed in January 1974 against Pittsburgh Corning Company, another manufacturer, which settled for $20 million.[37] Then, in a case against Johns–Manville filed in Pittsburgh,

Dr. Kenneth Smith, the Canadian who had been so instrumental in the company's coverup, agreed to talk to one of the plaintiff lawyers, in a deposition taken in Windsor, Ontario, where he had retired. Smith was undergoing a change of heart, and out came much of the material about the policy of concealment. The company promptly settled the case for $150,000, which kept the Smith deposition under wraps, at least for a while.

A gaggle of lawyers acting in these matters formed the Asbestos Litigation Group, to exchange information and tactics, and Smith was deposed again, and this time all the litigation lawyers were able to get at the information. The dike continued to crumble. In 1974, the annual report of Raybestos–Manhattan, another manufacturer, unwittingly revealed that that company had known about the dangers of asbestos as early as 1930 and had commissioned internal studies to show the extent of the problem. It was currently defending cases on the basis of blissful ignorance. That was embarrassing. So was the discovery, in another of the myriad cases now launched, of the personal papers of Sumner Simpson, who had been president of Raybestos.

In these papers, Simpson described a meeting with officials of Johns–Manville in Manhattan. At this meeting, company officials referred to studies conducted years earlier, pointing to the damage done by their products. Worse still, there was discussion of a report given to the companies in 1931, by Metropolitan Life, which showed that, of 126 workers employed for more than three years, 67 had developed asbestosis and 39 showed signs of the disease.[38] That put the incidence of injury at 84 per cent. The report concluded that "prolonged exposure to asbestos dust causes a pulmonary fibrosis" and that "it is possible for uncomplicated asbestos to result fatally."[39]

Another case turned up the minutes of the Asbestos Textile Institute, a trade association formed in 1944, which referred to steps taken trying to undo the damage back in 1946, and to studies which established the link between asbestos and cancer in 1952.

The companies were now settling suits by the hundreds, to keep this material out of the public eye, but on April 26, 1978, Joseph

Califano, the secretary of Health, Education and Welfare, issued a statement, which was duly reported in the *New York Times*, that asbestos was a carcinogen and that his department estimated that between four million and eleven million workers had been exposed to it.[40]

One of the reports prepared for the industry turned out to be an embarrassment to a number of the expert witnesses the companies had hired to show how ignorant they were. This was the Hemeon Report, prepared for the Asbestos Textile Institute in 1947, and it indicated that the standards being cited for safe exposure to asbestos dust in the late seventies had been shown, three decades earlier, to be dangerous to workers. The industry had done such a good job of hiding this information that the expert witnesses didn't know about it, and they were destroyed in cross-examination.[41]

More information came rolling out when Johns–Manville sued its insurance companies in 1980, claiming that it was owed indemnification that the companies had refused to pay. There was an interesting, and expensive, legal point involved, which had to do with the "occurrence" of the injury. Suppose an insurance company carried a policy for a company from 1970 to 1975, and then refused to renew. Suppose a worker sued the company in 1976, citing injury which he claimed had occurred over the past decade, but which was not manifest until 1976. Was the insurance company liable or not? Was coverage triggered during the time of a claimant's exposure to asbestos – the "exposure theory" – or not until the time asbestosis was discovered – the "manifestation theory?" Which was the "occurrence" that made the insurance company fork over?

In this instance, the exposure theory eventually won out in court,[42] but in the meantime, the cases were creating a public fuss which did not do the companies any good. Home Insurance, one of Johns–Manville's insurers, contended that the company had fraudulently concealed the asbestos hazard from Home's underwriters, who would not have issued the coverage if they had known what they now knew Johns–Manville had known all along.[43] This was the company's own creative-ignorance argument; they should have sued for breach of copyright.

Throughout all the personal-injury cases, Johns–Manville fought a rearguard action by, among other things, claiming that two witnesses the plaintiff lawyers wanted to interview were dead – they were duly produced in court – denying the existence of documents subsequently discovered, ignoring orders of the courts to produce evidence, and refusing to admit the authenticity of documents.[44] Thousands of other documents referred to in company minutes, including the results of studies at Saranac Lake, had mysteriously disappeared.

But, by this time, enough of the early material had come to light to convince juries that the company was not merely careless, but malicious, and, in 1981 and the first part of 1982, punitive damages of more than $6 million were racked up against Johns–Manville in ten cases, an average of $616,000 per case.[45] Under the insurance the company carried, punitive damages were not covered, and claims were being filed at the rate of five hundred a month. The company was not likely to win many of these; one appeal court had already cited Johns–Manville's "wanton disregard" for the users of its products and its "reckless disregard for human life."[46] Kind of hard to ignore in future trials. Johns–Manville was going to be nailed, hard, and the regrettable thing was that juries were becoming a mite peeved with the way the firm made every plaintiff go through years of agony and expense, fighting every step of the way.[47]

Johns–Manville was now a major international corporation, manufacturing a wide variety of building materials; asbestos products were only one of its lines. So, the company reinvented itself in 1981, about the time the first punitive-damage case was won against it, hiving off all the asbestos into a single division, called Johns–Manville, and renaming itself the Manville Corporation.[48] Johns–Manville Company Ltd. ceased to exist. It couldn't even do this without lying about the reasons. In a press release, the reason given for the change was to produce a "coordinated policy for the successful continuation of the asbestos business." But what McKinney told the board of directors who approved the move was the exact opposite – the reason was "to remove from Johns–Manville Corporation the non-asbestos-related assets and the people associated with those assets and thereby insulate them from the negative impact of asbestos litigation."[49] If a lawsuit succeeded against the former Johns–Manville Company Ltd., the plaintiffs could only collect from whatever assets remained in the asbestos division and not from the parent company.

Then the company commissioned a report by Epidemiology Resources Inc. of Boston which estimated that 48,000 new lawsuits would be filed between 1980 and 2009 and that the company's future liability for these would come to $1.9 billion, give or take a few million.[50]

You would think the time had come to throw in the towel, but not Manville, where the watchword is "stand fast." The corporation brought forward a strategy it had been working on in the background for some time and turned its lobbyists loose to sell it. This was an argument that, since the boys up top hadn't known about the dangers of asbestos until 1964, QED, and since it took a long time for the disease to manifest itself, the federal taxpayer should pay the freight. Asbestosis was a "social problem," not a problem with manufacturers; the profits belonged to them, but not that other nonsense.

Two bills were deposited in Congress, based on this theory. One came from Representative Millicent Fenwick, a Republican from New Jersey, whose district included the town of Manville, the manufacturing centre of the conglomerate. It was called the Asbestos Health Hazards Compensation Act and sought to bar victims from bringing product-liability or other common-law tort actions against the asbestos industry, the tobacco industry, or the federal government. Victims would, instead, be compensated from a centrally-administered fund, topped up by the taxpayer.[51] The maximum benefit to be paid to a completely disabled worker with a spouse and two children under this act would have been about one thousand dollars a month.

George Miller, a Democrat from California, described this bill as "a clear message to every industry in this nation which produces hazard-ous or toxic substances" that "the federal government is willing to pay for your recklessness."[52] Ironically, it was the inclusion of the tobacco companies in the pool that doomed this one; it alienated powerful congressional members from tobacco states.[53]

Then there was the Asbestos Hazards Compensation Act, intro-duced into the Senate in 1980 by Senator Gary Hart, after Johns–Manville moved its world headquarters from New York to Denver, in his backyard. Hart's bill, drawn up after consultation with Manville, not only proposed to block victims from filing suits, but left the level of compensation, and the administration of claims, in the hands of the states, where uneven, and often monstrously unfair, doctrines were applied.

Both of these bills died without coming to a vote, and it was their non-passage that allowed McKinney, in his guise as chief executive officer of Manville Corporation, to blame Congress for his company's plunge towards bankruptcy. You have to admit the logic of his claim. If your company has been killing and maiming hundreds of thousands of people for a few decades, and you haven't known about it or at least haven't admitted it in court until absolutely compelled to do so; and if juries are beginning to get a trifle irritated with your lies and evasions and wanton disregard for life; and if the lawyer for one of the plaintiffs against you calls you, in open court, "the greatest corporate mass mur-derer in history," which attorney Ronald Motley had done,[54] and which you will have to admit doesn't do much for the old public image; and then the government refuses to pay off the claims that are forming around your corporate head like, say, a cloud of asbestos dust, you are going to have money problems. What could be clearer than that?

It was on the basis of this history that the Manville Corporation, *pauvre petit*, ducked behind the comforting skirts of Bankruptcy Court Judge Burton R. Lifland. All of the cases against it were instantly transferred from federal and state courts, where there is a right to trial by jury and punitive damages, to bankruptcy court, where there is not.

Moreover, these claims would rank behind those of any secured creditors. Finally, no new claims could be filed against the company after it had been in bankruptcy for six months. The validity of the claims of people who were suffering and dying was to be determined by a calendar. As one of the plaintiff lawyers, Edward R. Greer, put it, "Manville will escape the suits of tens of thousands of people who will be discovering their asbestos-related illnesses in the years to come."[55]

One of the committees of creditors in the bankruptcy was the Asbestos Health Claimants Committee, the group of lawyers with all the cases. They tried to get the bankruptcy set aside as fraudulent, but Judge Lifland mowed them down.

Manville's protection lasted for four and a half years, as Judge Lifland kept giving it extensions on the time in which it had to file a plan of reorganization. During this time, the company's retained earnings increased by $200 million; it was making a substantial profit out of bankruptcy.[56]

The corporation offered to pay set amounts for its creditors out of its "free cash flow," that is, future profits in excess of those needed to fund Manville's operations. This money would be split evenly between health claimants and other unsecured creditors; if accepted, this provision would have cleared the company entirely of any current costs, but it couldn't get past the various creditor committees.[57] However, filing the plan helped to drag out the process, during which time Manville was coining profits, the lawyers were earning fees, and the victims were sickening and dying. Plaintiff lawyers began to take videotapes of their clients giving testimony, because it had become clear that many of them would be dead before they could ever get to trial.[58]

Judge Lifland dismissed as in bad faith a series of countermotions to get the bankruptcy ended and accepted Manville's arguments almost entirely.

The most important argument against the defendant was raised by Robert Sweeny, representing over three hundred litigants from Ohio, who said, "I just don't think a company can walk into a bankruptcy court with more than $2 billion of assets and hundreds of millions of dollars worth of insurance coverage and say, 'Your Honor, please excuse me from these claims.' As a matter of equity, it just doesn't wash."[59] Equity, Judge Lifland quickly showed him, had nothing to do with it. He ruled that there was no need to be insolvent to get Chapter 11 protection,[60] following already established precedent. He also accepted Manville's argument that it would not be able to meet future claims, and left the management to get on with running the business, freed of the noisesome worry of all those lawsuits. He even issued an order to prevent the litigants "from proceeding directly against the Company's insurers in pending asbestos-health lawsuits."[61] The cloak of bankruptcy protection had now been dropped over the insurers, who were not bankrupt, broke, or likely to become either. Finally, Judge Lifland passed his magic wand over "present and former directors, officers and employees of the Company."[62] They, too, were immune from legal proceedings which might be brought by some of the dying who might have been presumptuous enough to think that the people who made the decisions should be required somewhere, somehow, sometime, to explain themselves.

It was only after three years of much legal, but no real, action that Judge Lifland finally became a trifle impatient with the slow pace of the reorganization. He set up a "legal representative," who would represent all future health claims, and who became, in effect, the most powerful creditors' committee of all.

This turned out to be a silver-haired, silver-tongued New York attorney, Leon S. Silverman, who ignored everybody else and set about reorganizing the company for purposes of making it into one that could raise cash on Wall Street. He started things off by saying that he did not speak for future claimants, never had, never would. Judge Lifland didn't seem to mind.[63] Later, in one of those humorous twists for which the legal system is known, a victim of asbestosis filed a suit for damages, and his claim was rejected on the grounds that Silverman was the sole representative of claimants. No others need apply.[64]

Silverman proposed a trust against which all health claims were to be filed and which would operate separately from Manville. The company would put in $200 million to start the trust, and then add $75 million annually, out of its profits, during the fourth to twenty-fifth years of the trust, to which the insurance companies would also contribute about $650 million. To make up any shortfall in funding, the trust would hold 50 per cent of Manville's stock, which it could sell to raise money. It would also hold preferred shares in the company, which could be converted to stock and sold, if necessary.[65]

This arrangement would provide money, over time, to claimants, but it would also disenfranchise the current shareholders, of whom there were thousands all over North America. They promptly filed a lawsuit, demanding a shareholders' meeting – since Judge Lifland would not permit one. Manville went to court to get an injunction on the grounds that the shareholders were using an illegal method to force themselves into the discussions from which they had been excluded for three years, and, of course, the injunction was granted.[66] This is a rather neat example of what the economic texts mean when they talk about "shareholder democracy." The pushy bums, trying to horn in on the action of the firm they owned. All this took until late in 1986, by which time McKinney had retired from the company.

In the end, two trusts were established, one to deal with property claims arising from the need to replace asbestos in buildings, and the other to meet the avalanche of personal-injury claims, which had eventually reached 130,000.[67] The first trust was established with $125 million from Manville, and that money was accepted by the property claimants against an estimated $80 billion in damages. The settlement was less than 0.1 per cent of the claims. The second trust was made up of $250 million from Manville and $650 million from the insurance companies. In return, Manville got $100 million in tax refunds and an estimated $750 million to $900 million in future tax benefits, because it would be able to carry forward paper losses against future profits.[68] The trusts, with insurance money and continuing payments, would contain more than $2 billion U.S., which sounded like a huge sum, but which meant that each of 130,000 plaintiffs – the final total – stood to collect an average of $15,384, minus legal fees, which would certainly eat up at least half. Not quite so huge.

Judge Lifland approved this arrangement, and so did the secured creditors, who were able to collect all that was owed to them by an increasingly profitable company. The health claimants also voted for the plan, reasoning that, after a five-year delay in which they had received nothing, this was the best they were likely to get. The shareholders opposed the plan, but it was crammed down on them anyway, by the judge. In effect, they lost 80 per cent of the value of their stock as new shares were created to put into the trust, and Manville emerged from bankruptcy protection on December 22, 1986, freed of all lawsuits arising from the use of asbestos. The new corporation was established as a world leader in forest products, paper, cartons, plywood, fibreglass, home insulation, and lighting fixtures.

In 1986, the newly furbished company had sales of $1.9 billion and profits of $91 million,[69] 51 per cent higher than back in 1981, when the process began.

The health-claimants trust began operations in 1988, mailed its first cheques late that year – that is, after the victims had been waiting a minimum of six years – and reported in 1989 that it was running out of money. In 1990, Manville announced that it would put another $520 million into the fund, over a period of seven years.[70] We'll see what happens if it goes broke again.

None of the health claimants can collect punitive damages against the company, nor, indeed, anything more than token payments from the fast-eroding trust funds. The average claimant faces a wait of somewhere around twenty years to collect, with the very good possibility that, in most cases, he will be dead long since.[71] And, of course, no claims filed later than six months after the bankruptcy protection was extended will ever be accepted.

You will be happy to know, however, that some people collected immediately, and in full measure. Silverman, for one. He billed the bankrupt estate $2.3 million, and Judge Lifland thought he had done such a good job that he gave him another $2.3 million, as a bonus.[72] Then, there were the lawyers. Judge Lifland approved more than $100 million in legal fees, which were paid out at once. Lawyers acting for Manville Corporation got $45,308,234. No legal fee came in at less than $750,000.[73]

Manville had managed to shed all the health and property claims against it, shield company officers from any investigation, much less action, for their personal culpability for hundreds of thousands of injuries and deaths, and pick up hundreds of millions of dollars in tax benefits. Today, it is going along as well as, or better than, ever, although the same cannot be said for its victims. It no longer has any asbestos mines; the Jeffery Mine in Quebec, its largest, was sold to an investor group in Montreal in 1983, for $117 million.[74] It retains one Canadian manufacturing plant, at Innisfail, Alberta, owned by Manville Canada Ltd.

All in all, Manville Corporation's dash for shelter has to be accounted a success, from the company's point of view. Just the same, it was not a perfect Chapter 11 operation. The personal-injury trust holds theoretical control of the company, even if management continues to run it, and dividends are being paid into the trust. Some of the profits of this adventure in creative capitalism had been allowed to escape.

This regrettable result would be avoided in another, even more horrific case, that of the A. H. Robins Company and the Dalkon Shield.

CHAPTER NINE

The Shield of Bankruptcy

"Companies that had injured so many people, making adequate compensation difficult, could turn to bankruptcy to settle the gross liability, set it aside and, if possible, sell the company at a handsome profit."
– Laurence H. Kallen, 1993[1]

$

Karen Hicks of Richmond, Virginia, who did not want to get pregnant until later in her new marriage, went to her doctor for the insertion of an intrauterine device – an IUD – in 1971. Her doctor recommended a Dalkon Shield, which he described as the "Cadillac of contraception." For the next seven years, she was in constant pain, and a series of doctors told her she was neurotic, unstable, unbalanced. Finally, in 1978, a new gynaecologist removed the device, but she continued to be ill, she had no energy, her marriage broke up.

In 1984, she married again, and, this time, she and her new husband hoped to have a child quickly; she was thirty-five and he was forty. It was not to be; within three days of the marriage, she was back in hospital with an acute case of pelvic inflammatory disease (PID). She had a complete hysterectomy, and then, and only then, did a doctor suggest to her that the trouble might have been caused by the Dalkon Shield, all along. By this time, the Shield was the subject of a great many lawsuits, so Hicks joined the queue. But the joke was on her; before her case could come to court, the A. H. Robins Company, manufacturers of the Shield, had ducked behind a protective judge, filing a Chapter 11 bankruptcy petition, and her suit, like every other – there were more than fourteen hundred of them – was frozen.[2]

In 1974, a woman whom we will call Joan Smith, after long and searching conversations with her husband, a law officer in a Midwestern U.S. city, decided that, although as practising Catholics they were opposed to contraception, they could not afford to add any more to the five children they already had. The solution they came up with was for Joan, like Karen Hicks, to be fitted with a Dalkon Shield. She had read about it in a woman's magazine, and it sounded wonderful; it was said to have an incredibly high success rate against pregnancy and was advertised to be safe ("Anatomically engineered for maximum comfort and contraceptive effectiveness"[3]). That was the one for her.

Several months later, there were two unexpected developments; the first was that she became pregnant, the second that she was suffering constant pain, a "terrible burning in my gut."[4] Her doctor told her the Shield was causing a pelvic infection and would have to be removed; he suggested an abortion. However, having once become pregnant, she resolved to save the child if she could; she was opposed to abortion. "It's always a baby. It just is always a human life," she said.

In February 1975, she was given a general anaesthetic and the Shield was removed, but it came out with placenta tissue clinging to it. The fetus had to be removed as well. For years afterwards, she had mental and marital problems and considered suicide. Then, following an episode on the television program "60 Minutes" called "The Dalkon Shield Disaster," she learned that she was not alone; she learned that the Shield was neither good at preventing pregnancies, nor safe, nor comfortable, and that thousands of other women like her had begun lawsuits against Robins. She got in just under the wire; her suit was settled along with 197 other cases, for a total of $38 million, an average of $191,919 each. [5]

Thousands of other women who went through similar agonies, whose legal cases seem just as strong as hers – like Karen Hicks – have never collected a dime. Others died, in horrible agony. Others lost the ability to have children forever. But, by the time these cases had been gathered together and hurled at the heads of the A. H. Robins executives, whose benign neglect or gross misconduct lay at the root of all these tragedies, the company had skipped away into bankruptcy protection. Their punishment was to make hundreds of millions of dollars out of the subsequent sale of their shares, while their victims went on suffering – go on suffering – to this day.

The Dalkon Shield was patented by a Baltimore firm, based on a new IUD formed of plastic roughly in the shape of a police officer's badge, and called a "Shield." It was invented by Hugh J. Davis, who worked for the Johns Hopkins University School of Medicine, where he taught, researched, and helped to run a public family-planning clinic. However, Davis, an unduly modest man, did not put his name on the patent, which was instead taken out in the name of a close friend and business partner, Irwin S. Lerner, who worked for a firm that sold hospital supplies.

Lerner had a company called Lerner Laboratories, and he suggested some modifications to Davis's invention, which appeared in the patented version. After acquiring the Shield, Lerner dissolved into a new company, jointly owned by Lerner, Davis, and their friend and attorney, Robert E. Cohn. This firm was called the Dalkon Corporation. Davis later denied that Dalkon was made up of the last names of the three partners, but he never did say where the name came from. Davis had one of those trick memories you hear about. When he testified that he had no financial stake in the Dalkon Shield, whose wondrous properties he promoted from every medical pulpit in the land, he plumb forgot that he had received somewhere over $700,000 U.S.

through the firm. The other advantage in not making too much of his connection with the Shield was that if he had invented it by himself, he would have had to share some of the money with his employer, Johns Hopkins. This way, he got to keep it all.

However, that was nothing to the advantage of being able to turn out articles in medical journals and women's magazines, and even an entire book, *Intrauterine Devices for Contraception,* singing the praises of IUDs in general and the Dalkon Shield in particular, without ever remembering to mention that every single one sold put money in his pocket.

Davis and his pals manufactured the first Shields through their own company, but then they took in a partner, Thad J. Earl, a general practitioner in Defiance, Ohio, who ran a family-planning clinic there and became an enthusiast for the device – to the extent that he bought into the Dalkon Corporation and then went out and sold the patent rights to the A. H. Robins Company.

Robins was a venerable pharmaceutical manufacturing firm, with roots reaching back to 1866 in Richmond, Virginia, and a number of product lines, including Robitussin, a cough medicine, and Chap Stick, a lip treatment, that were doing very well, indeed. The company had gone public in 1963, but control remained firmly in the hands of family members, who owned 40 per cent of the stock. E. Claiborne Robins, Sr., the chairman, a staunch Baptist, was a God-fearing and generous man, who had given $50 million, mostly in company stock, to the University of Richmond, his alma mater. In turn, the president of the university, E. Bruce Heilman, pronounced Robins to be of the Lord's "most essential instruments."[6] Heilman happened to be on the board of directors of Robins at the time he made this pronouncement, but he was no doubt sincere. As you know, or maybe you don't – there is a lot of ignorance about these days – you don't get to be an essential instrument without spreading around the money, and the A. H. Robins Company, while well endowed with the stuff in 1971, when the Dalkon Shield first got going, could always use some more.

The company had never sold an IUD, knew nothing about IUDs,

except that you could make them for very little – nine cents, in this case – and sell them for rather more – $4.35.[7] But IUDs had another advantage, in that those nosy parkers up at the Food and Drug Administration in Washington, who were always demanding that things be tested before they go on the market, had no jurisdiction over them. This was because IUDs were a "device," not a drug. According to law, the FDA could not interfere unless and until the things began to do real damage – until there was "sufficient cause" according to the wording.

The only testing that had been done on the Dalkon Shield was that an early version of the device had been used at the Johns Hopkins family-planning clinic in 1968-69. In all, 640 women had been fitted with this version and, in an article in the *American Journal of Obstetrics and Gynaecology* for February 1970, Hugh Davis, while shyly concealing his connection with the Shield, boldly staked out its success: "Pregnancy rate, 1.1 per cent."

If true, that was stunning, better than twice as good as the rival Lippes Loop, which had a failure rate of 2.7 per cent. Actually, it wasn't true, although that would not prevent the A. H. Robins Company from using the same figure for years. Davis wrote that his data was gathered from "3,549 woman-months of experience," which sounded impressive, but what it meant was that, spread over 640 women, the average length of use was 5.54 months, not nearly long enough to test the efficacy of the device. The real failure rates would turn out to be anywhere from 5 per cent to more than 10 per cent, but that would be the least of the problems.

The Dalkon Shield had a couple of other unique qualities. To hold the device in place, there were ten wicked little barbs, five on each side, to grip the lining of the uterus. On insertion, the Shield folded down, then, once implanted, expanded again, with the barbs clinging to the lining of the uterus to prevent accidental expulsion. This aspect caused another pharmaceutical company, Schmid Laboratories, which had been approached before the arrangement with Robins was struck, to reject the Shield because, "We thought of it as a grappling hook."[8]

The consequent pain caused quite a few women to faint during the insertion process, but this was not really a marketing problem. It was considered more a female-weakness problem. Robins would meet it by blaming hamfisted doctors for the suffering and repeating its nice line about the Shield being "anatomically engineered for comfort."

The other unique quality possessed by the Shield involved the string that was attached to the bottom of the device and led out of the uterus through the vagina. It was there so that the wearer could be sure the Shield was in place, and to aid in its removal. All IUDs have such a string, but, because of the Shield's wicked little wings, a single string would not suffice. It would break before the IUD could be pulled out of place. The solution was a multifilament tail, one with 450 little strings bound together within a nylon sheath. However, the trouble with this solution was that the air spaces between the filaments would allow bacteria to travel up the string through the cervical canal, in a process known as "wicking." The result was likely to be pelvic inflammatory infection (PID), which causes horrible pain, and, in those cases where the Shield didn't do its job and a pregnancy occurred, may cause spontaneous abortions, septic abortions, permanent sterility, and death. This would turn out to be more than a female-weakness problem, but it still wasn't a marketing problem, because very few people knew about it. The FDA, which would never have allowed such a device on the market, wouldn't know about the wicking until thirteen years later, and, except for the women who began to be first infected and then killed, neither did anybody else in the rude general public.

A. H. Robins paid the Dalkon Corporation $750,000 U.S. for patent rights to the Shield on June 12, 1970. The money was split among the four partners, according to their shares in the company; Davis got $242,812.50. He also got a consultant's fee of $20,000 per annum, and Dalkon got a royalty of 10 per cent of net sales in Canada and the United States, which Davis shared, as well. That 10 per cent came to $1,840,640 between June 1970 and March 1974. Davis got $382,527 of this, plus consulting fees and witness fees. This did not prevent him from swearing in court that he had "never received any royalty from the Dalkon corporation" and didn't know if he had ever owned stock in Dalkon.[9]

Two days before the deal was concluded, W. Roy Smith, the director of product planning for Robins, who had never heard of the device before Robins bought it, wrote a memo in which he raised an ethical question. The Shield that had been purchased contained copper sulphate mixed into the plastic, which was intended to enhance its effectiveness; the one Davis had tested at Johns Hopkins had not. Copper sulphate might leach into the body and have a "deleterious effect," Smith pointed out. He thought doctors ought to be told about the addition of copper sulphate.

Like every other caution, warning, and scream of rage that would be landed in front of the Robins executives over the years, this one was ignored, although it indicated, among other things, that the Shield that was being sold was not the same device for which the 1.1-per-cent pregnancy rate was being claimed. Never mind. Robins went ahead with plans to produce the Shield at its Chap Stick plant in Lynchburg, Virginia, where the wage rates were even lower than in Richmond and the profit to be made correspondingly higher.

Seventeen days after Robins bought the patent rights, R. W. Nickless, the product-management coordinator for the pharmaceutical division of Robins, wrote in a confidential internal "orientation report": "The string, or 'tail,' situation needs a careful review since the present 'tail' is reported (by Mr. Lerner) to have a 'wicking' tendency." That's as far as it went.

This memo was sent to thirty-nine Robins executives at the middle and high levels and brought no response whatsoever, except a later, collective amnesia, when no one could remember having seen the darn thing.

The Dalkon Shield was unleashed on January 1, 1971, and hyped to a fare-thee-well with ads in the medical journals, glossy brochures for doctors, and, everywhere, the studious features of Hugh Davis, a member of the Johns Hopkins medical faculty, writing, lecturing, and shilling, always with his own customary modesty about his share of the take. In a hearing into contraceptive devices before Congress, Davis built the market for IUDs by inciting fears about the birth-control pill, which he said could cause breast cancer. He was asked, during that hearing, whether there was any truth in a report that he had recently patented an IUD. He replied, "I hold no recent patent on any intra-uterine device." Of course he didn't; the patent was held by Dalkon. He just happened to own a chunk of Dalkon, but why bother busy congressmen with a detail like that?

He was asked, "Then you have no particular commercial interest in any of the intrauterine devices?"

"No," he replied.[10] This was a fib.

In pushing the Dalkon Shield by exaggerating its effectiveness, Davis also forgot to mention that the best results were obtained when a contraceptive foam was used with the device. In an article for *Good Housekeeping*, Davis claimed that the Shield would be "virtually 100 per cent effective in preventing pregnancies," again leaving out the contraceptive foam and the real pregnancy figures.[11]

Davis's book, *Intrauterine Devices for Contraception*, was published in September 1971, just in time to keep the kettle boiling. It was described by an official of Laboratoires Martnet, a firm retained by Robins in Europe, as an "excellent book of propaganda."[12]

Based on the extraordinary claim of a 1.1-per-cent pregnancy rate and the vigorous shilling – A. H. Robins produced five million pieces of literature for doctors – the Dalkon Shield took off, and, by the end of 1971, more than 800,000 women were wearing it. Complaints began almost at once – complaints of pregnancies, of difficulty inserting the Shield, of women passing out from the pain of insertion, of pelvic inflammation. Robins responded by citing poor insertion and removal techniques, oddly shaped uteruses, and unclean sex practices among the customers, but, right from the beginning, the company knew there was much more to it than that.

In March 1971, twelve weeks after sales began, a Robins salesperson wrote in to say that he had been told, "The inner core acts as a wick to induce [*sic*] infection into the uterus."[13] No response. In August, the

Robins representative in Tokyo raised the same concern and got the same result. A letter from London, England, was also brushed off. Apparently, Robins was not interested in finding out whether there was a wicking problem; when Robert W. Tankersley, Jr., the company's head of microbiology, proposed a simple test to find out if wicking was taking place, and asked for ninety dollars to fund it, he was turned down.

Just the same, the problem would not go away. E. Wayne Crowder, the quality-control supervisor at Chap Stick, wrote a memo in March 1971, in which he noted a number of safety concerns about the Shield, including the fact that the sheath surrounding the tail was very often broken in the process of tying it on. It was knotted, by hand, in two places: at the base of the Shield itself, and further down, in what was called a "locator knot," where the string entered the vagina. These ruptures would allow bacteria into the uterus. In one quality-control study, Crowder reported that 9.94 per cent of 64,000 Shields that had passed inspection had defects, more than half of which were "broken string sheaths."

Crowder was also concerned about the wicking problem. He conducted a crude experiment of his own, clipping off a piece of the string below the attachment knot on a Shield and letting it dangle down into a beaker of water. Several hours later, he removed and dried the submerged portion, and was able to squeeze a drop of water out of it; clearly, this water, since it could not have come through the nylon, had travelled up the inside of the sheath. He also established that water bypassed the locator knot; presumably, so would bacteria. He proposed sealing off both ends of the multifilament tail by applying heat, a process that would have cost five cents per Shield. Julian W. Ross, Chap Stick's research director, told him this wasn't his responsibility and to leave it alone. Persisting, Crowder raised the issue with Daniel French, the president of Chap Stick, pointing out the danger of infection. French, Crowder later testified, told him that the company already had "too much time and money invested in the present configuration."

On July 28, 1971, Crowder wrote another memo, reiterating his concerns about infection, and this drew a stiff rebuke from his boss, Julian Ross, who told him that "my conscience didn't pay my salary" and warned him that "if I value my job, I would do as I was told."

By this time, French, the Chap Stick president, had become concerned enough to communicate with his immediate supervisor in Robins, Oscar Klioze, who replied that Robins's research committee had concluded that "the Shield will continue to be manufactured according to present specifications until management directs otherwise."

This brought a reply from French that deserves a place in the Hall of Fame for corporate crawl-downs:

> As I indicated in our telephone conversation, it is not the intention of the Chap Stick Company to attempt any unauthorized improvements in the Dalkon Shield. My only interest in the Dalkon Shield is to produce it at the lowest possible price, and, therefore, increase Robins' gross profit level.[14]

No one would know for years that Robins was aware of the danger of the wicking process, although an extensive series of tests outside the company showed, time and again, that wicking was taking place. Crowder's constant complaints were dealt with, in the end, by firing him during a "departmental reorganization." He had been with the firm for fifteen years and was earning $13,500 annually at the time. He sued on the basis of an "improper retaliatory discharge," but waited too long to file his suit, and it was dismissed.

In the meantime, sales of the Shield, which had become the fastest-selling IUD on the market, were beginning to flag, as more and more reports came in of pregnancies and pelvic infections.

On June 23, 1972, Thad Earl, the part-owner of Dalkon and the Shield's biggest booster, wrote to Robins to say that six women in whom he had implanted the device had become pregnant, and that five of them had had spontaneous infected abortions. He urged Robins to investigate the problem and said that he was warning physicians to remove the Shield as soon as a patient was found to be pregnant, because of the danger. This information was contained in a letter in which he said that he had had remarkable results, otherwise, and claiming a pregnancy rate of 0.5 per cent. Earl's letter was widely circulated within Robins, and his claimed pregnancy rate was used in a the company's eight-page Shield advertisement, but the warning was ignored. Again, Earl's part-ownership of the company that was collecting royalties was omitted from the literature boasting of his remarkable results.

Reports of PID, pregnancy, and other problems continued to pour in. Lindsay R. Curtis, an obstetrician and gynaecologist from Ogden, Utah, came to the Robins offices, accompanied by a medical student, to report that he had seen three cases of severe PID in Shield wearers and had stopped recommending the device. He said that his own daughter, the wife of the medical student with him, had become pregnant, and severely infected, while wearing the Shield, and had nearly died. She gave birth to a premature, stillborn child. Curtis later received a letter from Ellen J. Preston, Robins's liaison with physicians, saying that she was "disappointed to hear that your experience has not been entirely favorable."[15]

On the marketing front, things were going well; in the doctors' offices, not quite so well. Six weeks after the sales campaign began, Robins received a letter from a doctor that read, in part, "I have just inserted my tenth Dalkon Shield and have found the procedure to be the most traumatic manipulation ever perpetrated upon womanhood."

Another doctor, a gynaecologist, said, "I have seen a number of women pass out from Dalkon Shield insertion. If that is designed for comfort, I would hate to see one that was not designed for comfort." A third, a female gynaecologist, Dorothy I. Lansing, wrote to the company's medical director to complain about "those vicious spikes" and to decry the Shield as "an instrument of torture."[16] There was not at that time, or ever, a gynaecologist on the Robins staff. A. H. Robins met these complaints by blaming the doctors; it was not until the Shield had been in use for two years that the company began to advise doctors to use a local anaesthetic when implanting or removing the device.

Very soon after the complaints about the pain associated with the Shield began, reports came in of startlingly higher rates of pregnancy than those claimed in the Robins ads. The company responded, once more, by blaming doctors for improper insertion and stepping up the glossy ads in medical journals. An eight-page "progress report" on the Shield purported to show, among other things, a pregnancy rate of 1.9 per cent and a rate of removals for medical reasons of 14.9 per cent. Actually, these figures were derived from the first nine months of an eighteen-month survey that showed a pregnancy rate of 5.1 per cent and the removal rate for pain and or bleeding at 26.4 per cent.[17]

The *British Medical Journal*, in July 1973, reported a pregnancy rate among Shield users of 4.7 per cent.

In October 1973, Allen J. Polon, the newly installed Shield project coordinator for Robins, wrote an internal memo repudiating the claims of 1.1 per cent and asking for the destruction of all pieces of literature because they contained "statements which are either incomplete or invalid." Robins kept mum about this to the medical profession and the FDA, and, a year later, ran a full-page ad in *The Australian & New Zealand Journal of Obstetrics & Gynaecology* repeating the 1.1-per-cent figure and claiming a removal rate of 6 per cent.[18] The company met the threats to its marketing strategy in the usual way, by mounting another vigorous advertising and PR campaign to plant articles in friendly magazines, newspapers, and television programs.

On May 30, 1973, in a hearing before the Intergovernmental Relations Subcommittee of Congress on the safety of medical devices, Dr. Russel J. Thomsen, a major in the Army Medical Corps, who had studied the Shield and its marketing, described the level of deception in its promotion as "amazing."[19] Robins sent a delegation up to Washington to reply, on June 13. They simply denied the charges of fraudulent advertising, without going into specifics, and that was that.

It was not until the Center for Disease Control in Atlanta reported on an extensive survey it had done in 1973 that the FDA began to contemplate action. That survey of 35,544 physicians nationwide showed that, where women became pregnant despite wearing an IUD, the ratio of complications was twice as high with the Shield as with "all other (including unknown) types of IUDs."[20]

The FDA held a series of meetings and asked Robins to supply information on the Shield's construction and physical characteristics, but not a word was mentioned, in Robins's reply, about the wicking problems that it had been concealing for four years. The company insisted that the Shield was perfectly safe. Nonetheless, the rising toll of septic abortions had become too great a hurdle to overcome, and Robins was asked to withdraw – but not recall – the device from the market "for a lack of demonstrated safety."[21] It would not have to bring in Shields which were already in place; it just couldn't sell any more.

In fact, lower-level bureaucrats in the FDA had wanted a recall program, but that was turned down at the executive level, and Robins was finally allowed to suspend sales voluntarily, on a temporary basis. The company considered this a major victory, because, if it had had to recall the Shields, it would have been admitting that it was at fault, and lawsuits were already beginning to pile up. Moreover, it would cost a lot of money; let women who wanted the thing taken out pay for the removal themselves.

During the temporary suspension, the FDA intended to look into the safety factor, to see why the Shield had such a horrible record, so it told the company to deliver its research on the subject. Thousands of documents were gathered in the Robins offices, not a scrap of which was ever seen by the FDA. Many cartons of this informational material were simply thrown out.

The FDA continued to be puzzled by the higher infection rates among Shield wearers, which it could observe, but not explain. Their records now showed two hundred septic abortions and eleven fatalities caused by the Shield, but they still had no idea that the multifilament tail was to blame.[22]

The attendant publicity caused a continuing fall in Shield sales, and the device was finally, gradually, removed from the market, though not recalled, between January and August 1975. Robins blamed "unfair" negative publicity. The removal ended the FDA's curiosity about the Shield, which was no longer its legal concern.

Then the lawsuits began to go sour.

Morton Mintz, whose cry of rage, *At Any Cost: Corporate Greed, Women and the Dalkon Shield*, has blazed a trail through the thickets of documentation surrounding the Dalkon Shield, has provided a blow-by-blow description of how the Robins company responded to the threat of lawsuits. It was the same hard-knuckle strategy Johns–Manville invoked. Women who sued were blocked by the company's refusal to produce documents, by its lies, by the porous memory of its officers, by concealment, evasion, and the destruction of evidence, and by the strategy of revictimizing the women who dared to sue. Their private lives were exhumed, examined, and condemned. If a woman had had an extramarital, or premarital, affair, that was hauled out, sniggered over, and made, somehow, to seem to be at the root of the problems she suffered through the Dalkon Shield. A woman in Iowa who was afflicted with PID and lost her ovaries and womb began a case against Robins, and then was confronted with questions about her sexual relations before her marriage, ten years before she was fitted with a Shield. Her lawyer advised her not to go ahead with the suit, and she didn't.

In another case, Brenda Strempke of Little Falls, Minnesota, brought an action for PID and impaired fertility, and she and her husband were put through an embarrassing ordeal about their sexual habits, although Robins never produced a shred of evidence to suggest that her problems had anything to do with her private life. This couple were willing to settle for $195,000; Robins offered them $15,000 and the promise of a long, hard, expensive trial. They persisted with the case, and a jury eventually ordered punitive damages of $1.5 million and compensatory damages of $250,000. The case cost the Strempkes more than $1 million to pursue.[23] There is no way of knowing how many injuries Robins was able to dispose of by frightening off potential litigants, but, as more information seeped out, the company knew it had to settle cases, because trying them was bringing out more and more of the hidden story.

Robins responded by making it a condition of the settlement of cases that the lawyers involved agree not to provide information to other litigants, or work for other clients against A. H. Robins. This practice happens to be against the lawyers' code of professional responsibility, but that did not prevent it from being followed.

The way Robins was able to use lawyers to shut the mouths of the experts does not accord with what we see on "Perry Mason". When, for example, a test of wicking done by Stanford University provided devastating testimony, which the company could never refute in court, Robins settled, with the stipulation that the results were to be destroyed and the scientists who had conducted them agreed never to testify in a Dalkon case.[24]

The collective memory lapses of senior Robins personnel also played an important part in the lawsuits. E. Claiborne Robins, Sr., the company chairman, swore that he was unable to recall ever having discussed the Shield with his son, E. Claiborne Robins, Jr., the chief executive officer and president of the company. He didn't even know that PID could take lives.

He was asked by one plaintiff's lawyer, "You certainly knew, when you started marketing this device, that pelvic inflammatory disease was a life-threatening disease, did you not?"

"I don't know that. I have never thought of it as life-threatening."

Asked if he knew PID could cause sterility, he replied, "Maybe I should, but I don't know that. I have heard that. I am not sure where."

In another case, he said he had no knowledge of the wicking problem, and then, when pressed, finally admitted that it "had been brought to my attention over the last thirteen years," but he "didn't know what it meant."

Ernest L. Bender, senior vice-president for corporate planning, was asked, "Did the thousands of lawsuits and claims make you wonder at all . . . whether there might be something wrong with the device?"

"No, it doesn't make me wonder. I have no reason to believe that there is anything wrong with the device."[25]

Other senior officers, who might otherwise have been held accountable for their failure to take action, were just as ignorant and just as incurious.

Carl D. Lunsford, the company's director of research and its highest-ranking executive with specific jurisdiction over the Shield's safety, could recall no "expressions of concern" by any company official about the dangers of pelvic infection, had not personally reviewed any studies of the Shield's safety or effectiveness in preventing pregnancy, and had no curiosity as to why the company was paying out millions of dollars in lawsuits. He had never asked subordinates how many women were injured by the device.[26] He didn't even know, he swore, that there were hundreds of filaments in the Shield's tail.

Ellen J. Preston, the company liaison with doctors, was asked, "You don't know to this day whether or not the Dalkon Shield tail string deteriorates *in situ* do you?"

"I think I have a pretty good idea that it does not."

What did she base this on?

"I think there are documents around, but I don't know where they are."[27]

When I say the company took no action as a result of the avalanche of complaints and lawsuits, I misspeak myself. In fact, they did take some action: to cover their collective behinds, passing a resolution, in 1984, to amend the corporate charter so that the company would pay the fines, penalties, attorneys' fees, and other costs of any officer or director who was held liable "for gross negligence or wilful misconduct in the performance of his duties."

"More bluntly," writes Morton Mintz, "the two Robinses – the 'control persons' who voted enough of the stock to accomplish whatever they wanted – and the other directors, most notably E. Bruce Heilman, arranged that the company, not the perpetrators, would pay for proven 'gross negligence and wilful misconduct.'"[28]

Even though Robins was winning about half the cases that survived the gauntlet of legal obstructions and got to court, once more, as with Manville, the sheer volume of the cases began to bear the company down, and each shred of information gained could be used to try to pry out more secrets.

One of the big breaks came in 1975, in a way worthy of a television drama, although the scene took place not in a courtroom but at the Robins headquarters, where attorneys were squabbling over the production of documents for an upcoming trial. The Robins strategy had been to claim that most documents requested were privileged, and therefore it didn't have to produce them. When that didn't work, the company either lied about the existence of the documents, or destroyed them, so it could say that no such document existed.

However, in this case, on behalf of a plaintiff named Connie Deemer, this strategy blew up when a Robins employee dumped a file on the table where the lawyers were sitting, and out slipped the memo, written before Robins had bought the Shield, which showed that the company knew that the claimed 1.1-per-cent pregnancy rate was invalid. Bradley Post, counsel for the plaintiff, saw it and demanded a copy. Roger Tuttle, one of the inhouse lawyers for Robins, later explained, "Before I could do anything about it, he had seen it."

That memo was produced at the trial and led a jury to bring back the first award for punitive damages against A. H. Robins, a meagre $75,000.[29]

But there were other fallouts from this incident. The first occurred when Tuttle, the Robins lawyer, was called in by William E. Forrest, vice-president and general counsel of the company, who told him, according to Tuttle, "That if I had done the kind of job that I was being paid for, the (paper) would never have been produced." His comments were to the effect that, "He didn't ever want that to happen again, and that the only way it wouldn't happen again would be if documents were no longer in existence. . . . And I said I couldn't be aware of that which had been withheld from me." Then, Tuttle swore, Forrest ordered him to arrange the destruction of hundreds of "troublesome" Shield documents.

By accident, a measure of justice had been allowed to creep into the case. For this, after a discussion between Forrest and Aetna Casualty and Surety, the company's insurers, Tuttle was fired. When he appealed the firing, he was reinstated, but taken off all Dalkon Shield cases, which were handed over to outside counsel.

Thoroughly alarmed, Tuttle raised the issue of criminal culpability with his superiors and was told "it was not for me to worry about it, it was for me to follow orders." Instead of resigning – "With a wife and two young children, I'll have to confess to you that I lacked the courage to do then what I know today was the right thing" – Tuttle saved some of the most important documents, including the Nickless memo, which raised the concern about the wicking properties of the Shield, and the Roy Smith memo, which cited his concern about copper sulphate. Tuttle then got a job – I like this part – as a teacher of legal ethics at Oral Roberts University. He later accepted a subpoena to appear in a Dalkon Shield case, bringing along his documents. Robins tried to have him disbarred entirely from the practice of law, but the attempt failed, and his appearance laid out the whole sorry story of Robins's document-destroying spree.

There is no way of knowing how much material disappeared. One lawyer threw out twenty cartons of documents, which a court order had ordered conserved, while "spring cleaning" his garage. He explained it as "just one of those things."[30]

But there was too much under wraps to stay there. Another break occurred when Dalkon and its insurers, Aetna Casualty and Surety, got into a battle about who would pay what. Aetna informed the company that it was dropping its insurance, because it had enough information to work it out that Robins was about to take a bath. As in the Manville litigation, there was the all-important question of when did the liability begin? Was it when the Shield was inserted, or only when the injury became manifest? If it was the former, Aetna was on the hook for every case; if the latter, it was freed of claims brought after the insurance was dropped. Robins sued Aetna in circuit court in Richmond, in a case that dragged on until the two sides made a deal which side-stepped the entire issue of timing. The insurer would pay compensatory damages in all the cases, but no punitive damages.

This deal became a matter of public record when it was registered in court and showed that both firms had known for years that the Shield was damaging its wearers. As Dale Larson, a plaintiff lawyer, put it in January 1984:

> The agreement dramatically reveals that Aetna has evidence that A. H. Robins was intentionally causing injury by its product and its conduct way back in the mid-1970s. As part of the agreement, Aetna gave up its right to deny coverage on these grounds – but in so doing Aetna acknowledges both its secret knowledge and evidence of that conduct.[31]

Robins's delays, dodges, destructions, and intransigence led judges in five states to complain about the company's tactics of frustrating, delaying, and denying justice, but getting anywhere in court was still uphill work. In case after case, women declined, after being interviewed by Robins's counsel, to go on with their complaints. Still, the cases kept rolling in, so the company also mounted a lobby campaign to have their problems lifted from their shoulders by act of Congress – again as in the Manville case. What Robins asked for was a law saying that, wherever a company was hit with punitive damages as a result of its actions, it would only have to pay the damages on the first case. In the Dalkon Shield disaster, this would have limited Robins's liability to $75,000, the award won by Connie Deemer. This proposal hung around for years, but was never enacted. In the meantime, the Dalkon Shield cases continued to crawl through the courts.

And then along came Miles W. Lord.

Lord was the chief judge of the District of Minnesota, an activist, a hellraiser, and the man to whom twenty-one Shield cases were assigned in Minneapolis on December 9, 1983. You will recall from the last chapter that he handled one of the crucial asbestos-injury cases.

Lord was a rare radical on the bench. "If you just don't read the law-books," he told a reporter from the *Los Angeles Times*, "you can get lots done."[32]

He was outraged by Robins's tactics, and ordered two special masters of law, Thomas Bartsh and Peter Thompson, to go to Richmond to expedite discovery in the lawsuits and dig out concealed documents. Robins responded by demanding that the court remove Lord from the case, so he stepped down, temporarily, until the appeals court could uphold his jurisdiction. In the meantime, he sent a magistrate, Patrick J. McNulty, to Richmond, to oversee the work of the special masters, and McNulty was soon reporting the presence of "an impenetrable wall" erected by the Robins company. "The documents in these files," McNulty wrote, "have not only escaped production during twelve years of litigation, but A. H. Robins has not to date even searched these files to ascertain what they contain."[33]

When the company was ordered not to destroy documents, it claimed it had been "insulted" by the order, which added a nice touch; it had already destroyed thousands of them. By the time the special masters had completed their work, several months later, the index to documents which the company claimed were either nonexistent or covered by privilege, and which the special masters decreed should be made available, came to 568 pages and included more than one hundred thousand documents. The masters also reported that they believed there was a case for criminal fraud against the company, although it was never pursued. They wrote that "Robins officials knew that the results of the studies were inaccurate and misleading," and that Hugh Davis "in our view is neither a credible witness nor a scientist,"[34] based on the hidden documents.

Now all the material showing that Robins had known about the dangers from the beginning, had misrepresented the effectiveness of the Shield, had privately commissioned, and then concealed, university studies that conclusively proved the wicking effect of the multifilament string – all these and more were coming onto the public record.

Robins moved to settle fourteen of the cases before Judge Lord, agreed to a package settlement of the seven other cases that were in front of him, and was proposing to settle another three hundred cases in various courts.

Before he would sign off on one package of seven cases, however, Lord ordered three top Robins executives – E. Claiborne Robins, Jr., president, Carl Lunsford, senior vice-president for research and development, and William Forrest, general counsel – to appear in court in Minneapolis on February 29, 1984, and he laid before them a statement that he wanted them to read. When they had read it, he began to ask them questions about, among other things, the company's practice of inquiring into the private lives of women who brought suit against them. The three men stood mute, refusing to answer, and Robins counsel Charles Socha objected to the proceeding.

Lord then read his statement aloud. It was a brutal reprimand, with thunderbolts in every paragraph, which said, in part:

> It is not enough to say, "I did not know," "It was not me," "Look elsewhere." Time and again, each of you has used this argument in refusing to acknowledge your responsibility and in pretending to the world that the chief officers and the directors of your gigantic multinational corporation have no responsibility for the company's acts and omissions. . . .
>
> Gentlemen, the results of these activities and attitudes on your part have been catastrophic. Today as you sit attempting once more to extricate yourselves from the legal consequences of your acts, none of you has faced up to the fact that more than nine thousand women have made claims that they gave up part of their womanhood so that your company might prosper. It is alleged that others gave their lives so you might so prosper. And there stand behind them legions more who have been injured but who have not sought relief in the courts of this land.
>
> I dread to think what would have been the consequences if

your victims had been men rather than women, women who seem through some strange quirk of our society's mores to be expected to suffer pain, shame, and humiliation.

If one poor young man were, by some act of his – without authority or consent – to inflict such damage upon one woman, he would be jailed for a good portion of the rest of his life. And yet your company, without warning to women, invaded their bodies by the millions and caused them injuries by the thousands. And when the time came for these women to make their claims against your company, you attacked their characters. You inquired into their sexual practices and into the identity of their sex partners. You exposed these women – and ruined families and reputations and careers – in order to intimidate those who would raise their voices against you. You introduced issues that had no relationship whatever to the fact that you planted in the bodies of these women instruments of death, of mutilation, of disease. . . .

Your last financial report boasts of new records for sales and earnings, with a profit of more than $58 million in 1983. And all the while, insofar as this court is able to determine, you three men and your company still engage in the selfsame course of wrongdoing in which you originally commenced. Until such time as your company indicates that it is willing to cease and desist this deception and seek out and redress victims, your remonstrances to Congress and to the courts of this country are indeed hollow and cynical. The company has not suffered, nor have you men personally. You are collectively enriched by millions of dollars each year. . . .

Under your direction, your company has in fact continued to allow women, tens of thousands of them, to wear this device – a deadly depth charge in their wombs, ready to explode at any time. We simply do not know how many women are still wearing these devices because your company is not willing to find out. The only conceivable reasons that you have not recalled this product are that it would hurt your balance sheet and alert women who have already been harmed that you may be liable for their injuries.

Mr. Robins, Mr. Forrest, Dr. Lunsford: I see little in the history of this case that would deter others from partaking of like acts. The policy of delay and obfuscation practised by your lawyers in courts throughout this country has made it possible for you and your insurance company, Aetna Casualty and Surety Company, to delay the payment of these claims for such a long period that the interest you earn in the interim covers the costs of these cases. You, in essence, pay nothing out of your pocket to settle these cases. What other corporate officials could possibly learn a lesson from this? The only lesson could be that it pays to delay compensating victims and to intimidate, harass, and shame the injured parties. . . .

Another of your callous legal tactics is to force women of little means to withstand the onslaught of your well-financed, nation-wide team of attorneys, and to default if they cannot keep pace. You target your worst tactics for the meek and the poor.

If this were a case in equity, I would order that your company make an effort to locate each and every woman who still wears this device and recall your product. But this court does not have the power to do so. I must therefore resort to moral persuasion and a personal appeal to each of you. Mr. Robins, Mr. Forrest, and Dr. Lunsford: You are the people with the power to recall. You are the corporate conscience.

Please, in the name of humanity, lift your eyes above the bottom line. . . .

Please, gentlemen, give consideration to tracing down the victims and sparing them the agony that will surely be theirs.[35]

While he read the statement, several victims in the court wept. Indeed, it was a statement no one could listen to unmoved, and the

Robins executives were moved. They were moved to have Judge Lord charged under the Judicial Conduct and Disability Act, a 1980 law passed to provide recourse against judges who have problems such as alcoholism, drug addiction, and senility, or who engage in conduct "prejudicial to the effective and expeditious administration of the business of the courts."

On October 29, 1984, eight months after Lord's pleas to the senior executives, Robins announced a program to remove the Shield. Four days later, the appeal court ordered Lord's reprimand expunged from the record, denouncing it as a "governmental attack" on the three executives, "on their good name, reputation, honour and community standing." The appeal judges did not explain how a judge's statement became a governmental attack. They found no fault with the company and removed the offending "So Ordered" from the settlement, though the settlement itself stood.

A panel of judges heard the judicial complaint case against Lord, but dropped it after the appeal court ruling, on the grounds that the matter was now closed. It cost Lord more than $70,000 in legal fees to defend this action. Robins's costs, of course, were paid out of the company coffers.

But it was too late. Lord's statement was in newspapers and magazines – *Harper's* ran it in full in June 1984 – the damning documents concealed for so many years were in the hands of plaintiff lawyers, and Robins's intransigence, and refusal to recall the Shield, simply caused juries to bring in more and larger claims against the company. Things went from bad to worse when, in January 1985, the Eleventh Circuit Court of Appeals found that Dr. Louis Keith, one of the doctors Robins liked to trot out at its trials to say that everything was fine with the Shield, had given "false testimony," with the "complicity of counsel"[36] in his description of favourable tests on the device.

Not long after, a Wichita jury awarded a woman $7.5 million in punitive damages, and a Wichita judge ruled that a *prima facie* case had been established "for the purpose of the crime of fraud" against Robins.[37]

The company had to create a reserve fund of $615 million to pay future Shield claims, and, for the first time in its history, it was losing money. There was the minor compensation that, while the reserve would be paid out over many years, it could be claimed against income at once, which meant that American taxpayers would pick up $126 million on Robins's behalf.

Still, A. H. Robins had been stripped of its defences, humiliated, and threatened with destruction. Before the Shield was finally pulled from the market, 4.5 million of them had been distributed in eighty countries. There were tens of thousands of reported PID infections, and, in the United States alone, at least 110,000, or 5 per cent, of the wearers had become pregnant; 66,000 of these had miscarried, most by spontaneous abortion, others by septic spontaneous abortion, and there were fifteen deaths attributed to the Shield, along with hundreds of premature stillbirths, and grave congenital defects, including blindness, cerebral palsy, and mental retardation.[38]

It was all going to be very embarrassing when this parade came through the courts. By June 30, 1985, there had been 14,330 suits filed, and Aetna had paid out $378.3 million plus $107.3 million in legal expenses. By Robins's own calculations, its IUD had damaged 87,000 people worldwide by this time.[39]

On August 21, the company asked Judge Robert R. Merhige, Jr., of Richmond to extend Chapter 11 protection because of "the continuing burden of litigation," and he was happy to comply. Judge Merhige, it turned out, was a neighbour of E. Clairborne Robins, Jr. He denied that Robins was a friend, but described him as "a fine man." He immediately granted an order freezing all legal action against Robins, so that it could reorganize under the sheltering embrace of Chapter 11.

Even before a creditors' committee could meet, Judge Merhige issued a series of orders establishing April 30, 1986, as the last date on which any health claimant could file a claim against the estate – although it sometimes took many years for the symptoms to become diagnosed – ordering all injury lawsuits transferred to him and enjoining the entire world from suing Robins, Aetna, or their directors or officers in any court in the land.

The stay increased profits for Robins, because they no longer had to make interest payments, and the executives rewarded themselves with bonuses that came to $1.7 million. The only way for an injured party to collect, now that the courts had been cut off, was to file a claim in the bankruptcy court, but the filing process was incredibly complicated, five thousand claims were disqualified because they weren't correctly done, and nobody knows how many legitimate claims were not made at all.

A claimants' committee was set up, with thirty-eight members, most of them lawyers for the people suing Robins, but it was dismissed by the judge, for squabbling, and he put in its place a "blue ribbon" panel of five, with no plaintiff attorneys on it. [40] The men and women who had picked up expertise over the years of battling Robins were replaced with academics and bureaucrats, who were quieter.

Then S. David Schiller got into the act. He was a lawyer for Internal Revenue, which had a claim for $61 million, and he said that Robins was cheating the general creditors and the court, by paying out $6 million to pre-bankruptcy creditors, including the bonuses to the Robins bosses. He declared that "a raid on the estate's assets by corporate insiders cannot be tolerated." He asked the judge to replace Robins management with a trustee, because of "fraudulent conduct, dishonest dealings, incompetence and gross mismanagement." [41]

Judge Merhige found the company in contempt, but refused to replace the senior officers by a trustee, and there was no finding against any of the officers. "Now is not the time to impose sanctions," he said. He didn't say when, if ever, such a time would come. There were also more goodies for the company, including a ruling, in the late summer of 1986, that Robins could ask a sampling of claimants about their sexual practices. The nightmare Judge Lord thought he had banished was to return. Judge Merhige also ruled that any claimant who got sick after the filing for bankruptcy would be treated as if she had been afflicted before that time; the effect would be to sharply limit their claims through the company's plan of reorganization, because they would become part of the pre-bankruptcy gaggle of creditors. Then, he threatened to impose sanctions on lawyers who had brought a motion to challenge the makeup of the blue-ribbon claimants' committee and forced them to drop a class-action suit against Aetna, Robins's insurer. [42]

Robins's profits for 1986 came to $81 million, and, by the end of the year, cash reserves were up to $193 million. In the meantime, none of the claimants was receiving a dime.

It remained only to steer the firm through a plan of reorganization, shed of its debts. This turned out to be a long and complex process, in part because the company's owners kept trying to carve themselves a better deal. In July 1987, the Robins family signed a letter of intent to sell to the Rorer Group, a conglomerate that made, among other things, Maalox and Ascriptin. Rorer proposed to give Robins shareholders stock in their own company worth $735 million, to pay off commercial and trade creditors, and to set up a trust fund of $1.65 billion to pay off the Dalkon Shield claimants. This money would be raised by selling junk bonds, which would be paid off out of future profits. [43] It was a good deal, from the company's point of view, but the Robinses apparently felt they could do better; after all, A.H. Robins, shed of its lawsuits, was a valuable property.

Theoretically any suitor could have grabbed off the company, but Judge Merhige provided an answer to that, too. He protected Robins with an "exclusive period," during which no plans of reorganization would be accepted except the company's, and no other firm could try a takeover. The exclusive period lasted until the end of the bankruptcy. This meant that A. H. Robins could continue to seek higher offers, while safe from the danger that an outsider might step in and scoop the loot.

But finally, in late 1987, even Judge Merhige got fed up with the company's tactics and fined E. Claiborne Robins, Jr., $10,000 for his failure to act to collect back the improper bonus payments the company had made earlier.

There was a court hearing to decide how much money would be required to meet all the claims, which now numbered three hundred thousand. Estimates ranged from $698 million – by the Robins company itself – to $7.1 billion – by the Dalkon Shield Claimants Committee. Judge Merhige struck his own figure: $2.47 billion. This was the amount of money that would have to be placed in trust to pay off all the injured women and to earn Robins a discharge from bankruptcy.

The corporation that came up with the right offer to buy the company turned out to be American Home Products, a multinational conglomerate that produces, among other things, Jiffy Popcorn and Chef Boyardee. American Home offered to give Robins shareholders $29 in AHP shares for every share in Robins. The Robins shares had been trading at $8 when it plunged into bankruptcy protection.[44]

Two trusts were created, one to deal with the women victims who wanted to collect from Robins, another to provide for claims against doctors and hospitals. The first would be funded by $75 million from Aetna, $5 million from the Robins family, and $2.255 billion from the two companies, American Home Products and A.H. Robins. This would be raised by selling bonds. Aetna was also to put up an insurance policy, worth $250 million, which would be used when the fund ran out. The second trust would also contain a Robins contribution of $5 million, along with another $45 million from the company, and another insurance policy, this one worth $100 million, from Aetna.

In return for their $10 million, the Robins family would get $280 million for their shares. The sale price of the entire company was $700 million.

This arrangement had to be approved by a vote of the creditors, and in this respect, the Dalkon Shield claimants were in the same position as a trucking company owed for deliveries, or a supplier for goods. The claimants' committee sent out a notice urging acceptance, and the victims voted for the deal. On July 26, 1988, a month short of three years after the filing for bankruptcy, the plan was approved. The judge threw out any claims for punitive damage against the company and extended the injunction barring suits to cover Aetna and members of the Robins family, a highly unusual protection.[45]

If I were still capable of surprise, I would register surprise that no Robins executive has ever been charged with any of the actions the company took over the years, and, to this day, none has ever said he was sorry, or admitted that the Dalkon Shield was defective.

Claimants were persuaded to settle cheaply by rumours that the fund would soon run out, and by the fact that their only recourse, now, was to sue the trusts, and be back to where they had started, years earlier, and still without a dime in recompense. More than seventy thousand of the claimants accepted $725, on the average, from the trust, but nobody got any money until 1990, five years after the bankruptcy, nineteen years after the suffering began.[46] It is still trickling out of trust headquarters in Richmond, Virginia.

Moreover, as in the Manville case, the companies creating a trust to pay for massive injuries can deduct everything set aside as a business expense in the year the trust is funded, rather than waiting until it is actually paid out. Bankruptcy lawyer and author Laurence Kallen calls this "the taxpayers' unwitting contribution to the welfare of mass toxic tortfeasors."[47]

The Shield was sold in Canada for eleven years, and Canadian victims were in the same position as those in the United States or elsewhere, except that many of them were unaware that there was some meagre compensation awaiting them, in time, if they could get through the complex process set up by the bankruptcy. They were required to file for compensation by April 3, 1986, and on that date, NDP MP Neil Young asked the then health minister, Jake Epp, if the government would consider compensating women who had missed the deadline. Epp replied, bluntly, "Since 1981, the Health Protection Branch of my Department has advised users of the Dalkon Shield to stop its use . . . I can give no commitment on compensation."[48]

The Nation magazine (February 13, 1989) called the bankruptcy reorganization "HOW TO REWARD THE CRIMINALS," but of course, these were not criminals, they were just a bunch of guys trying to make the most of the American way.

The shareholders of Robins did much better than those of the Manville Corporation; instead of losing most of their stock into the trust fund, it was bought from them at a handsome profit. Bankruptcy had become a bonanza.

I have dealt with the Robins case in such detail because it represents the most outrageous example I know of in which bankrupts blossomed while their victims suffered, and I think Canadians ought to know about it. (Despite Morton Mintz's book, we don't.) It is one of dozens of cases where we are blindsided by American law. Furthermore, it represents what I fear could be our future. This case probably could not be duplicated in this country, yet, because our bankruptcy law is not yet quite as bizarre as Chapter 11, and we do not have a separate bankruptcy court, which could offer the shelter provided for the A. H. Robins company. I like to think that, in Canada, had Robins been a Canadian firm, another court would have stepped in, at some point. But maybe I'm kidding myself.

One thing is clear, and that is that we are moving in the same direction as the Americans. When I interviewed lawyers for this book, they constantly referred to "the Bankruptcy Court" or "the Bankruptcy Bench." Then, when I would say that we don't have such a thing, they would reply, "Yes, yes, but you know what I mean." Indeed I do; the specialists on the commercial list of our provincial courts are turning themselves into a bankruptcy court, and making law, in exactly the same way that our other judges are aping American precedent and making law in other fields. The law they are making follows American law, and even cites American law, as we will see in Chapter Twelve.

We haven't had an A. H. Robins case yet, but it looms just over the horizon.

CHAPTER TEN

First Move to Florida, Then *Go Broke*

"Bankruptcy is essentially the way you divide up the pie, when there isn't enough pie to go around." – Gordon Marantz, lawyer, 1993 [1]

$

I have dealt at length with business bankruptcies, both because they have a far greater impact on the economy generally than personal bellyflops, and because it is in this area that the most dramatic and dangerous changes have taken place. Still, personal bankruptcies outnumber those in the commercial field, even if the amounts involved are much smaller, and no account of bankruptcy can ignore them. We now know that the evolution of our law has turned the old standards on their head; the time has come to consider whether a parallel change has taken place in those failures that involve not some giant conglomerate but the store on the corner, your plumber, perhaps you yourself. This chapter will therefore step aside from the corporate world to note how, in a much less damaging way, personal bankruptcy is following the same evolution as the corporate kind, before we move on to consider a subject where there is no law, good or bad, that means anything – global bankruptcy.

Consider the case of a Toronto couple we'll call Tim and Mona, in their mid-forties, married for two decades, but with no children. He worked as the manager of a clothing store in a mall, she as a real-estate salesperson. In 1986, they decided, in accord with the current wisdom, that their best long-term chance to make money, real money, was not to work for other people, but for themselves. They would start with one clothing store of their own and gradually expand to a chain. Everybody has to have clothing, right? How could they lose? They decided to set themselves up – also current wisdom – with borrowed money, and they went to the bank – one of the ones that carries those ads about helping out the little guy – for the money. They needed, they figured, about $300,000 for the store lease, renovations, stock, and an advertising blitz to get them going. They knew they wouldn't take in much during the first few months, so they budgeted for salaries, too, so that they could collect a weekly stipend out of the company. They would start with only themselves in the store and hire staff as needed when the, ho, ho, expansion got under way.

The bank manager was not the ceaselessly smiling gent you see on TV. He was polite, but sceptical, and tough. Well, so he should be. That was fair enough. However, he wanted them to put themselves rather further out on a limb than they intended to go. Their idea was that they would form a limited company, put about $50,000, which they had saved up over the twenty years of their marriage, into the company, and let it handle the risk. If the whole venture went bust, they would be out $50,000, but that's all. The bank financing would be secured by the $50,000 and by the assets in the company – the stock, the receivables, even the shelving.

The bank manager didn't see it that way. He wanted them to put their house into the pot. They owned a house in North Toronto that they had bought a decade earlier for $128,000 and which was now worth, on a robust market, about $300,000. The bank manager said they could increase the mortgage, which they had whittled down to

$41,000, and use that money, or simply pledge the house as collateral for their loans, which would consist of a lump sum of $95,000 and a line of credit.

They said nuts; this way, they could lose everything, the hard-earned product of years of saving. So, they went to another bank, and another, and another, and they all said more or less the same thing: put the house in the pot. They went back to the numbers they had been agonizing over for months and worked them all over again. They calculated, conservatively, how much they could expect to take in over the first two years, how much the lease would cost, the cost of stocking the store, interest on the bank loans, everything they could think of. And then they rolled the dice. To accumulate, you have to speculate, they told themselves. Mona had read a story in one of the business magazines about a couple just like themselves who had started from less than they had and were now millionaires. Sounded good to them; the magazine article contained a photo of the woman standing beside a brand-new BMW. That's the stuff.

The final deal they made with the bank turned out to be quite complicated, but, in essence, they were borrowing about $140,000 at 12-per-cent interest (the renovations cost more than budgeted) and had a line of credit for another, similar, amount at whatever the rate happened to be when they had to draw it down. The loans were demand notes; the bank could call them at any time, which is the usual practice in Canada, but they were well covered, they calculated, by the $50,000 in savings they started with, plus, of course, the money that would come in as they went along. They used the house as collateral for the loans.

You know the rest. The economy went into a tailspin – although interest rates stayed high longer than anything else – and, within a few months, they were in trouble. Within a year, they were in deep trouble, and, within two years, the bank had yanked its loan and was demanding its money, plus owed interest. Failing which, it would exercise its agreement, sell the house, and pay off the notes. The bank manager, whose last smile they had seen the day they signed the papers, asked if they had any other assets, and Tim mentioned a cottage they owned in Muskoka, north of Toronto, which they had inherited from Mona's parents. The bank suggested they sell it, or mortgage it, and Tim promised to think about it, but he knew Mona would never agree; he didn't even bother to mention the suggestion to her.

Tim and Mona went to a lawyer, who sent them to an accountant specializing in insolvency, and he advised them to go bankrupt; not just the company, because that wouldn't do any good with the house pledged as collateral. He advised that they go personally bankrupt and save what they could from the wreckage. They refused. Bankruptcy sounded so drastic, so humiliating. There would be one of those ads in the newspaper, and all their friends would nudge each other and say, Too bad, with inner enjoyment. Tim had made rather a thing of being his own boss, president of his own company, when he left his former job; he was going to get the needle.

They managed to stave off the bank by signing another piece of paper that pledged their personal assets to back another infusion of cash. The bank took their word for what they owned – the car, the T V set, furniture, Mona's fur coat – and that turned out to be a good thing.

They hung on for several more months, cashed in their R R S P s, tried to borrow from friends, grew frantic, and got nowhere. Every now and then, they would have a good week at the store and think that, thank God, they were turning the corner at last. But they weren't, and one of their creditors, a clothing supplier, finally served them with the deadly papers. They were being petitioned into bankruptcy for the usual reason: they could not meet their financial obligations generally as they came due.

It was at this point that Tim and Mona got mad. And sneaky. They were going to lose the house, their furniture, their car, everything. The Ontario Exceptions Act, like most such provincial legislation, sets out the amounts a bankrupt can shield from his creditors, and it isn't a whole lot (we will look at the list later), but it wouldn't help them much, anyway. They had secured their last loan extension against personal assets, and that took them outside the protection of the Exceptions Act.

So Tim and Mona emptied the house of everything but the bare essentials before the inevitable bankruptcy sale. They hired a truck and, late at night, loaded it up and took the stuff up to their cottage; the big colour TV (they left behind the fourteen-inch model from the den), the best couch, the good dining-room set (they replaced it with the worn old stuff from the cottage), a collection of Inuit carvings Tim had collected in the sixties, when he did a lot of travelling in the north, and several valuable prints they had bought when they were first married. (They had moved this stuff up into the attic when the bank's assessors were going through the place before the sale. Climbing up to collect it, Tim stepped off a rafter and put his foot through the ceiling in the master bedroom. They just shoved the plaster back in place and left it.)

The law frowns on this sort of thing, and they knew it, but they no longer cared. They saw themselves as victims, especially when the house and contents were sold out from under them at distress prices. These fetched about $180,000, which should have cleared their debt and left them with a few thousand dollars, but, what with the costs of bankruptcy, and the forced sale, and interest charges, and penalties for being late in their payments, they got nothing. The day before another couple, much younger, moved in, Tim and Mona took out every lightbulb in the house. Let the buggers stumble around in the dark. Mona, in a final gesture of defiance, even took the toilet paper out of the two bathrooms. Then they slammed the door and drove off to rented digs in North York. They not only lost Mona's fur coat, they lost their car, a nearly new Ford LTD, which they replaced with an ancient, secondhand Chevvie. (They missed a trick there; some bankrupts surrender their car to the trustee and then buy it back, at a very good price, from their own estate.)

They received their discharge from bankruptcy about a year later. Tim found a job as a security guard, and Mona went to work as a clerk in a small art shop. They are struggling back now; Tim has an offer to manage another store, and Mona is selling real estate on the side – she held onto her licence – but they are starting all over again, and they are both bitter. Mona's normal route to work would have her driving past their old house, but she goes out of her way to avoid it.

Personal bankruptcy is quite another matter from the corporate kind; it is so, well, *personal.* For some people, it's not so bad, but that's because they don't have much and don't care much. We even have bankruptcy junkies, people who are constantly getting in over their heads, usually through credit cards, and go bankrupt five, six, even seven times over a period of years. They still get by. It is easy to check up on bankruptcies, now that they are on a government computer, but our credit-crazy age doesn't fuss its head with such things, and discharged bankrupts can usually get new credit, anyway – although they may pay higher rates than normal. Credit-granting agencies are always warning us to pay up or "you will ruin your credit rating," but I once got into a huge war with American Express, who yanked this particular chain in vain to try to get me to pay them money I didn't owe them. In the middle of our exchange of lawyer's letters, I received one of those chummy missives from the same folks, telling me that I was such a sound chap that I had been pre-approved for a Gold Card; all I had to do was fill out the form and bung it in. Allan A. Parker, whose excellent little handbook, *Credit, Debt and Bankruptcy*, leads the reader by the hand through the entire process, writes, "Debtors are often given unrealistic warnings about never getting credit again if they go bankrupt."[2] Oh my, yes.

Just the same, for the average Canadian, it is traumatic, draining, humiliating. Corporations may sail through the process, whistling a happy tune, and emerge out the other side more profitable than they were before, but ordinary people, with ordinary feelings, have to regard personal bankruptcy as a measure of failure. In my opinion, this is as it should be; whatever else it is, bankruptcy is not a good-conduct medal, although it is, and is meant to be, a resolution, not a punishment. The purpose of the law is to allow the debtor to exchange most of his or her assets for having the debts wiped out.

If you have assets that are worth more than the debts, this is not the way to go. Tell your creditors frankly that you are in trouble and make arrangements to pay off the debts over time. You have more leeway than you think, because, if they turn you over to a collection agency, which is what they are always threatening to do, they are going to lose at least 30 per cent of the money collected to the agency; 30 per cent buys a measure of patience.

There are financial counselling agencies, and there are government advisory bodies in all the provinces, who will shower you with advice, but you may not find it a whole lot of use. Spend your money wisely, they will say; always save a little something; don't pay off one credit card with another; be forthright and honest with your creditors. All perfectly true, but no substitute for cold cash.

If a few minutes with a pencil and paper tell you that there is no realistic possibility of paying off your bills as they come due, then bankruptcy is the only way to get a fresh start. A typical case is that of a Toronto woman who lost her job with a banking firm and could only find work with a temporary-employment agency, at seven dollars an hour. Her debtload had been acquired at a much higher salary, and, even saving every dime she could, she could not keep up the interest payments, much less the principal. She went to a financial adviser, who told her to go bankrupt, and she did, but she still feels badly about it. She need not; it is precisely this kind of circumstance that the law is intended to cover.

Under the new Bankruptcy and Insolvency Act, the process is not very complicated and not very expensive. If you don't know a lawyer or accountant, you can find firms that specialize in this business in the yellow pages. You cannot run yourself through the system; you must, by law, go through a trustee in bankruptcy, who is an accountant licensed by the superintendent of bankruptcy, and through the official receiver for your area or province, who is there to make sure the law is followed, by you and by the trustee.

You can either go to the official receiver first (the telephone number is under "Bankruptcy and Insolvency" in the government, or blue, pages of the telephone book) or go to the trustee first (this is simpler; I called the government number and waited for seventeen minutes before hearing a human voice; three trustee offices answered before the third ring). Trustees are in the yellow pages, under "Bankruptcy – Trustees." The trustee will interview you, usually for no charge, and take the matter in hand, including contacting the official receiver's office, which will, in turn, appoint the trustee to look after your case. You may be advised that, in your circumstances, you should make a proposal, which is an offer to all your creditors, either to discharge the debts at so much on the dollar, or to extend the period in which they have to be repaid. You will be required to draw up a schedule of repayments, and keep to it. If you meet all the terms of the proposal, you will in due course be discharged; if not, you will be shoved the further step into the soup and put into liquidation.

Under the old act, proposals could not be made by individuals; there is some debate as to whether the change is an improvement. Some practitioners argue that it is, because it allows the debtor to straighten out his finances without having to go through liquidation; others contend that it makes for too many "soft settlements," in which the debtor is able to walk away with only a small payment of the amount owing, because the creditors don't want to be bothered waiting months to collect.

If you are going belly up voluntarily, you will make an assignment of your assets – "the estate" – to the trustee, who will sell them, gather together the money, and pay off the creditors in order of precedence, starting with secured creditors, of course, who get paid in full before anyone else collects. The essential document is a one-pager which you fill out, with the trustee's help, that sets down your financial position, the assets, the debts, and the monthly income and outgo, and which reveals, with cruel clarity, just how broke you are. That is the petition that sets the wheels in motion. You are, by and large, much better off to file a voluntary petition of this sort than to hang on too long and be petitioned into bankruptcy by one of your angry creditors, or have a secured creditor sell the collateral out from under you. Once you are officially within the process, and the assignment to the trustee has been made, you are protected against a lawsuit, by a creditor or enforcement of a judgment in a lawsuit that has already taken place.

One of the nice ironies of this business is that you need money to go bankrupt. The trustee does not work for free, and he gets paid first, before any unsecured creditor, which is only fair. He didn't go broke, or borrow the money, or even lend it. He may be able to collect from the estate itself, if there are any free assets, or one of the creditors may be willing to pay him in order to collect at least something from the remnants, but if you can see bankruptcy looming and can siphon off about a thousand dollars before the fatal day to put some money into the hands of the trustee, you will be well received, you should pardon the expression. The amounts the trustee can charge your estate are all set out in law, and you can ask for them to be "taxed," that is, explained in some detail before an official. In general, the costs are reasonable, and the tribe of accountants have a much better reputation than, say, lawyers.

The trustee is the trustee for the estate, and he acts on behalf of the creditors, as well as serving as an adviser to the debtor. It is the trustee who informs the creditors what is going on, including the fact that they must now deal with the trustee, not the bankrupt, to collect.

The trustee will submit a statement of affairs to the court, along with a recommendation as to how much the bankrupt should be allowed to keep out of the estate, to get by on. We will return to this subject; for now, it is enough to note that, in Canada, the allowance permitted the bankrupt depends on how much he had before going bust. What Gordon Marantz, the Toronto insolvency lawyer, refers to as "my rich bankrupts" are able to hold onto much more of their incomes than ordinary debtors.

The federal law does not say anything about what assets are exempt from inclusion in the estate; that is a matter for provincial legislation, and there is considerable variation from province to province. In

Ontario, the law exempts $2,000 worth of household furnishings, $1,000 worth of clothing, and $2,000 worth of "tools of trade," which may include a car or other vehicle if it is necessary for work. These figures have not been revised for years, and most bankruptcy trustees argue that they should be higher. Uwe Manski, for example, believes that $5,000 is a more reasonable figure for household furnishings.

Most of the provinces have exceptions at about the same level as Ontario, but in Alberta, things are much, much better for the debtor. The Alberta Exemptions Act holds back:

(a) the necessary and ordinary clothing of the execution debtor and his family;

(b) furniture and household appliances to the value of $4,000;

(c) cattle, sheep, pigs, domestic fowl, grain, flour, vegetables, meat, dairy or agricultural produce, whether or not prepared for use, or such of them as will be sufficient either themselves or when converted into cash to provide

  i. food and other necessaries of life required by the executive debtor and his family for the next twelve months. . . . [3]

It goes on. The debtor who happens to be in the farm game is well looked after; he keeps horses and farm machinery, a tractor, seed grain, and "the homestead," up to one quarter section (160 acres). Not the house, though, if it is worth more than $40,000. In that case, it will be sold, although the "execution debtor" – a rather grisly phrase – is still entitled to keep $40,000 from the sale. This applies whether he is a farmer or not. In addition, any bankrupt in Alberta gets to keep a car worth less than $8,000 or "one motor truck" (no value is stipulated, it could be anything); as well as "the books of a profession," tools of the trade, to the value of $7,500, and a mobile home, if he lives in it, and it is worth less than $20,000. [4] If it worth more than that, he gets the $20,000.

Clearly, Alberta is the place, within Canada, to go to go broke, especially for a farmer. Not only is the law itself friendly to the debtor, the courts are less cruel than elsewhere. For example, a piano fits within the term "household furnishings,"[5] and the courts have held that a debtor could pool together several land-holdings for protection, as long as they came within the 160 acres.[6] The same bankrupt, who had done exactly the same things, could hold onto assets worth well over $100,000 in Alberta, or about a tenth of that in Ontario. We call it equity.

However, the state laws south of the border are even more widely variable than our provincial statutes, and some of them are astounding. In Texas, for example, the bankrupt can shelter $60,000 worth of personal property and any house, of whatever value, along with 1 acre of land, within a city; the house and 200 acres are exempt, outside city limits.[7]

In Florida, laws passed during the last century allow outsiders to move in, buy up to 160 acres in real estate, plus whatever mansion there happens to be on the real estate, go bust, and shelter it all from the creditor. Thus, when Bowie Kuhn, the former baseball commissioner and New York attorney, found that his Manhattan law firm was headed for the ditch, he moved to Florida, bought a five-bedroom house at the Marsh Landing Country Club in Ponte Vedra Beach for $1 million, and settled down, secure in the knowledge that no one could seize it. In New York, he could have sheltered $10,000, no more, in the way of housing. One of his law partners, Harvey Myerson, bought a $1.75-million ocean-front home in Key West, leaving behind a $3.1-million claim against himself and Kuhn filed by Marine Midland Bank. The *New York Times* quoted Frank Maas, a Marine Midland lawyer, remarking sorrowfully that, "It has been my experience over the years that people from all sorts of places seem to move to Florida once they know they are in trouble with the law."[8]

But my favourite of the expatriates now benefiting from Florida law is Marvin Warner, once of Ohio, more recently a resident of the clink, who was sentenced in April 1991 to three and a half years for various violations in connection with the collapse of his savings and loan empire. The former U.S. ambassador to Switzerland has more than

$4 billion in claims against him, but his pesky little troubles did not prevent him buying a horse ranch worth several million dollars near Ocala, which is out of the reach of his creditors,[9] and awaits his return.

In addition to home shelter, bankrupts who file in Florida get an exemption for all of their wages, and any annuities, pension plans, life insurance, or profit-sharing plans, without limit. Their cars, boats, and jewellery, however, are up for grabs. In Delaware, by contrast, the exemptions come to $500.[10] Period.

Or, to put it briefly, Canadian law is variable and American law is screwy, and both leave local legislatures in charge of what is held back in the case of a personal bankruptcy. In both countries, the combination of bad economic times and easier laws has vastly increased the number of filings (see the tables in the Appendix).

Three major changes were made in the Canadian law in 1992 affecting consumer bankruptcies, which is the label that covers most personal bankruptcies. The first was the change already discussed, which allowed individuals as well as corporations to file proposals. The second greatly simplified the process of "summary administration" of small personal bankruptcies. This applies to estates where, in the opinion of the official receiver, by the time the secured assets have been paid out, there will be less than $500 left in the estate.[11] In this case, there is no longer a requirement for a meeting of creditors at all; if the creditors ask for one – they sometimes have some curiosity to know what became of their money – they are entitled to it, but if they don't ask, the law assumes that they accept the proposal made by the bankrupt, and, once the court okays it, the deed is done. In the ordinary case, under the new law, discharge from bankruptcy is virtually automatic after a year, if the insolvent person has stuck reasonably to the rules, and budget, approved by the court.

Finally, the law no longer requires the bankrupt, in a summary case, to take out a newspaper ad telling all his friends that he fell over the cliff; it suffices to stick a notice in the *Canada Gazette*, where official notice of bankruptcy must be recorded.[12] The trustee informs the creditors, by ordinary mail, and anyone else who wants to know can check in the computer. (In Toronto, anyone can walk in off the street to the bankruptcy office at 145 Queen Street West, stand in line – there is always a line – and punch a name into a computer. If the subject has filed for bankruptcy, the dates of filing and discharge will pop right up. If you want a printout, though, it costs $17.)

Under the new law, there is actually an advantage in *not* making a consumer proposal, which is the way an insolvent person can deal with his debts without going bankrupt. Uwe Manski finds this discouraging. "We're trying to encourage people to do the honourable thing and settle with their creditors, but if they do, the debts are usually discharged over a period of three years. If they hold out and go bankrupt, the debt is usually gone after nine months. There is really no reward for doing a consumer proposal. In fact, you pay a penalty."

Manski gives us one example of the way this works in practice. "Say you want to lease a car. If you have gone bankrupt and been discharged within a year, the lessor knows you are free and clear of debt. If you are working out a three-year proposal he knows, on the contrary, that you have a load of debt hanging over you."[13] It is easier for the person who goes bankrupt, after paying off a portion of his loans, to get credit than it is for the person who strives to pay off every dime.

Another bizarre aspect of the law is the way in which debtors are treated by the courts while in bankruptcy, a subject touched on briefly above. The law allows the debtor to receive, from the estate, an amount of money that will support "a reasonable standard of living" based on his station in life. This turns out to mean the station in life he has reached; the poor youth who has struggled into wealth by one means or another, even if the means are dubious in the extreme, is entitled to a higher standard of support than his neighbour, who never stole, and never got rich. The courts have interpreted this not just to mean that a busted banker needs more to live on than a ditchdigger, but that the insolvent is entitled to keep on pretty well, not as he began, but at the level he reached before he went belly up.

In one case, two dentists, husband and wife, who made a series of unwise investments and went into bankruptcy, were able to draw enough money to keep their son in an expensive private school; they were able to shelter more cash for school fees than many bankrupts would be allowed to draw *in toto*. It doesn't matter how the bankrupt got into trouble in the first place. Consider what happened in the case of Vernard "Len" Gaudet (pronounced, appropriately, "go-debt"), the leading light in a nasty little company called Osler Inc.

Osler Inc. was a Toronto brokerage house owned by Gaudet, Paul Cohen, and Tony Chesnutt, which collapsed in December 1987, with losses of $30 million. Gaudet is a balding, bespectacled, pugnacious gent, who was born on a farm in Prince Edward Island, dropped out of high school after Grade 10, and moved to Toronto, where he got a job with the brokerage firm, Burns Fry. A hustler who generated large commissions, he wound up as a bond trader at the century-old firm of Osler Inc. and gradually accumulated a controlling 41-per-cent share.

By late 1986, Gaudet, as Osler's chairman, had turned the company into one of the biggest dice-rollers on Bay Street. They did things up brown; when the receivers moved in they found, in the firm's opulent Toronto offices, a sixteen-place setting of fine English china, 150 items of crystal and glassware, expensive chandeliers, and receipts for an $18,000 Christmas party the boys threw themselves a week before the company collapsed. It featured a belly dancer, who was no doubt explaining the gyrations of the stock market to bemused executives.

Besides Lenny, the other major shareholders were Cohen, the president and chief operating officer, and Chesnutt, the executive vice-president. A subsequent hearing by three commissioners of the Ontario Securities Commission (OSC)[14] turned up some practices that might have won a respectful nod from some of the S&L operators south of the border, including the payment of large sums of money to Len Gaudet, which somehow wound up translated into assets owned by his wife, Noreen.

In a pattern that has now become familiar, Osler Inc. first got into difficulty soon after Gaudet got control in 1986, when it lost

$1.7 million worth of trading bonds.[15] To cover up these losses from auditors and regulators, the company created paper transactions designed to hide the fact that it was so broke that it was in violation of the capital requirements imposed by the Toronto Stock Exchange, its main regulator. And, along the way, the three principals scooped money out of the till for themselves.

In the OSC hearings, Robert Mitchell, a witness from the accounting firm of Ernst & Young, identified thirty-eight transactions involving the three men in April 1986 and March 1987 that had the effect of "diverting over $3.2 million from Osler to the benefit of the account holders."[16] He acknowledged that there may have been more diversions that he didn't find.

The 1991 investigation – four years after the collapse – found that Osler had used "an astonishing variety of schemes"[17] that enabled the company to stay in business by hiding the fact that it was insolvent, and ended with the company nearly ten times as badly off as when the process began.[18] Osler employees filed false reports, wrote fake letters about the firm's finances, kept fake internal books, created fake trading tickets showing nonexistent, profitable trades, kited cheques, and used clients' assets to secure loans. False journal entries were created to show deposits or transfers of funds into Osler's account with the Bank of Nova Scotia: "One such false entry, for instance, had the effect of routing to Mr. Gaudet the sum of $1 million."[19] What he did was startling in its simplicity; once the million had been wished into being, Gaudet took it out of the firm's cash flow as an "employee advance."

I always thought these schemes were complicated; not at Osler. For example, when the three principals, and Osler itself, lost money in trading, "Tickets showing a nonexistent but profitable trade or trades would be prepared retroactively for that account so that the loss would be off-set, or even more." In one of those slip-ups that can happen anywhere, Kevin Cooke, an Osler bond trader, "got the steps backwards so that he put a fictitious loss into his account instead of a fictitious profit," and the process had to be reversed.[20]

The OSC concluded that "while the actual dirty work was carried out by hired hands . . . it is beyond any doubt that the three principals knew exactly what was being done and were in complete charge of the various schemes being carried out on their behalf." [21]

The big loser in the collapse was the Canadian Co-operative Credit Society Ltd. (CCCS), the central bank for the Canadian cooperative movement. Through the CCCS money-market trader, Tom Bourne, the co-op wound up lending Osler $335 million, on the basis of security worth less than $300 million. This money kept Osler going, and the firm paid Bourne $121,250 on the way past. However, in late 1987, when the brokerage couldn't repay this loan, CCCS discovered, for the first time, that it had been plunged into a sea of debt, and blew the whistle. The co-op lost $35 million, but the National Contingency Fund of the Investment Dealers Association picked up $10 million of this. In all, Osler was $60 million short when it was pushed into receivership.

The OSC charged twenty-four Osler employees with various counts; seventeen of them reached settlements with the stock cops, and seven others were dealt with in the longest OSC hearing on record, which included forty-one days of testimony taken between February 15, 1990, and October 31, 1991. The three principals were banned from trading for life. As the court said:

> Faced with such overwhelming evidence of the dishonesty of the three principals of Osler, we have concluded that the public interest demands that none of them should ever again be allowed to participate in the capital markets of this country in any way. [22]

The other four were banned for periods of from one to twenty years. We are talking about bad people who did wicked things, and finally got caught. Now take a peek at what happened to the architect of all this, in bankruptcy.

When the balloon went up, the OSC put Len Gaudet and his wife, Noreen, into a "conservatory receivership." This was an extension of the Osler receivership; it was not bankruptcy, but it was next door.

Noreen had been an employee of Osler when they met, and she was included in the receivership, because, by the time her husband's company had gone into the garborator, she seemed to own most of the assets. These assets included a Toronto mansion, valued at $4.5 million, a Georgian Bay ski chalet, an art collection valued at $2.2 million, which was transferred from his ownership to hers shortly before the bankruptcy, a $700,000 condominium in Florida, where they kept an Aston Martin worth $140,000, and a lot of personal assets (among them, a wine cellar full of very ordinary wine from the Albany Club in Toronto). The court ordered Clarkson Gordon, the accounting firm that was handling the case, to pay the Oslers $5,000 a week as an allowance,[23] although that was later cut to a meagre $3,300, or $171,600 per annum. This was based on the fact that Gaudet's pre-crash income had topped $1 million, so it was a punishment, when you come to think of it, when he and Noreen had to scrape by on $171,600 and drink that Albany Club wine.

There was one very embarrassing moment on the lifestyle front. Gaudet had a Mercedes 560 on lease, and he had not been able to keep up the payments, so he was advised to leave the chariot in the garage, or it would be grabbed. However, one day, Noreen was going to meet a friend at Pearson airport, and she went in the Mercedes. She drove up to the arrivals area, jumped out, and went into the lounge. The repo lads, who had been following close behind, moved in and scooped the car, and when Noreen came back out with her friend, it was gone. The friend was the wife of Joe Ghiz, the former premier of Prince Edward Island, where the Gaudets started out.[24]

Noreen was released from receivership, but Gaudet was pushed the further step, into bankruptcy, on January 27, 1989. So, he climbed into a Mercedes – another Mercedes, which he owned – and drove downtown to apply for legal aid.[25] He needed it because, one of the lessons we have already learned is that, in every bankruptcy, the professional fees are staggering.

Jerry Levitan, Mrs. Gaudet's lawyer, put it rather neatly when he said, "The lawyer grabs as much as he can. That's how he gets paid. That's the system we have."[26]

The Gaudets' estate, for example, was relieved of $1.2 million in the first twelve months, by five accounting firms, eight law firms, and eighteen lawyers.[27] The charges included $165 for writing a letter, $55 for a memo, and $1,000 for an hour of telephone talk between two lawyers.[28]

By the time a deal had been approved by the court, the bill for fees had risen to $2 million,[29] Gaudet had lost his assets, and Noreen was left with about $1.2 million. They moved to Boca Raton, Florida, to the condo, where Len went back into business. In return, his business partners picked up many of his bills, including $3,500 for a skiing trip to Aspen, Colorado, a trip to the Turks and Caicos, and credit-card bills. Price Waterhouse, on behalf of the creditors, wanted the court to consider censuring Gaudet for failing to disclose the existence of a company called AG Family Trust, created in May 1988 – after the crash. This trust in turn owned Avalana Management Inc., which paid car-leasing bills of $2,045 a month for Len and signed a consulting deal with him for $40,000 – which he apparently never got.[30] The point Price Waterhouse wanted to make was that, the way it worked, about $74,000 was released to Gaudet to pay his creditors in the period while he was in receivership and before his bankruptcy, but part of this "did not find its way to them."[31] The complaint was duly noted.

Gaudet was discharged from bankruptcy on January 15, 1992. So far as the bankruptcy process was concerned, he got off lightly. It remained for the criminal courts to make life unhappy. In February, the three Osler principals, Gaudet, Chesnutt, and Paul Cohen, were charged with twenty-two counts of fraud, theft, and possession of stolen property. They were released on bail. The case has not yet gone to court, and I wouldn't hold my breath.

Kevin Cooke, the bond trader, was convicted on twenty-one counts of security violations in April 1992 and sentenced to sixteen months in jail,[32] but an appeal court in 1994 cut the convictions to thirteen and the sentence to six months.[33]

Equity, in these matters, is adjustable, but if you are going to go into personal bankruptcy, you would not be wise to count on an allowance in the $3,000 to $5,000 per week range, just because Gaudet got it.

Presuming you behave yourself in a more-or-less reasonable fashion while in bankruptcy, you can expect to be free and clear, as already indicated, within a year. (Gaudet's discharge took three years, but he was naughty.) The trustee prepares and files a report with the court and sets a discharge hearing date. The creditors are notified of this hearing, which is normally held before a registrar in bankruptcy. If no one demurs, the discharge goes through automatically. If any of them objects to the debtor being released – because not enough was done to pay down a loan, for example – the case goes before a judge. In many cases, a creditor or creditors will argue that the bankrupt is now doing well enough that he can make partial payment in the future. The judge might then give the bankrupt a "conditional discharge," under which he would be required to keep paying until, say, fifty cents of every dollar of debt had been repaid to every creditor. The discharge becomes absolute if the judge ignores the complaint or when the condition has been met. This is what happened in the case of Michael Chodos, mentioned in Chapter One. He was naughty, but he got a discharge, anyway, simply by signing a consent judgment to pay a fraction of the amount he owed.

Personal bankruptcy is treated differently in law because it is seen as a social as much as an economic problem. The aim of the process is to relieve the insolvent of a crushing debt, and that is a worthwhile aim. The question remains, though, whether, as in corporate bankruptcy, we may not have gone too far, and set up a system in which the advantages go to those who regard debt as a mere nuisance and bankruptcy as a means of ridding themselves of the nuisance.

CHAPTER ELEVEN

Going Broke Globally

"Global financial systems have been constructed without the global coordination and laws needed to keep them honest. The existing patchwork of financial regulations is decades behind the times – and the crooks." – James Ring Adams and Douglas Franz, 1992 [1]

$

In 1991, two of the largest bankruptcies in world history took place, and they are both very much with us today. In July 1991, the Bank of Credit and Commerce International (BCCI, also known as the Bank of Crooks and Criminals International) was seized by the financial authorities in eighteen nations in a well-coordinated swoop; in November, Robert Maxwell toppled off, or was pushed off, or jumped off, the deck of his luxury yacht, the *Lady Ghislaine*, into the Atlantic Ocean, near the Canary Islands, and carried Maxwell Communications Corporation into the briny deep with him. There are a number of parallels between the two cases. Each company was a huge international conglomerate built on a tower of debt; each had a series of layers of ownership and control; each was the creation of a singular mind;

each was run on principles not taught (I hope) at the Harvard Business School; each was looted into insolvency; and, most importantly for the purposes of this book, each represented the kind of bankruptcy nightmare that is going to become as much a part of the global economy as selling Pepsi-Cola in Moscow and Toyotas in Toledo.

Our economists are terrifically proud of the global economy, which allows companies to whisk billions around the world in a nanosecond, which allows textile workers in Quebec to compete with the labourers of Mexico and the automatons of Taiwan – while the profits float out, tax free, to the Isle of Man – which persuades the multinationals to plant their corporate feet under whichever sheltering palms suit them best, and which allows them to enjoy all the advantages of modern finance while avoiding many of its responsibilities.

The collapse of these two global firms presents a morality tale for our time; regrettably, the moral is that we have no method, and we are not close to having a method, either of controlling global corporations or of efficiently tidying up the messes they leave behind when they go belly up.

The BCCI was founded in 1972 by a Pakistani with a gentle smile named Agha Hasan Abedi. He was fifty years old at the time and had extensive banking experience; he was self-effacing, but brilliant, courageous, and genuinely moved by the plight of Third World nations starved for decent, affordable banking services. He was a Shiite Moslem, born in 1922 into a middle-class family in Lucknow, India, where his father worked as an estate manager for the Raja of Mahmoodabad.[2]

After graduating from Lucknow University, Abedi moved to Bombay and joined the Habib Bank, a new institution created by the Moslem Chamber of Commerce, which was itself the creation of Mohammed Ali Jinnah, head of the Moslem League, and a fierce advocate for a separate Moslem nation to be formed when India achieved independence. Because banking in British India, like almost everything else, was dominated by Hindus, the Moslems wanted their own bank to serve their own people, founded on their own principles. (One of these prohibited usury, which was interpreted as charging excessive interest.)

This was a time of great turbulence and opportunity. On August 15, 1947, Jinnah was one of the winners, when India was partitioned into two nations: India and Pakistan, with the two parts of Pakistan, East and West, designated as the homeland for the Moslems. During 1947, some twelve million refugees crossed the borders of India and Pakistan, seeking shelter with their own religions, and about two hundred thousand of these were slaughtered in communal fighting.[3] It was a rough time for the people, a better time for the banks. Habib Bank moved its headquarters from Bombay to Karachi, in West Pakistan (East Pakistan became Bangladesh in 1970, after a civil war) and grew to be the new republic's largest financial institution.

Abedi, by now a rising executive with the bank, knew he would never become its president, so he started his own financial house, United Bank Ltd., to compete with Habib and the government-run National Bank. United Bank was the first in Pakistan to computerize its records. Under Abedi's direction, it also opened scores of new branches in areas of rural Pakistan that had been ignored by the larger banks. United Bank did well, but it lacked the capital base for the kind of expansion Abedi had in mind, and, in 1966, he chartered an aircraft and flew off to the Middle East to round up funding from Saudi Arabia and other rich Moslem lands.

He struck, um, oil in Abu Dhabi, a tiny sheikdom on the Persian Gulf, and one of the seven petroleum-soaked mini-states that make up the United Arab Emirates. The ruler of Abu Dhabi, and president of the Emirates, was, and still is, Zaid ibn Sultan an-Nahayan, an illiterate, but shrewd, man, who had just seized power from his brother in a coup organized with the help of British agents. (The British didn't like the brother, who was not merely illiterate, but backward; he kept the national treasury under his bed, and $2 million worth of bank notes were nibbled into confetti by the palace rats;[4] we can't have that.) Zaid allowed Abedi to open a branch of United Bank in Abu Dhabi and later became the most important investor in the BCCI.

That bank was founded – according to James Ring Adams and Douglas Franz, authors of *A Full Service Bank*, one of the many books written about the débâcle – in part because Zulfikar Ali Bhutto, Pakistan's dictatorial president, decided in 1972 to nationalize all the banks and put all the bank presidents, including Abedi, under house arrest while he thought it over.[5] Abedi did some thinking of his own while confined to quarters and came up with the notion of a global bank, run by Pakistanis, which would serve the Third World and at the same time operate as a bridge to the First World, and which would fulfil the Moslem requirement for a business operated not merely to make a profit, but to address social concerns, as well. Abedi was going to build a planet-straddling bank that would have a heart, as well as vaults, of gold.

When he was sprung from house arrest and given his passport back – Bhutto had changed his mind about taking over all the financial institutions – he flew off to New York, where he persuaded the Bank of America, then the world's largest bank, to invest a cautious $2.5 million in the shares of a new venture he was founding, the BCCI. Chicken feed, for the Americans, but the kind of chicken feed that allowed the BCCI to put the Bank of America logo on its letterhead and present itself as the fulfilment of Abedi's dream. The Bank of America owned 24 per cent of the outstanding shares in return for its money, but the business was entirely run by Abedi and his friends. the BCCI did not have any stake in America, as yet, but America had a stake in the BCCI.

Although the bank would begin its operations in Abu Dhabi – the entrée to the oil lands, which was why the Bank of America invested – Abedi decided to incorporate it in Luxembourg, as BCCI Holdings, SA. The secrecy laws are strict in the duchy, while other regulations are evanescent, taxes are negligible, and there was no chance whatsoever that the bank would be nationalized or its president bunged into house arrest, again. Later, another corporate headquarters was established in Georgetown, Grand Cayman, and a third in Gibraltar, giving the shareholders three places to play where the constituted authorities are singularly incurious about what goes on in the vaults.

By the mid-seventies, the BCCI – financed by Arab money, started in Abu Dhabi, incorporated in three other nations, with a solid connection to the United States – was off and running. Pakistan was the second major centre of expansion, after Abu Dhabi, but soon the bank was popping up all over the Middle East, the Far East, then Africa, then Europe, and, before it was done, there were four hundred branches in seventy-three countries, all lending away like crazy. It became involved in a lot of noisesome, not to say crooked, operations, floated out loans based on not much more than a promise and a prayer, and indulged in some unusual giveaways to the customers – prostitutes in place of pop-up toasters, for example. This was not the usual course of banking, but we know enough now to know that the BCCI was not unique; having seen the S&Ls in action, we know that, except for their scale and international reach, the BCCI operatives were treading in well-worn footprints.

Abedi believed that the most important element in lending was trust and that mere collateral was pretty poor stuff. He ran seminars on mysticism for his employees, during which he got off lines like, "Western banks concentrate on the visible, whereas we stress the invisible."[6] Loan repayments, as it turned out, fell into the latter category. In the circumstances, it is not surprising that Abedi's managers tended to lend money to well-connected financial figures who told them that they had a wonderful little deal going here in real estate or oil shares, or possibly a cure for cancer, and how about it? Sounds a lot like Charles Keating, or, come to that, Donald Cormie.

A bank that is willing to shove the stuff over the counter with only a cursory glance at the collateral does not have any trouble finding customers, and the BCCI blossomed. Prakesh Desai, who was one of the forensic accountants flown from Toronto to Grand Cayman to try to clean up the mess, recalls that "some of the loan files had very little information in them, in some cases, not even the recipient's current address."[7] Not hard to rack up business that way.

Along with the line about the importance of the invisible, BCCI employees were given to understand that whatever the customer wanted, he should get. Thus, the Pakistan subsidiary organized hunts for the great houbara bird of Pakistan and delivered prostitutes from the red-light district of Lahore, along with the (minimal) paperwork, to borrowers at their hotels. Sign here please, hi, my name is Peaches.

There were also – and again, this is not unusual, although it is written about in most of the accounts as original sin – a number of occasions on which the various incarnations of the bank made generous donations where they would do the most good. There was, for example, a £3-million gift to a foundation favoured by Sunny Jim Callaghan, the former British prime minister, who became a paid consultant to the BCCI[8] and who said a lot of nice things about what had become the largest foreign-owned bank operating in the United Kingdom. U.S. President Jimmy Carter was introduced to Abedi by his own director of the Office of Management and Budget (OMB), Bert Lance, and, after his defeat in 1976, Carter received $500,000 to help establish his library and the Carter Center in Atlanta. Over the years, Carter's Global 2000, a project to bring health care to Third World countries, received between $6 million and $8 million from the BCCI and its affiliates.[9]

This kind of generosity engenders warm feelings in the hearts of the recipients, whether it is the BCCI giving money to Carter's undoubtedly worthy causes in stricken nations or the Royal Bank forking out for the Liberal and Progressive Conservative parties here in Canada. That is why the money is given. Ask Charles Keating, or anybody.

The favour-granting game certainly worked for the BCCI. The bank lined up a buyer to take the National Bank of Georgia off Bert Lance's hands, when he was forced to divest himself in order to take over the OMB job in the White House. During the process, he ran into a spot of legal bother and was represented by two of Washington's top lawyers, Clark Clifford and Robert Altman, who soon after became the most important American lawyers for Abedi and the BCCI. Clifford, a former defence secretary and a lobbyist so potent he was known in Washington as "Mr. Connections," was a useful chap to have on your side.

For a time, the BCCI could not own an American bank, because it was connected with the Bank of America, in California, and would have run up against interstate banking prohibitions, but the B. of A. had had an audited look at its partners' loan portfolio in 1977 and thereafter headed for the exit.[10] It sold its shares late that year, but did not feel called upon to tell anyone else, including the bank regulators, why it was bailing out. That would have depressed the price of the shares it was now trying to unload. You can go to the regulators and say, "Hey, these guys are a bunch of crooks!" or you can sell your shares at a good price. Not both.

However, even after the B. of A. departure, the BCCI could not get the one thing Abedi most wanted, control of an American bank, because the U.S. regulators were not satisfied with the information provided by the company and because, as the years rolled along, a rather noxious stink was beginning to emanate from the BCCI, due to various of its operations coming to light. For one thing, it had laundered quite a lot of drug money for various unsavoury characters, among them Manuel Noriega, the Panama dictator, well-known for his pockmarked face, previous chumminess with the Americans, and key role in the business that shoved cocaine up many American noses. Quite a number of banks have laundered drug money over the years, and some of them have known about it, and some of them have not. The sin of the BCCI was that it was caught knowing about it and had to plead guilty to charges in that connection.

The drug dealers brought cocaine into the United States, sold it, deposited the take in the BCCI accounts in low-denomination money orders and certificates of deposit, to make tracing more difficult, and then wired the cash offshore. The bank collected handling fees. In addition, satchels of cash were shipped to Saudi Arabia, turned into gold, and plugged back into the system to finance more goings-on. When the BCCI was caught by officers of the U.S. Customs, you might have thought that that would have blown the lid off the entire racket, but it did not. Customs referred its evidence of the drug rackets and their financing to the Justice Department, and the marvellous incuriosity that so often accompanies the misdeeds of the well-connected came into play; the BCCI was allowed to plead guilty to money-laundering charges and paid a $15-million fine. Among the many bits concealed from the public during this process was the fact that the BCCI owned First American and five other U.S. banks.[11] It now appears possible that the hush-hush treatment was applied because the U.S. government wanted the BCCI's cooperation in the prosecution of Noriega, whose nation the Americans had just invaded in order to arrest him on drug charges.

The BCCI also got into gun-running, financing the sale of arms into South America out of an office in Boca Raton, Florida, bankrolling the sale of helicopters to Guatemala, and putting up the cash for an abortive attempt to ship prohibited materials from the United States to Pakistan, to help with its nuclear-weapons program. The Pakistan-born Canadian, Arshad Pervez, who arranged this last deal, was arrested in Philadelphia before it could go through.[12]

The CIA, which actually used the BCCI to pay off its operatives, had submitted a report on the bank in 1986, pointing to money-laundering and other illegal activities,[13] and, while the details were hidden, there was, let us say, a general air of uneasiness about the BCCI among regulators even then. If the bank was going to own an American financial house, it would have to go about it in a snaky and indirect fashion. So the BCCI, using the Clark Clifford–Robert Altman connection first established in 1976, bought control of First American through sham nominees, and First American bought shares in a number of U.S. banks, including Bert Lance's old institution, the National Bank of Georgia. Abedi was exactly where he wanted to be, at the head of a global bank, with sixteen thousand employees, branches all over the world, and assets listed at more than $20 billion U.S. The money was poured in through the Middle East, the bank's main operation centre was in England, but its corporate headquarters were split between Luxembourg, Grand Cayman, and Gibraltar. No national regulator was willing, or able, to take responsibility for what it got up to.

But, alas, it was now going bust. The BCCI had always been run in an expansive way; the buildings were beautiful, and the stationery heavy, and the business luncheons plentiful, and it all costs money. There was also the fact that many of the large loans were going sour, some because the assets against which they were borrowed, such as real estate, had lost much of their value, and some because the loans were fraudulent from beginning to end, or, at the very least, somewhat porous. The Gokal shipping family of Pakistan owed the BCCI over $700 million in a series of transactions that slipped through the bank's offices in Grand Cayman and for which a subsequent audit could discover only $65 million in security.[14] The bank was kept afloat in the now-familiar way: new money is sucked in at high interest rates to cover the bills as they come due, piling up more debts, while the yokels were constantly assured that everything would work out in the end. In Canada, we call it the federal budget.

Abedi had a heart attack in 1988, and not a moment too soon; he was given a heart transplant at Cromwell Hospital in London in February 1988, and, while he recovered, he was removed from virtually all banking operations, which became even more frantic, and less profitable, with the absence of this key figure. Its problems were about to be visited on the regulators, like it or not.

In March 1990, Robin Leigh-Pemberton, governor of the Bank of England, was handed an audit report prepared by Price Waterhouse that showed that the BCCI was in such severe financial trouble all over the world, because of fraudulent and imprudent loans, that it would require $1.78 billion in new funding to stay afloat.[15] The American authorities demanded, and received, a copy of this audit and began digging into their old files on the BCCI.

Over in Abu Dhabi, Sheik Zaid was persuaded by Swaleh Naqvi, a longtime friend and associate of Abedi, who had taken over his role in the bank, to pump in another $600 million U.S. to prevent imminent collapse; later, he loaned another $400 million. Abu Dhabi now owned 77 per cent of the BCCI. Abedi resigned from the bank, as did Naqvi, his successor; a Pakistani named Zafar Iqbal, the BCCI manager for Abu Dhabi, took over and cooperated with the British and American investigators, who had now evinced some interest in what was going on. With Abedi out of the way, the bank's senior staff finally began to provide some of the hard information on soft loans that had been concealed for so long.

But the bank was kept going, and the extent of the damage was concealed, for fear of causing a run on deposits. Leigh-Pemberton would later justify this course of action in a quote that should be stitched in needlepoint on the pillow-sham of every institutional investor: "If we closed down a bank every time we had a fraud, we would have rather fewer banks than we have."[16]

Possibly this did not provide much comfort for anyone who bought BCCI shares between the time the Bank of England knew it was up to its hamhocks in disaster and the time of its demise. You will be glad to know the governor got his comeuppance; the severe criticism rained on the Bank of England for its sloth in connection with the BCCI was followed by a pay raise of 17 per cent for the governor in May 1991.[17]

Still, two new audits into the bank's operations were ordered; one by the BCCI itself, another by and for the Bank of England. These turned up enough evidence to spur criminal investigations in both Britain and the United States, showed that the bank was in debt to the tune of at least $5 billion U.S. – and perhaps two or three times that – proved beyond all doubt that the BCCI owned First American (this would come as a terrible shock to Robert Altman and Clark Clifford), and revealed that, while the bank's annual reports showed robust earnings until the late eighties, it had possibly never earned a profit in its entire history.[18]

On July 5, 1991, bank regulators in eighteen countries seized the assets of the BCCI in a coordinated shutdown, and bank branches were restricted in forty-four other lands. The accounts of 1.25 million depositors were frozen, businesses were paralysed all over the globe, ships were stranded in ports, factories shut their doors, and thousands and thousands of paycheques turned into useless little slips of dirty paper in the hands of people who had never had anything to do with the BCCI except to work for a company that kept its accounts there. In a score of cities, customers massed in front of the closed bank branches, demanding their money, in vain. Deposit insurance applied in only a handful of the nations where the BCCI operated, so most of its depositors were left to the mercy of bankruptcy proceedings; they will probably never collect a penny.

Canada was one of the nations that cooperated in the shutdown; the Office of the Superintendent of Financial Institutions took over the four BCCI branches here, and the depositors were paid off in full. It was about the only part of the mess that reflected any credit on us. The government had been receiving tips, some of them anonymously, from BCCI employees, and from the Canadian Bankers Association, warning that the bank was operating in a wicked way, since the early eighties.[19] The complaints were passed along to the then minister of finance, Donald Mazankowski, but nothing happened. It was all put down to sour grapes, one of the crops in plentiful supply in the financial community. However, after the cracks in the BCCI's structure began to appear abroad, and the Canadian subsidiary began to leak losses, it was put on a short leash, with a charter limited to three months of operation at a time. That was the situation when the Bank of England and the U.S. Federal Reserve System hauled out the handcuffs in mid-1991. It was then that our lads sprang to with a will and slammed the doors of the four Canadian branches.

Other countries were not so cooperative. In Pakistan, three branches were kept going by government order, and in Abu Dhabi, the collapse was not even reported, and accounts in foreign newspapers were cut out as they arrived, but, in fact, the BCCI was finished. No one would deal with a bank whose assets had been frozen, and there was nothing to do but call in the liquidators, under a score of different insolvency rules, to see what could be salvaged.

Teams of accountants were flown out to Grand Cayman, Luxembourg, and Gibraltar to take control of the headquarters' operations and attempt to gain control over the branches on behalf of the liquidators, so the assets could be pooled and divided with some semblance of order. It never happened.

One of those who went was Prakesh Desai. He was born in Zambia, educated in England, and then moved to Canada with Deloitte & Touche, the international accounting firm. Young, handsome, intelligent, and soft-spoken, Desai remembers the excitement of the call that sent him flying off to Grand Cayman. "We had not been married that long, and were expecting a baby, and I didn't want to be away, but my wife and I talked it over, and we thought it was too good an opportunity to miss. Besides, it was only to be for a month or so."[20] He raises an unbelieving hand, wags it, chuckles. He stayed eighteen months – his wife and child came to join him – and left when it became clear that, as he puts it, "The initial proposals pertaining to the dividend payout anticipated the process to continue for almost twenty-five years." Or, to put it another way, a quarter of a century. It will take even longer to clean up the BCCI mess than it took to create it.

Desai mentions one of the problems – ring-fencing.

"Where the bank had certain good assets in a particular country, that country's government would not allow the pooling of those assets with the assets of other countries. In some instances where the government was legally challenged by the liquidators, the government threatened to change its country's legislation to facilitate the ring-fencing of the good assets."

A number of African countries ring-fenced assets, and in other countries, the threat of similar action made the job of the liquidation well-nigh impossible. Desai says, "The situation in France was quite classic. The division of BCCI there was a branch, owned by the Grand Cayman office. The Grand Cayman liquidators took the position that the assets of the Paris branch, wherever they be, belonged to the Grand Cayman head office. But no cooperation was offered by the French liquidator. Any attempts by the Grand Cayman head office to secure assets noted on the Paris branch's books were blocked by the French liquidator.

"Ring-fencing, to some extent, was politically motivated. Individual governments did not wish to be blamed for the financial loss suffered by the depositors in their countries following the collapse of the bank."

In nations where there was no deposit insurance, the government was not going to win any Brownie points for handing over assets which would promptly be shipped away to pay off paper in some far-away land, while the locals got nothing. In Pakistan, the government invoked a section of the Companies Act to merge the BCCI with the Habib Bank, thus blocking any shift of assets out of the country. In India, where the collapse led to rioting in the streets, the government was able to exert its influence, so that, while BCCI assets were sold, they remained, as Desai puts it, "Closer to home than they would have been if they had simply been sold on the open market."

These complications came on top of all the other problems – trying to identify the assets, evaluate them, find out who owed what, based on what collateral, and realize on the assets, in the unlikely event that they could be found, identified, seized, and sold. Most of the money that was coming in went right out again, to pay for the process. Going broke is not always a profitable process, but looking after the bankrupt estate always is, and in the case of the BCCI, it was made more interesting by the fact that the accountants doing the job were paid at marvellously different rates. Prakesh Desai notes that, "If living costs in the various countries were to be disregarded, the variance in the partner charge-out rates was significant; in the U.K., it was about $500 to $600 an hour, here, about $300 on average; in Bombay, $20 an hour, and they are all doing exactly the same work."

When Desai came back to Canada in mid-1992, the BCCI was in chaos. It is still in chaos. When it went into limbo, the worldwide assets were at $1.4 billion U.S. (they had been listed at $23.4 billion not long before) and liabilities were more than $10 billion. This was a $9-billion embarrassment. If all the assets could be pooled – and, with ring-fencing, they could not be – the creditors would get about ten cents for every dollar owed.[21] This was not likely to be accepted anywhere, and so the teams of liquidators went to work to get the principal shareholders, in Abu Dhabi, to slide a few more doubloons into the till, in return for getting out of some of the claims that were likely to be launched against them by various creditors.

After months and months of labour, the deed was done, and in late 1992, a deal was approved by the majority shareholders in Abu Dhabi, and the liquidators in Luxembourg, Grand Cayman, and Gibraltar. Under this deal, Abu Dhabi would put in an additional $1.7 billion. This would be used to pay something towards the creditors, including depositors in forty of the countries involved.[22] They would get, after the sale of assets and the Abu Dhabi contribution, perhaps thirty cents on the dollar.

The way it worked out, the new money put in would mostly come back to Abu Dhabi, since Sheik Zaid, the chief shareholder, was owed more than that by the bank and would collect ahead of other creditors. For Sheik Zaid, it was not such a bad deal, since the creditors would write off $4.75 billion U.S. as part of the settlement. As owner of 77 per cent of the shares, Abu Dhabi owed 77 per cent of the debt; that came to $3.65 billion. By putting in $1.7 billion, it got rid of more than twice that much in liabilities, and would get most of it back. Not bad. There would be another $4.5 billion or so still hanging around out there in contested claims, untouched by this particular arrangement, but sufficient unto the day are the debts thereof.

However, the whole thing came apart when some of the shareholders, not surprisingly, kicked and got a Luxembourg judge to uphold an appeal from another court, which had looked upon the settlement, and found it good, and accepted it. When the appeal was granted, George Baden, a court-appointed liquidator, told the press that, the way things were going, creditors would not receive any payment "for at least ten years."[23]

With any luck, this one will drag on until well into the next century and will die out only when all the assets have been distributed to lawyers and accountants, and nothing whatsoever wasted on the creditors. In one of the sideshows, Robert Altman and Clark Clifford were charged with taking bribes in exchange for helping the BCCI hide its illegal ownership of American banks, but a New York judge threw out the charges. Altman went on trial for scheming to defraud regulators and preparing false documents to conceal the BCCI's role in the take-over of the First American Bank, but a jury acquitted him in August 1993. Clifford, who is in ill health, will probably never be put on trial.[24]

In another sideshow, in December 1991, the BCCI agreed to forfeit all its American assets (estimated at $550 million U.S.) and pay a fine of $10 million to New York state on charges of fraud, racketeering, and lar-ceny.[25] You will notice that the effect of the seizure and fine is precisely the same as ring-fencing; the American assets are scooped into the judi-cial till, locally, before they can be frittered away in some foreign land, paying off a creditor. Then a class-action suit was launched in Califor-nia, on behalf of 1.1 million Americans who had a total of $12 billion U.S. on deposit with the BCCI. The defendants include Price Waterhouse, one of the BCCI auditors, Clark Clifford, and the government of Abu Dhabi, and the statement of claim runs to 550 pages.[26] That one should ensure that any money shaken loose in the United States stays there for another decade or so, even if the plaintiffs lose.

The BCCI débâcle was just getting nicely unfolded when "Captain Bob" Maxwell became submerged in the waters of the Atlantic, and all hell broke loose ashore. The 310-pound media mogul was one of the most fascinating characters of our age, intelligent, alert, aggressive, impressive, and as twisted as a spiral staircase. Born in 1923 into a poor Jewish peasant family in the Carpathian Mountains of Czechoslovakia as Jan Ludwig Hoch, he created – as well as printed – headlines for much of his life, and, to make up for a deprived childhood, he gobbled down caviar by the bucket in his later life and used Turkish towels for toilet paper.[27] One of the lads.

After the Nazis marched into his native country, Hoch signed up in the Czech Legion, fled to England, and joined the Pioneer Corps of the British Army, where he became a translator. He had learned nine, or perhaps it was eleven, languages while growing up. One of the problems with Maxwell, to which his biographers all attest, is that he was such a liar that it became almost impossible to sort out the truth from the various tales he wove about himself. It is clear that he was a war hero – there is a picture, in Tom Bower's *Maxwell: The Outsider*, of him receiving the Military Cross from General Bernard Montgomery himself in 1945, for bravery under fire.[28] He fought the war under four names: his original one, "Leslie du Maurier," a name he chose from a brand of cigarettes, and which he used to disguise himself from the Germans; "Corporal Jones," a name he thought more suitable to a British soldier; and, finally, "Ian Robert Maxwell," a name bestowed upon him by his commanding officer, a Scot, so that he would fit in better in England, after the war.[29] The "Ian" was an echo of "Jan."

It was as Robert Maxwell that he met Elisabeth Meynard in Paris, during leave. She was working as an interpreter, and Maxwell very quickly told her two things: that he wanted to marry her and that he wanted to make his fortune in England. He did both.

War's end found Maxwell in Berlin, as a translator, censor, press officer, and all-around expediter for the British army. After demobilization, he remained as a control commission officer, with the titular rank of "Captain," which he kept all his life. He built up a series of contacts in publishing, while, on the side, running a profitable trading operation, and, when he moved to England in 1947, he set up a company called "European Periodicals, Publicity and Advertising Corporation," which proceeded to make him quite a lot of money.

As the money rolled in, he rolled it back out again, into various business ventures that became increasingly complicated, interwoven, leveraged, and dodgy. Maxwell obviously believed in Andrea del Sarto's dictum – according to Robert Browning – that "a man's reach should exceed his grasp"; he was never satisfied with what he had, and had to trade it in for something larger, and more expensive, bought with leveraged debt. His multiple ambitions – among other things, he wanted to be prime minister of Britain – kept him thrashing around in finance, forever in debt, forever hovering on the edge of disaster, and pulling himself back, like the hero of one of the old movie serials, just as the runaway train was about to pass over his increasingly rotund body, roped to the tracks.

He had a number of outstanding successes, such as the purchase and rescue of the British Printing Corporation, the takeover of the Mirror Group of Newspapers, and the capture of Macmillan Publishing, which owned, among other things, Berlitz International. But his business methods were not nice; he lied quite a lot, wiretapped his own executives, betrayed his business partners, and got himself into trouble with authorities on both sides of the Atlantic for some of his stock manipulations. After one investigation, he was declared to be "a man who is unfit to be the steward of a public company";[30] it would take another twenty years for this truth to be driven home.

In politics an avowed socialist, he ran for the Labour Party and then attacked it for interfering with free enterprise. He campaigned with a lavishness that overwhelmed his Tory opponents and considerably annoyed his Labour allies. He was defeated in his first run for parliament, in North Buckinghamshire, near Oxford, where he had a palatial home, then made it, was re-elected, and then defeated. He took credit for the elections and blamed his handlers for the defeats.

By the late eighties, he had set up an empire with so many layers, interstices, and hiding places that it is doubtful if anyone understood it in its entirety. Maxwell himself had a better grip on it than anyone else, but when you had said that, you had said it all. There were more than four hundred companies,[31] and some of them were private, and some were public, and he used them all as his personal piggy-bank. Maxwell Communications Corporation (MCC) was the major public holding company, and when it became mired in debt during a $3.5-billion U.S. buying spree in which he scooped up Macmillan and the Official Airline Guides, he began, quite illegally, churning Maxwell stocks. He had used his shares to support his loans, and when the share prices began to droop, his entire empire was threatened, so he began nudging up the price by buying his own company's stocks through nominees.

When that didn't work, and his creditors were clamouring for overdue payments, he began to loot the pension funds of the Mirror

Group and other companies, which he controlled, and managed to pledge the stock of Berlitz International to nine different parties at once.[32] Oh, yes, and with the debt-level rising around his knees, he went out and bought the *Daily News* of New York in 1991, for a good deal more than it was worth, on more borrowed money.[33] At the time of his death in 1991, the accounting firm of Coopers & Lybrand were scheduled to do an audit of the looted funds, a Swiss banking corporation was threatening to report him to the Serious Fraud Office in England (isn't that a lovely name? Funny Fraud, we don't bother about), because he hadn't delivered some stock which he had pledged to deliver, but which, it seems, he had already carelessly turned over to another lender, and, to top it all off, Goldman Sachs, the international financial conglomerate, had unloaded a large block of MCC stock on October 31. This would become public knowledge on November 5, a few hours after Maxwell's demise at the age of sixty-eight.

When he took his unscheduled dip in the Atlantic, it was all coming apart, and one theory at the time was that he had committed suicide to avoid having to face the music. Either that, or he was murdered, possibly by Arabs because he was a Mossad agent, or, if you won't believe that, how about the KGB? Or, perhaps, he just slipped and managed to pitch over the rail. However it came about – and the mystery has never been solved – he was dead, his family was plunged into (comparative) poverty, and thousands of pensioners were plunged into real poverty, to say nothing of other shareholders in his various ventures, and his other creditors. Maxwell was given a state funeral in Israel and some fairly sharp obituaries. The *Daily Mirror*, which he happened to own, thought he was a fine fellow, but the *Independent* called him "a liar, a cheat and a bully," while, to *The Times*, he was "an egoist and monstrously improbable socialist."[34] In a way, he was well out of it, because of the chaos he left behind.

To meet the interest on his bank loans, it turned out, he had siphoned £448 million from the various pension funds, and, when MCC had to seek bankruptcy protection soon after his death, payment on these funds was suspended, leaving thirty thousand employees and former employees uncovered.[35] The Mirror Group of Newspapers agreed to put up the money to keep its own pensioners going, but that accounts for only twelve thousand of those involved;[36] the other eighteen thousand saw their monthly cheques truncated instantly. Pensioners in the Headington Pension Plan, who had worked for one of Maxwell's main holding companies, were cut to 30 per cent of the money owing; in some other cases, pensioners will have to wait their turn under liquidation proceedings.[37] The Mirror pension trustees launched lawsuits against the fund managers, and won an out-of-court settlement worth £40 million, or less than 10 per cent of the missing funds, in early 1994.[38] Price Waterhouse, the firm handling this part of the proceedings, now believes creditors, including the pension funds, will eventually recover somewhere between 28 and 43 per cent of their money,[39] but the legal battles over who should get what part of the remnants will doubtless go on for years. Who, for example, is entitled to the take from the sale of the multipledged Berlitz International shares? The banks say they should get the money, as secured creditors; the pensioners say it should come to them. By the time the courts finish with that one, there may not be enough left to fight over.

The usual expressions of civic dismay were placed on the record. There were months of parliamentary hearings – there are always months of parliamentary hearings – which showed three things:

1. The City, London's financial community, is a self-regulating body, whose role in the Maxwell imbroglio consisted in looking the other way and whistling a happy tune.
2. The Bank of England had known that something was rotten in the state of Maxwell for a long time, and did nothing, for fear of starting a run on the lending banks.
3. No government body was willing to take responsibility for monitoring pension-fund activities, up to and including scooping a few hundred millions out of the till.[40] The Investment Management Regulatory Organization (IMRO),

which was supposed to have checked into Maxwell's Bishopsgate Investment Management, through which he manipulated the funds, never got around to it.

Once its laxity had been made a matter of public record, the government offered to contribute £2.5 million to help Maxwell pension schemes, while the ownership of £100 million – all that Maxwell left in the funds – is determined by the courts. The £2.5 million, less than 1 per cent of the missing money, is not a gift, mind; the pension funds will have to pay it back.[41]

The bank lenders to MCC became infuriated when the company directors put it into Chapter 11 protection in the United States, in December 1991, and their objections led to a modest legal advance. On December 31, 1991, a British High Court approved a cooperative agreement, under which the systems of both nations were applied. The U.S. bankruptcy court accepted the appointment of Price Waterhouse as the administrator of MCC – in line with British practice. In return, the administrators agreed to consult the American court on asset sales and other key activities of the failed firm.[42]

This at least allowed the insolvency practitioners in the two countries to agree to a "scheme of arrangement," as it is called in England, and a "plan of reorganization" (same thing) in the United States, which was accepted simultaneously in British and American courts on August 5, 1993.[43] The nub of that scheme was to begin the long process of liquidating the assets, but at least there had been a measure of cooperation between the insolvency machines of two nations. However, that was an *ad hoc* arrangement, which future courts and administrators may follow or ignore as they wish. The ordinary creditors were expected to get about ten cents on the dollar under this arrangement.[44] Moreover, the most prominent feature of the Maxwell bankruptcy was not the modicum of international agreement that emerged, but the amount of money it is costing to supervise. In London, 302 professionals – lawyers, accountants, investment bankers – were paid about £60 million up until mid-1992. By that time, they had managed to round up and sell about £200 million in assets,[45] none of which went to the pensioners. In the United States, another $120 million had gone to the same groups. The costs of bankruptcy administration rolled in at $600,000 per working day, and one of the eyebrow-raising bills concerned the collection of $3 million U.S. in assets from Maxwell's personal holdings, at a cost of $2-million.[46] The accountants collected an average of £90 to £120 an hour, the lawyers £153 to £191.[47]

The Social Security Select Committee of parliament estimated that the British share of the bankruptcy costs will come to more than £100 million, and as much again will be spent in the United States, with smaller costs in France, Switzerland, and a dozen other countries where Maxwell had holdings.[48] Headington Investments was registered in friendly Gibraltar, and the Maxwell Charitable Foundation, which believed that charity began at home, in Liechtenstein.

After a seven-month police probe, two of Maxwell's sons who were active in the business, Kevin and Ian, were charged with fifteen offences, including conspiracy, theft, and fraud.[49] That case is expected to be heard before the end of 1995, or maybe after. This is more of the barn-door-slamming-as-the-horse-vanishes-over-the-horizon kind of law that has become a feature of modern finance.

I have picked the BCCI and Maxwell as examples of the most spectacular kind of international failure, but there are dozens of others to choose from, including Polly Peck, the giant food conglomerate, O&Y Developments, and, of course, Manville Corporation and A. H. Robins. In the latter two cases, the application of American law blocked victims from all over the world in attempts to collect from their tormentors.

But surely, you are saying, something is being done to deal with these globe-straddling failures. Of course. We have the European Insolvency Practitioners Association, formed in 1980, to deal with countries within the European Community, and Insol International, formed in 1982. They hold meetings.

Gordon Marantz, a cheerful, thick-set, bearded Toronto lawyer and expert on insolvency, is the president of Insol. He explains that, in these matters, "the problems are easy to identify – what set of rules do you use to reorganize or liquidate an enterprise with operations in more than one jurisdiction? Which court has the right to control the process? The court in the country where the company has its head-quarters? Or, where it operates?"[50]

Insol has been working away at this sort of question for thirteen years now. It has representatives in fifty-one countries, who, in turn represent six thousand individual insolvency practitioners.[51] Lawyers, accountants, bankers. Their work is all voluntary. Marantz, for example, puts in hundreds of hours a year towards Insol's stated objectives, which are:

- to hold global conferences every four years;
- to publish regular newsletters on insolvency;
- to produce an international insolvency review;
- to hold regional conferences in between the global conferences; and
- to encourage cooperation and communication between individual insolvency practitioners in various countries.[52]

That's it. This is all fine stuff, but, in terms of dealing with the crises brought on by these global flops, it is about as effective as meeting the forest-fire hazard by promoting seminars for fire wardens to teach them how to spit. The fact is that the European Community has been trying for more than two decades to frame a treaty that would bring some common order to bankruptcy practices within the EEC, utterly without success. In France, when there is a bankruptcy, the wages of employees head the list of those who will collect first from the estate; in Switzerland, repayment of the debt takes precedence over everything else. In Germany and Japan, two of the world's economic powerhouses, it is the custom, when a corporation gets into financial difficulties, for its lead bank to step in with a reorganization plan, which may include removing the current management;[53] this would create chaos in North America. And so it goes, from nation to nation, each, quite properly, enforcing its own rules within its own jurisdiction.

The European insolvency group now lists, as one of its major activities: "Negotiates with the European Economic Community and the Council of Europe concerning any bankruptcy convention that might be proposed."[54] If there ever is any agreement on a common thread to which an international insolvency guideline can be hung, the practitioners will jump into action. In the meantime, I asked Marantz, what rules are followed? "You make it up as you go along," he replied.

Not even Canada and the United States, with many shared practices, can agree on a common approach. A treaty which proposed to do this was drafted in the seventies, but shelved by the Reagan administration.[55] Thank God. The ideal would be a treaty that would settle claims according to the principle of "unity"; that is, one administrator would deal with all charges against the bankrupt estate, foreign and domestic. The far-more-likely practical principle would be that Canadian practice would be changed to accommodate the senior partner, as usual in North America. Chapter 11, with maple syrup. If we and the Americans cannot agree on a single approach, other nations are far less likely to do so.

In short, the capacity of rogues and rascals – and of rogue and rascal corporations – to develop new ways of fleecing the lambs continues to outpace any attempts to bring the buggers to heel, and there is no measure of agreement even on what to do when bankruptcy ensues. We have invented ways for companies to operate globally, but we are not within a country mile of inventing ways to control them.

The next BCCI, or Maxwell, or Polly Peck, or Olympia & York bankruptcy is already ripening, just offstage. When it happens, we will be no better able to deal with it than we were when Agha Abedi and Captain Bob sank in 1991.

CHAPTER TWELVE

Binding the Wounds

"The virtue of bankruptcy is that the untenable situation is brought to an end. But, when the miscreants get away with it, the smooth functioning of society breaks down." – *Economic Impact*, 1993[1]

$

The main thrust of this book's argument is that bankruptcy law, as it applies today, favours those who bend or break the rules. In an earlier time, the rogues and rascals went belly up, often in colourful ways, and lost their money; now, they keep it: they may even make more. This is a product of what began as a useful and sensible move away from punitive laws and towards rehabilitative laws in the world of finance. As often happens, the pendulum has swung too far, so that now, instead of merely allowing debtors to make a compromise with their creditors, they are enabled, more and more, to shed their debts, and responsibilities, onto the backs of others. Unfortunately, this is not confined to the rules of bankruptcy; rather, the beneficiaries of change are, to a large extent, the same beneficiaries who have gained so much in our steady tramp towards the global corporation. In the name of international

competitiveness, we have created a society in which "corporate conscience" is an oxymoron, in which growth and profit are not merely
the most desired ends of business activity, they are the only ends. Corporations who pollute fare better, by and large, than those who do not,
and they can hire PR firms to minimize the damage to the company's
good name. Tax-dodging companies – pardon me, companies that
operate at the most efficient level – do better than those who retain
some scruple about their accounting methods. Corporations who
treat their employees with fairness and humanity suffer on the bottom
line, with consequent criticism for the management, while there is
nothing quite so comforting as having a president who is known to
"stand up to labour."

Such quaint and old-fashioned notions as community, morality,
and equity have long since been excised from our financial vocabulary
and replaced by the notion that anything that isn't illegal is permissible. And if it is illegal, but profitable, we will hire a lawyer to prove
that it isn't against the law, or that we didn't do it, or, if we get caught,
to say that while we don't admit we ever did it, we promise not to do it
again. The company pleads *nolo contendere*, a Latin phrase meaning "I
am unwilling to contend," and walks away.

In such a world, to argue that we ought to run our bankruptcy system with more scruple is to invite a loud snort of derision. We ought to
run our world with more scruple. We cannot conduct business efficiently, either locally or globally, on the assumption that everyone we
deal with is a potential crook, that agreements mean nothing until they
have been tested in court, that legislation is merely a test to see how we
can avoid the intent of the law without getting caught.

That being the case, I cannot argue that what we have to do now is
to patch up a few potholes on the road to bankruptcy, and all will be
well. The ills that assail us in the business of going belly up are symptoms of the greater illness that pervades our society and threatens
to bring it down. My aim in this final chapter, then, is limited. I believe there are some obvious and concrete measures we can take to improve the situation in which we find ourselves, so far as it relates to

bankruptcy. Binding these wounds will not cure the body politic, but the process can't do any harm, might do some good, and is worth trying. Out of the preceding pages, I think we can see a baker's dozen of points worth consideration as the parliamentary committee, scheduled to begin study of the bankruptcy law in late 1995, and the attendant hordes of politicians, consultants, and practitioners, bend over the operating table in the next two years or so:

1. We know enough about Chapter 11 and its workings to know that we must not go any further down that pathway. In particular, we must avoid the three cardinal sins, which were the three huge corporate advantages of the Chapter 11 amendments, namely: the elimination of the need to prove insolvency in seeking bankruptcy protection; the establishment of special bankruptcy courts; and the removal of deadlines for the filing of a proposal while a company is under the protection of the court. Our law, with all its flaws, works better than their law when it comes to business bankruptcies, and we must resist the endless temptation to copy the Americans.

The class-action suits that have become so prominent and expensive a feature of U.S. law are now firmly established in Canada, under the Class Proceedings Act. This Ontario legislation came into effect in 1993, but will apply to corporations across the country, because most of them sell securities in Ontario.[2] The Class Proceedings Act provides for contingency fees, which means that we will soon have corporate ambulance chasers swarming over the financial sector, just as the Americans do. And because the Americans do. Why should it be any different in the bankruptcy business? Our corporations, which means, in the main, their corporations, will hanker after the seductive charms of Chapter 11, and, unless we make it clear that we reject this approach, it will be part of our law before you can say *res ipse locitur*. When you live in a country where the phrase "National Hockey League" defines a league in which the vast majority of the teams are American, you are advised to cling to anything that works, and our approach, with all its flaws, works better than Chapter 11.

2. There is nothing in present legislation or practice to prevent a

Canadian corporation in the same fix as, say, Johns–Manville or A. H. Robins from creating a special class of creditors out of injured consumers, or other victims of its blunders, who launch lawsuits. Whatever benefits there are in the class-action suit – and in my view, they are debatable – will be swiftly undone if all a company has to do is to go into bankruptcy and get rid of the plaintiffs by making them a single class of creditors, dividing the shortage with all other claimants. The Chapter 11 protection afforded giant corporations is an outrage, but we have to do more than reject Chapter 11 to keep our corporations from using the shield of bankruptcy. Personal tort-injury claims ought to survive the bankruptcy process in exactly the same way that court fines do now. A simple amendment to the law will take care of this.

3. The level of debt that can be used to trigger a bankruptcy should be raised from $1,000 to $5,000. When you have a threshold which coincides with the amount of money it costs to launch the simplest bankruptcy, you have a problem; it is simply too easy to shed debts. Bankruptcy trustees have told me of cases where people rack up as little as $2,500 in credit-card debt and dive into bankruptcy to get rid of it.

4. The federal statute should contain some minimum exemptions designed to make the provincial laws fairer and more uniform. For example, the $8,000 worth of household furnishings that Alberta allows to escape the auctioneer's hammer might make a fair national standard. If this presents insuperable constitutional barriers – most things do these days – the law could content itself with setting out a schedule of recommended exemptions and leave it at that. At least it's a start.

5. The Companies' Creditors Arrangement Act should be abolished. This nearly happened in 1992 and ought to happen now. If there are parts of the act that need to be kept, they ought to be incorporated in the general statute. In particular, the woolly vagueness that allows the court to supervise the operations of the bankrupt company – or, to put it another way, allows the management to keep doing what they do, shed of debt – should end. The CCAA is our Chapter 11. We don't need

it; let corporations go bankrupt under the Bankruptcy and Insolvency Act or provincial winding-up statutes.

6. As we saw in Chapter Ten, the way the law now works, there is no reward, and indeed, there is a penalty, for the debtor who makes a proposal to his creditors rather than going personally bankrupt. That is because proposals normally take three years to work off the debt, while the bankrupt is normally discharged in one year. We ought to make it more worthwhile to pay off the debts than to walk away from them, or at least to make the process neutral, either by extending the length of time before an automatic discharge is granted to three years, or adjusting the tax system to aid the debtor who is determined to repay his creditors.

7. A lawyer who speaks one of Canada's official languages ought to go through the act and rewrite it in terms that can be understood. As it is, years, and millions of dollars, will be spent trying to find out what the law is supposed to say. This is madness. It is also typical of most of our laws, but that is no excuse for avoiding the task of making this law intelligible. (It is not even clear, under the law's murky phrasing, whether a debtor can earn an automatic thirty-day stay of all proceedings against him – such as scooping his assets and selling them – just by filing a notice of intention to file a proposal. In Ontario, the court held that, since there was no chance of the proposal being accepted, it was just a stall, and they refused the stay. In Quebec, a debtor was given four extensions of thirty days each before it became clear that no workable proposal would ever be forthcoming. The law says a stay "may be granted," but gives no further direction.)[3]

8. We will have to put more teeth into the enforcement process, to make it more dangerous to cheat in bankruptcy cases. The law is perfectly clear, in this area; what is lacking is the money, and the will, to enforce the law. Uwe Manski describes one case that is symptomatic of what goes on:

Just before a bankruptcy, the owner of the company removed most of the valuable assets and hid them in a warehouse. When we asked about them, he said the landlord must have seized them, but the landlord didn't have them. Then a couple of ex-employees came to see us; they had driven the loaded truck to the warehouse. We reported this to the RCMP, who interviewed the men, seized the assets, raided the company owner's home, and found more assets there. It took two years and four tries to get him into court, with the ex-employees being flown back and forth from Newfoundland for several pre-trial hearings, and, in the end, the guy received a sentence of thirty days, to be served on alternate weekends. He spent one weekend in jail, and then appealed the sentence. Here is a guy caught red-handed and all he got was a slap on the wrist.[4]

9. The proposal for a Wage Claims Settlement Fund, which was sunk by Tory backbenchers in 1992, should be reintroduced, and passed. The proposal, you will recall, was that an employee who lost his or her job because of the bankruptcy of the employer would be covered up to $2,000 in wages and vacation pay per employee, plus up to $1,000 in expenses for travelling employees. If the assets in the estate could not cover this amount, it would be paid out of the fund established for that purpose and financed by a levy about ten cents per week per employee.

10. An underlying theme in many corporate bankruptcies is the laxity, sometimes even the complicity, of accounting firms. Corporations who cannot get their own auditors to go along with the games they want to play can switch auditors. Even the threat of a switch will sometimes bring the number crunchers into line. U.S. writer Mark Stevens notes,

> Not all the competition in accounting is over who does what best. Increasingly, clients are won and lost on the basis of a less noble criterion: Who is the most willing to sacrifice professional standards for audit fees. In accounting's version of musical chairs, clients dissatisfied with their audit, which, theoretically, should produce virtually the same findings regardless

of who performs it, shop the market for firms more willing to see things through their own eyes than through Generally Accepted Accounting Principles.[5]

One of the most notorious of these cases involved a company called OPM (it actually stood for "other people's money") in Chicago. It was started by two men who got into the computer-leasing business by borrowing the money to buy the machines in the first place, and then renting them out for very low prices. Computers are fine things to lease, because the current models are so quickly outdated by new ones that leasing makes more sense than buying. The other side of that coin is that the computers lost most of their value to the leasing company very early in the process; in effect, the more they leased, the more they lost. The business grew by leaps and bounds, losing money all the way. The losses were covered by more borrowing, using the same computers for collateral several times over, and creating fictitious leases for non-existent computers, and then borrowing against these leases.

The auditors of OPM, Fox & Co. of Denver, turned red ink into black by booking in the first year of a six-year lease all the income that would be received over the full term of the agreement.[6] When the firm went bankrupt, another accounting company was hired by the receiver, which discovered that, for example, in a year when Fox & Co. had OPM making $1.7 million, it had actually lost $17.8 million.

The whole thing came unravelled when a fictitious lease to Rockwell International was discovered by a Rockwell executive, and two OPM principals went to jail for fraud. Price Waterhouse, the firm brought in to clean things up, never said anything to cast aspersions on another member of the profession, although it did note that Fox's audits might have been improved by "inquiry into the existence of possible illegal acts."[7]

We saw in Chapter Seven how a profit of $5 million produced by Standard Trust turned into a loss of $59 million in a new audit by the same accounting firm when it knew it was being watched. There is a lesson here. Accounting, like so many other professions, is self-regulating; clearly there is need for outside regulation and stiff penalties. The present system doesn't even work well for the accountants, who increasingly find themselves on the receiving end of lawsuits when the client goes into bankruptcy. The accounting firms carry insurance against damage suits, so they get the writ.

11. Speaking of insurance, corporations carry all kinds of it; why not insurance that would cover them in the case of a bankruptcy? Or that would, at the least, pay off suppliers and employees not otherwise covered. The first thing managers do is to provide themselves with golden parachutes in case the craft goes down. It would be nice of them to fold up a little something for their workers, too.

12. We cannot meet the menace, or opportunity – take your pick – of the global corporation by changing bankruptcy rules. We can, however, recognize that the existence of widely differing rules all over the world multiplies the chances of chicanery and diminishes the prospects of equity for everyone, everywhere. This suggests that any group, such as Insol International, that is working on the problem should be encouraged by word and deed – that is, by some government funding – to get on with the job. Cocktail parties among volunteers in the ritzy hotels is not going to do it. We need treaties that persuade nations to recognize each other's bankruptcy practitioners, for a start. We also need an international code, which will have to be voluntary, to regularize the accounting and legal fees at a reasonable level.

I do not hold out much hope that these simple steps will be taken in the foreseeable future, and I don't see any chance that the practice of ring-fencing assets will be brought to a halt. Why should Pakistan surrender hundreds of millions of dollars in assets to a pooling of the BCCI's bankrupt estate so that bondholders in Britain and the United States can collect? Especially when the Americans have already grabbed hundreds of millions by using their own court system as a siphon? About the best we can hope for is that the courts of various lands will cooperate, as they did in the Maxwell case, to share knowledge and coordinate the process.

13. Finally, we must have some accurate measure of the costs of bankruptcy, not just under the BIA, but under the CCAA, the Winding-Up Act, and the provincial Corporations Acts. This is not a simple, or cheap, process; it requires amendments to all the relevant laws to make it mandatory, and it requires, sigh, a minimal bureaucracy to track the filings. However, to operate an economic policy that costs billions without even knowing how many billions is not an intelligent way to proceed.

We have come a long way from the days when people were treated as criminals when they couldn't pay their debts. It is just possible that we have come too far. A mixed economic system like our own, which gets most of its zip out of capitalism, and most of its balance out of state intervention, cannot be made to work unless profits are seen as the reward for risk. I am almost embarrassed to type that sentence; it seems so obvious. Without risk, there is very little progress; without reward, none. The very same giant corporations where this sort of stuff is etched on brass under a picture of the founder spend most of their time trying to avoid risk, by buying out the competition, if it can be worked, or in some other form of conspiracy against the general good.

Perhaps we cannot blame them for that; squeezing out the competition and then hiking prices comes as naturally to our corporate overlords as breathing, even more naturally than the speeches they make praising the competition through whose heart they have just driven a stake. Wherever there is competition, there is risk, and, from time to time, it is bound to result in business failures. Therefore, we need, we will always need, a system to allow businesses, and individuals, who get into financial trouble to get a new start. What we don't need, and what we are in danger of getting, is a system that allows businesses and individuals to use bankruptcy to slough off not only their debts, but their risks and responsibilities, to shelter from the consequences of their decisions at the expense of their customers and the general public.

There is a brief moment of opportunity available to us in the forthcoming examination of the Bankruptcy and Insolvency Act, beginning in the fall of 1995. This represents a chance to undo some of the harm we have already done and to rewrite the rules in a fairer way. If the process is left in the hands of the corporate lawyers, we will have an American-style bankruptcy system in place before the year 2000. We are already using the CCAA as a kind of Chapter 11 in snowshoes; we are creating, without any discussion, a bankruptcy court for which there is no provision in law, and which follows the American style; our courts are citing U.S. precedent to establish Canadian law, and we appear to have accepted, again without much public debate, the approach favoured south of the border in which the rights of the debtor appear to roll over those of creditors. Finally, although we have not gone nearly so far down the road as the Americans in allowing large bankrupt corporations to escape their debts and responsibilities, come what may, we are heading that way, and the increasing dominance of global corporations will push us further. Don't kid yourself; if the international bankruptcy practitioners ever do get their act together and produce a series of standards for global bellyflops, the rules will not be those made in Ottawa; they will be drawn up for, and by, the Americans.

If we don't act now, while the BIA is still open for reform, we will end up with an insolvency system which is financially suspect, socially backward, and morally bankrupt.

APPENDIX

Table 1
Canadian Bankruptcies*

Year	Number	Assets	Liabilities (figures in $ millions)	Deficit
1984				
Business	9,578	569	2,465	1,896
Consumer	22,022	299	1,243	944
Proposals**	389	177	355	178
Totals	31,989	1,045	4,063	3,018
1989				
Business	8,664	774	2,199	1,425
Consumer	29,202	363	850	4,862
Proposals	570	197	321	124
Totals	38,436	1,334	3,370	6,411
1990				
Business	11,642	1,437	3,342	1,906
Consumer	42,782	817	1,761	944
Proposals	1,355	475	596	121
Totals	55,779	2,729	5,699	2,971
1991				
Business	13,496	2,313	6,179	3,856
Consumer	62,277	1,606	3,265	1,659
Proposals	1,239	639	860	226
Totals	77,012	4,558	10,304	5,741
1992				
Business	14,317	2,044	7,374	5,329
Consumer	61,822	1,725	3,263	1,659
Proposals	1,133	396	456	603
Totals	77,272	4,165	11,093	7,591
1993				
Business	12,527	1,862	5,383	3,521
Consumer	54,456	1,615	3,181	1,566
Proposals	2,314	689	1,015	326
Totals	69,297	4,166	9,579	5,413

Between 1984 and 1993, all bankruptcies under the act went from 31,989 to 69,297, a rise of 216 per cent. The money owing went from $4,063 million to $9,579 million, up 235 per cent, and the deficit – the difference between assets shown and liabilities – went from $3,018 million to $5,413 million, up 179 per cent. Business bankruptcies went from 9,578 to 12,527, an increase of 130 per cent, while the liabilities in connection with these went from $2,465 million to $5,383 million, a jump of 218 per cent, and the deficit went from $1,896 million to $3,521 million, up 185 per cent.

*Source: Compiled from figures in the *Canadian Annual Statistical Summary*, Consumer and Corporate Affairs, Office of the Superintendent of Bankruptcy, Ottawa, various years. These are the failures reported under the Bankruptcy Act, now the Bankruptcy and Insolvency Act, and do not include those under the Winding-Up Act, the Companies' Creditors Arrangement Act, or the provincial statutes for dissolving corporations, which are nowhere recorded, although they are much higher than the numbers shown here.

**These are the cases in which an insolvent person or company made a proposal to creditors while in bankruptcy protection, which was accepted.

Table 2
What Was Left

	Assets	Liabilities	Realizations by trustee ($ millions)	Costs	Dividends	%*
1933	9.2	8.6	1.8	0.4	1.4	16.27
1984	814	2,603	133	67	66	2.53
1990	811	2,414	252	145	107	4.43
1992	1,866	4,414	329	209	120	2.71
1993	2,575	6,593	778	631	147	2.22

*The dividends paid out to creditors as a percentage of the total liabilities claimed by them from estates closed during the year.

This table shows the advancement of the accounting and legal professions. In 1933, at the height of the Depression, there were 2,604 bankruptcies in Canada, involving assets of $9,207,503 and liabilities of $8,629,393. The trustees managed to recover $1,882,014.70 (they kept track of the cents), of which the creditors were paid $1,458,181.80, and the costs of administration came to $423,832.99. The dividends represented 16.27 cents out of every dollar owed.

In 1984, out of more than $2,603 million owing, the trustees were able to recover $133 million, and the costs came to $67 million, leaving $66 million to be paid out as dividends. That was 2.53 cents on the dollar. By 1990, the money paid out soared up to just over 4 cents on the dollar, but by 1993, it was battened back down. That year, the liabilities were up to $6,593 million, of which $778 million was collected, at a cost of $631 million, leaving $147 million to be paid out as dividends. That is 2.22 cents on the dollar. Note that in 1993, a year of surging recovery in the economy generally, while the lawyers and accountants recovered almost $450 million more than they had in 1992, only $27 million more slipped through the cracks to the creditors. In 1992, they got back $120 million out of $329 million collected, but in 1993, they got a mere $147 million out of $778 million. Send your children to law school, or into accountancy. Note, too, that the assets and liabilities in this table differ from those in Table 1, because these represent estates that were closed during the year, not bankruptcy filings. Some bankruptcies take years to close.

Source: Compiled from figures in the annual report of the Superintendent of Bankruptcies, Table 7, various years.

Table 3
U.S Business Bankruptcies

	Business Failures	Liabilities ($ millions)
1983	31,334	16,072
1984	52,078	29,268
1985	57,252	36,914
1986	61,183	43,961
1987	61,384	34,818
1988	57,099	35,908
1989	50,361	42,328
1990	60,432	64,044
1991	88,140	96,825
1992	96,750	93,756

In the decade shown here, U.S. business failures increased from 31,334 to 93,756, or 299 per cent. The money involved went from $16,072 million to $93,756 million, or 583 per cent.

Source: *Survey of Current Business*, U.S. Department of Commerce, Washington, Table S5, various years.

NOTES

Chapter One

1. Sherman, Stratford P., "Bankruptcy's Spreading Blight," *Fortune*, June 3, 1991, p. 124.
2. "Gabereau," CBC, March 24, 1992.
3. From the judgment of Mr. Justice D. H. Carruthers, *Ontario Report*, 54 O.P. (2d), p. 672.
4. From the judgment of Mr. Justice Dennis Lane, Ontario Court (General Division), in the Matter of the Bankruptcy of Michael E. Chodos, File No. 31-232-607, p. 2.
5. Carruthers judgment, p. 672.
6. Lane judgment, p. 3.
7. Lane judgment, p. 14.
8. Lane judgment, p. 9.
9. Ibid., p. 9.
10. Ibid., p. 10.
11. From the consent judgment in the Matter of the Bankruptcy of Michael E. Chodos, p. 2.
12. This was his own estimate in testimony before the bankruptcy court.
13. See Table 2 in the Appendix. Below is a table prepared by Uwe Manski of the accounting firm of BDO Dunwoody Ward Mallette, who is president of the Canadian Insolvency Practitioners' Association. He has taken the figures for 1991 and broken them down, using the assets shown by debtors as a basis, rather than the liabilities. This seems generous to me; the money owed is not the amount the bankrupt has left in the estate, but what is owed to all legitimate claimants. In 1991, the trustees collected about 26 cents for every dollar of assets and the creditors got 4 cents.

Bankruptcy estates completed in 1991

Number of estates	38,102
Assets declared by debtors	$1,190,300,000
Assets realized by trustee	306,000,000
Realization percentage	25.7
Cost of administration	174,300,000
Creditors' claims	3,215,200,000
Dividends paid	37,700,000
Recover percentage for creditors	4.1

14. Attributed, undated.

15. See *Do You Sincerely Want to be Rich? Bernard Cornfeld and* IOS, *An International Swindle*, by Charles Raw, Godfrey Hodgson, and Bruce Page, London: Andre Deutsch, 1971.

16. Stewart, Walter, *The Golden Fleece*, Toronto: McClelland & Stewart, 1992, pp. 187-92.

17. *U.S. News and World Report*, April 8, 1991, p. 9.

18. Work, Clemens P., "Bankruptcy: An Escape Hatch for Ailing Firms," *U.S. News & World Report*, August 22, 1983, p. 67.

19. See Rothchild, John, *Going for Broke, How Robert Campeau Bankrupted the Retail Industry, Jolted the Junk Bond Market, and Brought the Booming Eighties to a Crashing Halt*, New York: Simon & Schuster, 1991.

20. Stewart, Walter, *Too Big To Fail: Olympia & York, The Story Behind the Headlines*, Toronto: McClelland & Stewart, 1993, p. 263.

21. *U.S. News & World Report*, April 8, 1991, p. 50.

22. Shannon, James, *Texaco and the $10 Billion Jury*, Englewood, N.J.: Prentice Hall, 1988.

23. Ibid., p. 515.

24. Kallen, Laurence, *Corporate Welfare, The Megabankruptcies of the 80s and 90s*, New York: Carol Publishing, 1991, p. 293.

25. *Globe and Mail*, September 22, 1993, p. C2.

26. *Panamericana De Bienes Y Servicos, S.A. (Receiver of) v. Northern Badger Oil and Gas Ltd.*, Alberta Court of Queen's Bench, Judicial District of Calgary, MacPherson J., December 20, 1989.

27. *Dominion Law Reports, Panamericana v. Northern Badger Oil & Gas Ltd.*, 81 D.L.R. (4th), p. 281.

28. *Globe and Mail*, October 16, 1990, pp. B1, 4.

29. See the Appendix, Table 2.

Chapter Two

1. Willes, John A., *Contemporary Canadian Business Law: Principles and Cases*, Second Edition, McGraw-Hill Ryerson, Toronto, 1986, p. 700.

2. Orsingher, Roger, *Banks of the World*, Macmillan, London, 1967, p. 38.

3. Stewart, Walter, *Towers of Gold, Feet of Clay: The Canadian Banks*, Toronto: Collins, 1981, p. 32.

4. Earle, Peter, in *The Lives of the Kings and Queens of England, edited by Antonia Fraser*, London: Futura, 1977, p. 66.

5. Willes, op cit., p. 701.

6. Coleman, Peter J., *Debtors and Creditors in America: Insolvency, Imprisonment for Debt, and Bankruptcy, 1607-1900*, Madison: State Historical Society of Wisconsin, 1974, pp. 3-4.

7. Ibid., p. 701.

8. Quoted in Ibid., p. 5.

9. There is a detailed description of the development of the limited corporation in Kierans, Eric, and Stewart, Walter, *Wrong End of the Rainbow*, Toronto: HarperCollins, 1991, pp. 33-56.

10. Coleman, op. cit., p. 9.

11. Playfair, Giles, *The Punitive Obsession: An Unvarnished History of the English Prison System*, London: Victor Gollancz, 1971, p. 105.

12. Ibid., p. 106.

13. Coleman, op. cit., p. 10.

14. Ibid., p. 11.

15. *An Act to Provide for the Relief of Bankrupts and the Administration of Their Estates*, Province of Canada, Legislative Assembly, 1851, Section II.

16. Ibid.

17. Ibid., Section XLIV.

18. *Our Bankrupt Law*, by "T.B.P.," Montreal, January, 1877, p. 13.

19. Ibid.

20. Attributed to Lord Chancellor Baron Thurlow, 1731-1806.

21. Bennett, Frank, *Bennett on Creditors' and Debtors' Rights and Remedies*, Third Edition, Toronto: Carswell, 1992, p. 528.

22. *The Bankruptcy Act, 1919, with Amendments*, The King's Printer, Ottawa, 1923, Part I, Section 3.

23. Ibid., Section 55(1).

24. Willes, op. cit., p. 702.

25. Manski, Uwe, "Bankruptcy Act Amendments," 1993.

26. Chapter B-3, *An Act Respecting Bankruptcy*, 1992. Hereafter, "The Act." Section 42(1).

27. Bennett, op. cit., p. 530.

28. The Act, Section 136.

29. Ibid., Section 136(1)(d).

30. Bennett, Frank, op. cit., p. 710.

31. Ibid.

32. Interview, August 31, 1992.

33. *Canadian Lawyer*, October, 1993, p. 37.

34. Bennett, op. cit., p. 541.

35. Bennett, op. cit., p. 536.

Chapter Three

1. Braudel, Fernand, *Civilization and Capitalism, 15th-18th Century*, Volume III, London: Collins, 1984, p. 115.

2. Posthumous, N. W., *The Tulip Mania in Holland in the Years 1636 and 1637*, originally published in the early eighteenth century, publisher and date not recorded, p. 437.

3. Ibid., p. 438.

4. Miller, Nathan, *The Founding Finaglers*, New York: David McKay, 1976, p. 105.

5. Schacner, Nathan, *The Founding Fathers*, New York, publisher not recorded, 1954, pp. 85-87.

6. Sobel, Robert, *Panic on Wall Street*, New York: E. P. Dutton, 1988, pp. 8-32.

7. Stewart, Walter, *The Golden Fleece*, pp. 46-52.

8. Quoted in McGrane, Reginald C., *Foreign Bondholders and American State Debts*, New York: Macmillan, 1935, pp. 59-60.

9. Ibid.

10. Ibid.

11. Walsh, Annmarie Hauck, *The Public's Business*, Cambridge, Mass.: M.I.T. Press, 1980, p. 19.

12. Cockburn, Henry, *Memoirs of his Time*, New Edition, Edinburgh: T. N. Foulis, 1910, p. 402.

13. See, for example, the entry in the *Oxford Companion to English Literature*, which makes Scott a broken, heroic figure done in by the machinations of his publisher.

14. Quayle, Eric, *The Ruin of Sir Walter Scott*, London: Rupert Hart-Davis, 1968.

15. Quayle, op. cit., p. 205.

16. Quayle, op. cit., p. 209.

17. This excerpt from Scott's personal journal is quoted in Quayle, p. 212.

18. Quayle, op. cit., p. 213.

19. Quayle, op. cit., pp. 213-214.

20. Quayle, op. cit., p. 209.

21. The *Oxford Companion to English Literature* says, in the Fifth Edition, "In 1826 James Ballantyne & Co. became involved in the bankruptcy of Constable & Co., and Scott, as partner of the former, found himself liable for a debt of about £114,000. He shouldered the whole burden himself and henceforth worked heroically, shortening his own life by his strenuous efforts, to pay off the creditors, who received full payment after his death." The only part of this that is true is that he worked heroically; the rest is all hokum.

22. Quayle, op. cit., p. 278.

23. Nicholson, Harold, *Helen's Tower*, London: Constable & Co. Ltd., 1937, p. 264.

24. Ibid., p. 67.

25. Ibid., p. 268.

26. MacDougall, Curtis D., *Hoaxes*, New York: Dover, p. 67.

27. Nicholson, op cit., p. 278.

28. Ibid., p. 276.

29. Shaplen, Robert, *Kreuger, Genius and Swindler*, New York: Alfred Knopf, 1960, p. 6.

30. MacDougall, op. cit., p. 69.

31. Ibid., p. 5.

32. Myers, Gustavus, *A History of Canadian Wealth*, Vol. I, Toronto: James, Lewis, and Samuel, 1972, p. 183ff.

33. Shortt, Adam, *History of Canadian Currency and Banking, 1600-1800*, Toronto: Canadian Bankers' Association, undated, p. 687.

34. Naylor, Tom, *The History of Canadian Business, 1867-1914*, Vol. I., Toronto: Lorimer, 1975, p. 127.

35. *Report of the Royal Commission Appointed to Inquire Into The Failure of Atlantic Acceptance Corporation Ltd*, 1969, Volume Three, p. 1,519.

Chapter Four

1. Bennett, Frank, op. cit., p. 554.

2. Kallen, Laurence, op. cit, p. 58.

3. Wyden, Peter, *The Unknown Iacocca*, New York: William Morrow, 1987, pp. 149-168.

4. Ibid., p. 156.

5. *Fortune*, March 23, 1981.

6. Franks, Julian, and Torous, Walter N., "An Empirical Investigation of U.S. Firms in Reorganization," in *Bankruptcy and Distressed Restructuring*, Edward J. Altman, editor, Homewood, Illinois: Business One Irwin, 1993, p. 363.

7. Kallen, op. cit., p. 59.

8. Kallen, op. cit., p. 55.

9. Kallen, Laurence, *Multinational Monitor*, January/February 1993, p. 14.

10. *Public Law 696* – 75th Congress, Chapter XI, Section 437(1), in *Bankruptcy Laws of the United States*, compiled by Gilmer G. Udell, Washington: U.S. Government Printing Office, 1972.

11. *The Touche Ross Guide to International Insolvency*, Chicago: Probus, 1989, Section 4, p. 6.

12. *Bankruptcy and Distressed Restructuring*, p. 412.

13. Kallen, op. cit., p. 56.

14. Kallen, *Corporate Welfare*, p. 134.

15. Ibid., p. 136.

16. Kallen, *Corporate Welfare*, pp. 138-139.

17. *Wall Street Journal*, July 10, 1985, p. 13.

18. Kallen, *Corporate Welfare*, p. 202.

19. *Wall Street Journal*, September 26, 1983, p. 1.

20. Ibid.

21. Kallen, op. cit., p. 215.

22. *Globe and Mail*, July 7, 1993, p. B2.

23. Ibid.

24. "Eastern: The Wings of Greed," unsigned article in *Business Week*, November 11, 1991, p. 35.

25. Ibid., p. 37.

26. Ibid., p. 34.

27. *Calgary Herald*, September 9, 1993, p. D3.

Chapter Five

1. *Fortune*, June 3, 1991, p. 124.

2. Interview, August 31, 1992.

3. Chapter C-36, Revised Statutes.

4. *Canadian Lawyer*, October 1993, p. 40.

5. Tay, Derrick, "Canadian Bankruptcy Reform," in *International Insolvency Review*, Spring 1993, Volume 2, Issue 1, p. 44.

6. *An Act to Amend the Bankruptcy Act* (hereafter BIA), Part III, Division I, Section 50.4(8).

7. BIA, Section (11)b.

8. Shorten, Lynda, "BIA: Help or Hindrance?" in *Canadian Lawyer*, October 1993, p. 37.

9. BIA, Section 58.

10. BIA, Section 50(1).

11. CCAA, Section 2.

12. Interview, November 6, 1993.

13. BIA, Section 50.4(8), (9).

14. Ibid., Section 65.2(2).

15. BIA, Section 50(1.4).

16. Ibid., Section 50(1.5).

17. CCAA, Part I, Section 6.

18. Ibid., Part II, Section 11.

19. *Globe and Mail*, March 11, 1992, p. B11.

20. *Daily Commercial News*, June 4, 1992, p. 1.

21. *Financial Times*, August 10, 1992, p. 12.

22. *Globe and Mail*, January 18, 1994, p. B25.

23. *Globe and Mail*, June 19, 1992, p. B13.

24. *Globe and Mail*, August 26, 1992, p. B1.

25. *Financial Post*, July 31, 1993, p. 1.

26. Quoted in the *Globe and Mail*, February 29, 1992, p. B5.

27. *Globe and Mail*, April 11, 1992, p. B5.

28. Stewart, Walter, *Too Big To Fail: Olympia & York, The Story Behind the Headlines*, Toronto: McClelland & Stewart, 1993.

29. Interview, February 4, 1994.

30. From the Order, Section 23(iv).

31. Ibid., Section 23(v), (vi).

32. From the Order, P C-5, Paragraph 18.

33. Farkas, Peter P., "What's Really Wrong with the Bankruptcy Act?" *CA Magazine*, June 1991, p. 39.

34. BIA, Section 92.

35. Annual Statistical Summary for the 1992 calendar year, Consumer and Corporate Affairs Canada, Office of the Superintendent of Bankruptcy, Table 3.

36. Stewart, Walter, *Too Big To Fail*, p. 306, note 11.

Chapter Six

1. Quoted in David Olive's *Just Rewards*, Toronto: Penguin, 1988, p. 24.

2. O'Shea, James, *The Daisy Chain*, New York: Pocket Books, 1991, p. 17.

3. *The United States Government Manual*, U.S. Government Printing Office, 1984, p. 506.

4. Schlesinger, Arthur M., *The Coming of the New Deal*, Cambridge: Houghton Mifflin, 1959, p. 443.

5. Mayer, Martin, *The Greatest Bank Robbery: The Collapse of the Savings and Loan Industry*, New York: Collier, 1992, p. 94.

6. Mayer, op. cit., p. 97.

7. Pusey, Allen, *New York Times Magazine*, April 23, 1989, p. 23.

8. O'Shea, op. cit., p. 294.

9. O'Shea, op. cit., p. 12.

10. O'Shea, op. cit., p. 34.

11. O'Shea, op. cit., p. 192.

12. O'Shea, op. cit., p. 105.

13. O'Shea, op. cit., p. 44.

14. *The World Almanac, 1990*, p. 83.

15. Adams, James Ring, *The Big Fix: Inside the S&L Scandal*, New York: Wiley & Sons, 1991, p. 206.

16. Greenwald, David, *Orange County Register*, March 30, 1990, p. 1. When his little stunt came to light, Christensen drove his Porsche into a highway abutment, leaving behind a grieving girlfriend and a life-insurance policy in her behalf, to ease the pain, for $10 million. Then she was convicted on twenty-two counts of racketeering and fraud. Darn.

17. *Globe and Mail*, July 4, 1990, p. B19.

18. O'Shea, op. cit., p. 149.

19. Mayer, op. cit., p. 125.

20. The phrase originated with Dallas real-estate lawyer Robert Feldman, according to John Saunders, *Globe and Mail*, September 4, 1990, p. B1.

21. *Wall Street Journal*, April 18, 1989, p. 1.

22. *Grant's Interest Rate Observer*, May 13, 1988, p. 1.

23. Mayer, op. cit., p. 168.

24. *Boston Herald*, July 11, 1992, p. 22.

25. O'Shea, op. cit., p. 211.

26. O'Shea, op. cit., p. 218.

27. O'Shea, op. cit., p. 285.

28. *The Universal Almanac 1993*, John W. Wright, general editor, New York: Andrews and McMeel, 1993, p. 250.

29. *Silverado Banking, Savings and Loan Association, Hearings before the United States House of Representatives Committee on Banking*, May 23, 1990, p. 532.

30. *Washington Post*, May 25, 1990, p. A2.

31. Adams, op. cit., p. 283.

32. Proxmire, William, "Take the Pledge, No More Special Interest Money," in *Roll Call*, September 17, 1990.

33. Adams, op. cit., p. 309.

34. O'Shea, op. cit., p. 308.

35. O'Shea, op. cit., p. 311.

36. *Globe and Mail*, April 11, 1992, p. B2.

37. *Boston Herald*, July 11, 1992, p. 22.

38. *The Universal Almanac 1993*, p. 251.

39. *Globe and Mail*, September 11, 1990, p. B11.

40. Bliss, Michael, *Report on Business* (column), March 1991, p. 27.

41. Mayer, op. cit., p. 20.

42. Ibid., p. 28.

Chapter Seven

1. *In the Court of Queen's Bench of Alberta, Judicial District of Edmonton, Action Number 8703-1633, In the Matter of the Companies' Creditors Arrangement Act, Chapter C-25, R.S.C. 1970, as Amended, and in the Matter of Associated Investors of Canada Ltd., and in the Matter of the Judicature Act, Chapter J-1, R.S.A. 1980 as Amended, Final Report of Inspector Code*, QC, July 1989, hereafter "Code Report," p. 58-59.

2. Most of the material in this section comes from a magazine article that James Fleming and I wrote for *Maclean's*, and which appeared in the

June 13, 1983, edition of that magazine, pp. 32-37. It won us two lawsuits and one business-writing award. The lawsuits died, and we spent the money, but hung onto the research.

3. Corcoran, Terence, and Reid, Laura, *Public Money, Private Greed: The Greymac, Seaway and Crown Trusts Affair*, Toronto: Collins, 1984.

4. Corcoran and Reid, op. cit., p. 350.

5. *Hansard*, November 6, 1990, p. 15,220.

6. *Toronto Star*, June 29, 1993, p. A6.

7. *Report of the Inquiry into the Collapse of* CCB *and Northland Bank*, Ottawa: Supply and Services, p. 12. (Hereafter the Estey Report.)

8. Ibid., p. 12.

9. Johnson, Arthur, *Breaking the Banks*, Toronto: Lester, Orpen & Denys, 1986, p. 244. Lester, Orpen & Denys later went bankrupt, too.

10. Ibid., p. 212.

11. *Canadian News Facts*, September 1-15, 1985, p. 3,310.

12. Estey Report, p. 502.

13. Ibid.

14. Ibid., p. 501.

15. Estey Report, p. 17.

16. Ibid., p. 5.

17. Ibid., p. 502.

18. Ibid., p. 5.

19. Ibid., p. 7

20. *Maclean's*, December 1, 1986, p. 36.

21. Estey Report, p. 530.

22. Johnson, op. cit., p. 245.

23. *Financial Post*, November 3-5, 1990, p. 1.

24. Code Report, p. 79.

25. *Globe and Mail*, January 23, 1992, p. A1.

26. Code Report, p. 29.

27. Ibid., p. 23.

28. Ibid.

29. Ibid., p. 24.

30. Ibid., p. 27.

31. Ibid., p. 33.
32. Ibid., p. 30.
33. Ibid., p. 34.
34. Ibid., p. 126.
35. Ibid., p. 127.
36. Ibid., p. 81.
37. Ibid., p. 50.
38. Ibid., p. 56.
39. Ibid., p. 65.
40. Ibid., p. 234.
41. Ibid., p. 84.
42. Ibid., p. 89.
43. Ibid., p. 346.
44. Ibid., p. 357.
45. Ibid., pp. 358-9.
46. Ibid., p. 418.
47. Ibid., p. 401.
48. Ibid.
49. Ibid., p. 418.
50. *Globe and Mail*, January 23, 1992, p. A2.
51. Fisher, Matthew, *A Matter of Principal*, Toronto: Seal Books, 1990, p. 13.
52. *Report of the Ombudsman*, Legislative Assembly of British Columbia, September, 1989, p. vii.
53. Ibid., p. i.
54. Report of the Ombudsman, Province of Saskatchewan, p. 56.
55. *In the Matter of the Regulation of First Investors Corporation Ltd.*, Report of the Office of the Ombudsman, Halifax, February 1990, p. 44.
56. Ibid.
57. *Globe and Mail*, April 6, 1990, p. B5.
58. Ibid.
59. Fisher, op. cit., p. 293.
60. *Financial Post*, April 22, 1991, p. 3.
61. Ibid.
62. *Financial Post*, April 20-21, 1991, p. 1.

63. *Toronto Star*, January 4, 1994, p. A12.

64. *Toronto Star*, January 4, 1994, p. A12.

65. He wrote a column on the subject in the *Toronto Star*, January 20, 1994, p. A23.

Chapter Eight

1. Brodeur, Paul, "Annals of Law: The Asbestos Industry on Trial. 1. Failure to Warn," *The New Yorker*, June 10, 1985, p. 50. Brodeur wrote four massive articles on the Manville Corporation, which became a book called *Outrageous Misconduct: The Asbestos Industry on Trial* published in New York by Pantheon in 1986. Like many books of solid worth and exemplary research, it has gone out of print. The single copy on the shelves of Toronto's Reference Library has disappeared. I have used the original articles, and refer to them by their dates of publication.

2. *New York Times*, August 27, 1982, p. A1.

3. Ibid., p. 22.

4. Ibid., p. D3.

5. *New York Times*, October 7, 1964, p. 24.

6. United States Bankruptcy Court, Southern District of New York, in *re* Johns–Manville Corporation, et al., In "Proceedings for a Reorganization Under Chapter 11, First Amended Disclosure Statement."

7. *Asbestos: The Dangerous Fiber*, edited by Melvin A. Bernade, Boca Raton: CRC Press, 1990, p. 3.

8. Sentes, Raymond Max, PH.D. thesis, *The Privileged Position of Business: An Analysis of Canadian Industry-Government Policies Pertaining to Occupational Health, 1887-1987*, p. 16. (Available in the National Archives and the University of Regina Archives.)

9. Ibid., p. 53.

10. Ibid., p. 16.

11. Stewart, Miller (my late father, actually) "Catholic Labor Wins a Strike," in *The Nation*, October 1, 1949, p. 15.

12. Kallen, *Corporate Welfare*, p. 232.

13. Ibid.

14. Quoted in CCF *News*, April 28, 1949, p. 5.

15. *Facts and Figures About Canadian Johns–Manville Company, Ltd.*, (undated, but filed in 1949) p. 10.

16. Ibid., p. 11.

17. Bernade, op. cit., p. 5-6.

18. Ibid., p. 7.

19. Brodeur, June 10, p. 58.

20. Brodeur, June 10, p. 50.

21. Ibid., p. 50ff.

22. Sentes, p. 57.

23. Brodeur, *The New Yorker*, June 10, 1985, p. 67.

24. Sentes, p. 74.

25. Sentes, p. 282.

26. Quoted in Sentes, p. 297.

27. Ibid., p. 298.

28. Ibid.

29. Sentes, op. cit., p. 89.

30. Ibid., p. 98.

31. *The Asbestos Report*, Winter 1976, p. 3.

32. Selikoff, I., "Asbestos-associated disease," in *Asbestos Litigation*, edited by W. Alcorn, New York: Harcourt, Brace, Jovanvich, 1982.

33. Brodeur, June 10, 1985, p. 67.

34. Brodeur, June 10, p. 80.

35. Ibid., p. 87.

36. Brodeur, June 17, p. 46.

37. Brodeur, June 17, p. 60.

38. Brodeur, June 17, p. 72.

39. Ibid.

40. *New York Times*, April 27, 1978, Section II, p. 1.

41. Brodeur, June 17, p. 87.

42. Court of Appeals for the District of Columbia, Keene *v.* the Insurance Company of North America.

43. Brodeur, June 17, p. 102.

44. Ibid., p. 109.

45. Keene *v.* the Insurance Company of North America, First Amended Disclosure Statement, p. 54.

46. Kallen, *Corporate Welfare*, p. 243.

47. Legal literature is now rife with Manville cases in which the company, having lost, kept appeals going for years. Among these are *Fischer v. Johns–Manville, Moran v. Johns–Manville, Jackson v. Johns–Manville Sales Corp., Hansen v. Johns–Manville Products Corp., Janssens v. Johns–Manville Sales Corporation, and Cathey v. Johns–Manville Sales Corporation.*

48. Kallen, *Corporate Welfare*, p. 232.

49. Brodeur, July 1, p. 41.

50. *New York Times*, August 3, 1982, p. D1.

51. Brodeur, June 24, p. 46.

52. Ibid., p. 48.

53. Delaney, Kevin J., "Control During Corporate Crisis: Asbestos and the Manville Bankruptcy," in the *International Journal of Health Services,* Volume 21, Number 4, 1991, p. 708.

54. Brodeur, June 24, p. 70.

55. *The Nation*, October 16, 1982, p. 361.

56. Kallen, *Corporate Welfare*, p. 259.

57. Ibid., p. 260.

58. Ibid., p. 273.

59. *New York Times*, August 27, p. D4.

60. In *re* Johns–Manville Corp. Chapter 11, Nos. 82B 11656-11676 (Bankruptcy, Southern Division, New York.)

61. Keene *v.* the Insurance Company of North America, First Amended Disclosure Statement, p. 55.

62. Ibid., p. 58.

63. Ibid., p. 278.

64. Ibid., p. 297.

65. Kallen, *Corporate Welfare*, p. 282.

66. Ibid., p. 287.

67. *Washington Post*, September 8, 1990, p. C1.

68. Kallen, *Corporate Welfare*, p. 293.

69. Ibid., p. 295.

70. *Washington Post*, September 8, 1990, p. C1.

71. *International Directory of Company Histories*, Vol 11, Chicago: St. James Press, 1991, p. 709.

72. Kallen, *Corporate Welfare*, p. 297.

73. *International Directory of Company Histories*, p. 706.

74. *Globe and Mail*, September 16, 1983, p. B1.

Chapter Nine

1. Kallen, Laurence, *Corporate Welfare: The Megabankruptcies of the 80s and 90s*, New York: Carol Publishing, 1991, p. 382.

2. Ibid., p. 370.

3. A. H. Robins advertisement, reproduced in Mintz, Morton, *At Any Cost: Corporate Greed, Women and the Dalkon Shield*, New York: Pantheon, 1985, p. 85.

4. Ibid., p. 11.

5. Ibid., p. 13.

6. Mintz, op. cit., p. 240.

7. "Manufacturing Proposal for the Dalkon Shield," A. H. Robins, December 16, 1970.

8. Mintz, op. cit., p. 40.

9. Mintz, op. cit, p. 176.

10. Kallen, *Corporate Welfare*, p. 308.

11. Ibid., p. 317.

12. Mintz, op. cit., p. 75.

13. Ibid., p. 133.

14. Ibid., p. 140.

15. Ibid., p. 154.

16. *House Subcommittee of the Committee on Government Operations, Regulations of Medical Devices (Intrauterine Contraceptive Devices)*, 93rd Congress, June 13, 1973, p. 118.

17. Mintz, op. cit., p. 81.

18. Ibid., p. 83.

19. Kallen, op. cit., p. 320.

20. Mintz, op. cit., p. 164.
21. Ibid., p. 165.
22. Kallen, op. cit., p. 325.
23. Mintz, op. cit., p. 196.
24. Kallen, op. cit., p. 329.
25. Mintz, op. cit., p. 148.
26. Mintz, op. cit., p. 18.
27. Ibid., p. 137.
28. Ibid., p. 52.
29. Kallen, op. cit., p. 327.
30. Mintz, op. cit., p. 214.
31. Ibid., p. 202.
32. *Los Angeles Times*, June 28, 1984.
33. Mintz, op. cit., p. 225.
34. Kallen, op. cit., p. 340.
35. This material is excerpted from the statement Judge Lord read in court on February 29, 1984, and reproduced in *Harper's*, June 1984, pp. 13-14.
36. Mintz, op. cit., p. 181.
37. Ibid., p. 245.
38. Ibid., p. 3.
39. Kallen, op. cit., p. 346.
40. Ibid., p. 354.
41. Ibid., p. 357.
42. Ibid., p. 361.
43. Ibid., p. 364.
44. *The Nation*, February 13, 1989, p. 193.
45. Kallen, op. cit., p. 373.
46. *Toronto Star*, November 7, 1989, p. A8.
47. Kallen, op. cit., p. 382.
48. *Hansard*, April 3, 1986, p. 17,787.

Chapter Ten

1. Interview, November 17, 1993.

2. Parker, Allan A., *Credit, Debt and Bankruptcy: How to Handle Your Personal Finances*, Toronto: Self-Counsel Press, 1988, p. 91.

3. Exemptions Act, c. E-15, Province of Alberta, 1985, Section 1(1).

4. Ibid.

5. Hotham v. Bright, 1923, 3 *Western Weekly Reports*, 94 (Alta.).

6. Prokopchuk v. Mandryk, 1942, 2 *Western Weekly Reports*, 577 (Alta.).

7. Graham, Mary, "Going for Broke," in *The New Republic*, June 8, 1992, p. 17.

8. *New York Times*, July 25, 1993, Section I, p. 1.

9. Ibid.

10. Graham, op. cit., p. 16.

11. BIA, Section 49(6).

12. Ibid., Section 155 (b).

13. Interview, November 16, 1993.

14. The Ontario Securities Commission, OSC *Bulletin*, Volume 14, Issue 47, November 22, 1991, "In the Matter of the Securities Act, R.S.O. 1980, Chapter 466, as Amended, and in the Matter of Osler Inc., and in the Matter of Thomas Henry Bourne, and in the Matter of John Joseph Campbell, and in the Matter of Patrick Anthony Chesnutt, and in the Matter of Paul Marion Cohen and in the Matter of Kevin Robert Cooke, and in the Matter of Allen Gaudet, and in the Matter of Venard Joseph Gaudet. Decision and Reasons."

15. Ibid., p. 8.

16. Ibid., p. 18.

17. Ibid., p. 9.

18. Ibid.

19. Ibid., p. 11.

20. Ibid., p. 12.

21. Ibid., p. 15.

22. Ibid., p. 18.

23. Lilly, Wayne, "Lenny's Billable Nightmare," in the *Financial Times of Canada*, June 11, 1990, p. 10.

24. Interview with one of the legal team, November 1993.

25. Lilly, op. cit., p. 10.

26. Quoted in the *Globe and Mail*, February 21, 1990, p. B5.

27. Lilly, op. cit., p. 10.

28. Ibid., p. 12.

29. *Globe and Mail*, February 21, 1990, p. B5.

30. *Globe and Mail*, July 18, 1991, p. B11.

31. Ibid.

32. *Globe and Mail*, April 28, 1992, p. B3.

33. *Globe and Mail*, February 4, 1994, p. B2.

Chapter Eleven

1. Adams, James Ring, and Franz, Douglas, *A Full Service Bank: How BCCI Stole Billions Around the World*, New York: Pocket Books, 1992, p. 348.

2. Ibid., p. 11.

3. *World Almanac and Book of Facts*, New York: Pharos Books, 1990, p. 718.

4. Adams and Franz, op. cit., p. 15.

5. Ibid., p. 16.

6. Brenner, Marie, "How They Broke the Bank," *Vanity Fair*, April 1992, p. 172.

7. Interview, December 10, 1993.

8. Adams and Franz, op. cit., p. 164.

9. "Carter Donors: Questionable Givers?," *The Atlanta Constitution*, April 14, 1991, p. 1.

10. Adams and Franz, op. cit., p. 42.

11. Ibid., p. 226.

12. *New York Times*, December 18, 1987.

13. Adams and Franz, op. cit., p. 134.

14. Adams and Franz, op. cit., p. 292.

15. *The Times*, July 21, 1991, p. 4A.

16. *Financial Times*, July 24, 1991, p. 1.

17. *The Times*, May 23, 1991, p. 4A.

18. *Washington Post*, August 6, 1991, p. 1.

19. *Globe and Mail*, September 27, 1993, p. B3.

20. Interview, December 10, 1993.

21. Fletcher, Ian F., "International Insolvency, The Way Ahead," in *International Insolvency Review*, Spring 1993, p. 9.

22. *Globe and Mail*, October 23, 1992, p. B2.

23. *Globe and Mail*, October 28, 1993, p. B4.

24. *Globe and Mail*, August 16, 1992, p. B1.

25. Brenner, op. cit., p. 168.

26. *Globe and Mail*, January 27, 1994, p. B8.

27. Klein, Edward, "The Sinking of Captain Bob," *Vanity Fair*, March 1992, p. 184.

28. Bower, Tom, *Maxwell: The Outsider*, London: Mandarin, 1988, p. 315.

29. Ibid., p. 25.

30. Bower, op. cit., p. 9.

31. *Time*, January 6, 1992, p. 42.

32. Klein, op. cit., p. 186.

33. Bower, op. cit., p. 513.

34. The *Independent, The Times*, both November 6, 1991.

35. *Financial Times*, June 2, 1992, p. 16.

36. *The Observer*, June 14, 1992, p. 35.

37. Reuters database, June 9, 1992.

38. *Toronto Star*, February 1, 1994, p. C14.

39. Ibid.

40. *Sunday Times*, June 2, 1992, p. 16.

41. *The Observer*, June 14, 1992, p. 35.

42. *The Economist*, January 4, 1992, p. 67.

43. Maxwell Communication Corporation PLC (In Administration), Legal Notice, August 5, 1993.

44. *New York Times*, July 12, 1993, p. D8.

45. *Sunday Times* (London), September 19, 1992, p. 3.

46. Montreal *Gazette*, November 15, 1992, p. B7.

47. *Sunday Times* (London), July 30, 1993, p. 25A.

48. Ibid., July 25, p. 25A.

49. *Globe and Mail*, January 19, 1992, p. B11.

50. Interview, November 17, 1993.

51. Turton, Richard, "L'Insol: Ovvero I Curatori Fallimentari Nel Mondo," in *Il Giornale del Dottori Commercialisti*, August-September, 1993, p. 13.

52. Ibid.

53. *The Economist*, April 27, 1991, p. 23.

54. Ibid., p. 15.

55. *The Economist*, January 4, 1992, p. 68.

Chapter Twelve

1. Quoted in the *Globe and Mail*, August 20, 1993, p. B4.

2. *Globe and Mail*, January 27, 1994, p. B8.

3. Shorten, Lynda, "BIA: Help or Hindrance?" in *Canadian Lawyer*, October 1993, p. 37.

4. Interview, November 16, 1993.

5. Stevens, Mark, *The Accounting Wars*, New York: Macmillan, 1985, p. 219.

6. Stevens, op. cit., p. 233.

7. Ibid., p. 235.

BIBLIOGRAPHY

RECOMMENDED FURTHER READING

Adams, James Ring, *The Big Fix: Inside the S&L Scandal*, New York: Wiley & Sons, 1991.

Adams, James Ring, and Franz, Douglas, *A Full Service Bank: How BCCI Stole Billions Around the World*, New York: Pocket Books, 1992.

Bennett, Frank, *Bennett on Creditors' and Debtors' Rights and Remedies*, Third Edition, Toronto: Carswell, 1992.

Bower, Tom, *Maxwell: The Outsider*, London: Mandarin, 1988.

Brodeur, Paul, *Outrageous Misconduct: The Asbestos Industry on Trial*, New York: Pantheon, 1986.

Code, William E., *In the Court of Queen's Bench of Alberta, Judicial District of Edmonton, Action Number 8703-1633, In the Matter of the Companies' Creditors Arrangement Act, Chapter C-25, R.S.C. 1970, as Amended, and in the Matter of Associated Investors of Canada Ltd., and in the Matter of the Judicature Act, Chapter J-1, R.S.A. 1980 as Amended, Final Report of Inspector Code*, QC, July 1989. "The Code Report."

Coleman, Peter J., *Debtors and Creditors in America: Insolvency, Imprisonment for Debt, and Bankruptcy, 1607-1900*, Madison: State Historical Society of Wisconsin, 1974.

Corcoran, Terence, and Reid, Laura, *Public Money, Private Greed: The Greymac, Seaway and Crown Trusts Affair*, Toronto: Collins, 1984.

Estey, Willard Z., *Report of the Collapse of CCB and Northland Bank*, Ottawa: Supply and Services. "The Estey Report."

Fisher, Matthew, *A Matter of Principal*, Toronto: Seal Books, 1990.

Johnson, Arthur, *Breaking the Banks*, Toronto: Lester, Orpen & Denys, 1986.

Kallen, Laurence, *Corporate Welfare: The Megabankruptcies of the 80s and 90s*, New York: Carol Publishing, 1991.

Kierans, Eric, and Stewart, Walter, *Wrong End of the Rainbow*, Toronto: HarperCollins, 1991.

Mackay, Charles, *Extraordinary Popular Delusions and the Madness of Crowds*, London: Noonday Press, 1932.

MacDougall, Curtis D., *Hoaxes*, New York: Dover, 1958.

Mayer, Martin, *The Greatest Bank Robbery: The Collapse of the Savings and Loan Industry*, New York: Collier, 1992.

Mintz, Morton, *At Any Cost: Corporate Greed, Women, and the Dalkon Shield*, New York: Pantheon, 1985.

Myers, Gustavus, *A History of Canadian Wealth*, Toronto: James, Lewis and Samuel, 1972.

Naylor, Tom, *The History of Canadian Business, 1867-1914*, Toronto: Lorimer, 1975.

Olive, David, *Just Rewards*, Toronto: Penguin, 1988.

O'Shea, James, *The Daisy Chain*, New York: Pocket Books, 1991.

Parker, Allan A., *Credit, Debt and Bankruptcy: How to Handle Your Personal Finances*, Toronto: Self-Counsel Press, 1988.

Playfair, Giles, *The Punitive Obsession: An Unvarnished History of the English Prison System*, London: Victor Gollancz, 1971.

Quayle, Eric, *The Ruin of Sir Walter Scott*, London: Rupert Hart-Davis, 1968.

Raw, Charles; Hodgson, Godfrey, and Page, Bruce, *Do You Sincerely Want to Be Rich? Bernard Cornfield and IOS, An International Swindle*, London: Andre Deutsch, 1971.

Rothchild, John, *Going for Broke, How Robert Campeau Bankrupted the Retail Industry, Jolted the Junk Bond Market, and Brought the Booming Eighties to a Crashing Halt*, New York: Simon & Schuster, 1991.

Shannon, James, *Texaco and the $10 Billion Jury*, Englewood, N.J.: Prentice-Hall, 1988.

Shaplen, Robert, *Krueger, Genius and Swindler*, New York: Alfred Knopf, 1960.

Sobel, Robert, *Panic on Wall Street*, New York: E. P. Dutton, 1988.

Stewart, Walter, *Too Big To Fail: Olympia & York, The Story Behind the Headlines*, Toronto: McClelland & Stewart, 1993.

———— *Towers of Gold, Feet of Clay: The Canadian Banks*, Toronto: Harper-Collins, 1991.

——— *The Golden Fleece*, Toronto: McClelland & Stewart, 1992.

Walsh, Annmarie Hauck, *The Public's Business*, Cambridge, Massachusetts: M.I.T. Press, 1980.

INDEX